⟦ WELCOME TO SHANGRI-LA ⟧

Above the town the Aurang split into a series of gentle cataracts where dim figures worked with long fishing sweeps. Terraces heavy with fruit bushes stepped toward heaven.

Neat narrow streets ran down to the Aurang and continued on the far shore, and water wheels turned steadily in the swift current. The buildings had flowerlike domes and elegant arches; graceful, winding walls connected the main structures; small towers bloomed amid the larger structures.

Bells and wind chimes were everywhere, dangled from windows and rafters and projecting beams. The tinkling and clanging and bonging were audible even above the rush of the Aurang.

"Isn't it magnificent?" Lyra was enraptured. Behind her the alien made an impolite noise.

By Alan Dean Foster
Published by Ballantine Books:

THE BLACK HOLE

CACHALOT

DARK STAR

MIDWORLD

NOR CRYSTAL TEARS

SENTENCED TO PRISM

SPLINTER OF THE MIND'S EYE

VOYAGE TO THE CITY OF THE DEAD

. . . WHO NEEDS ENEMIES?

WITH FRIENDS LIKE THESE . . .

The Icerigger Trilogy:
 ICERIGGER .
 MISSION TO MOULOKIN
 THE DELUGE DRIVERS

Pip and Flinx:
 FOR LOVE OF MOTHER-NOT
 THE TAR-AIYM KRANG
 ORPHAN STAR
 THE END OF THE MATTER
 BLOODHYPE

VOYAGE TO THE CITY OF THE DEAD

Alan Dean Foster

A Del Rey Book

BALLANTINE BOOKS • **NEW YORK**

For Daniel, with love,
for when he gets older and starts traveling. . . .

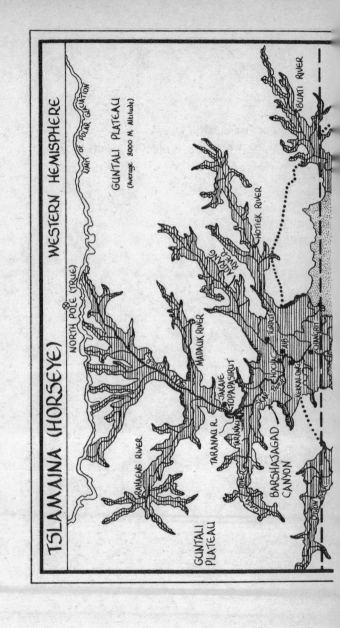

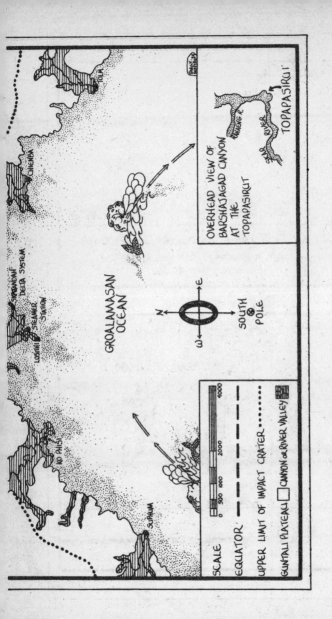

SCALE

EQUATOR

UPPER LIMIT OF IMPACT CRATER

GUNTALI PLATEAU   CANYON or RIVER VALLEY

0 500 1000   2000   4000

GROALAMASAN OCEAN

N
W   E
S
SOUTH POLE

OVERHEAD VIEW OF
BARSHAJAGAD CANYON
AT THE
TOPAPASIRUT

TOPAPASIRUT

KYAR RIVER

AMNYE R.

SUPHUR

KO PAHSI

LOSHII

SHIGUMO
STATION

SINGONDHI
DELTA SYSTEM

CHENIGA

TOLA

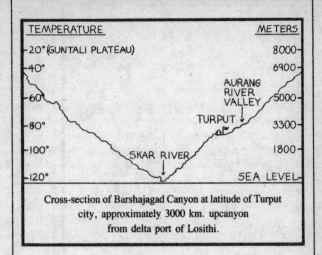

Cross-section of Barshajagad Canyon at latitude of Turput
city, approximately 3000 km. upcanyon
from delta port of Losithi.

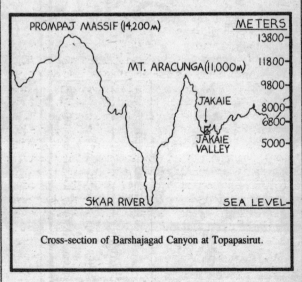

Cross-section of Barshajagad Canyon at Topapasirut.

[1]

They didn't call in the Guard because the intruder was already half dead. Still, they were upset.

Muttering angrily among themselves over the outrageous breach of protocol, the members of the Zanur looked to their leader for direction, but Najoke de-me-Halmur held his peace. It was up to the intruder to explain himself, and fast. Hands still hovered close to sheathed knives, although it was becoming apparent this was no assassination attempt—the intruder was too enfeebled to present a threat to anyone but himself. So Najoke stayed his hand as well as his lips. Seeing this, the other members of the Zanur calmed themselves.

Two unkempt servants attended the intruder, and they had their hands full keeping him on his feet. He was completely bald, as befitted his age, but more than age had been at work on that body recently. Pain was evident even in the movement of the eyes, and their owner was breathing as if he'd run a long ways, for all that two younger Mai supported him.

Several of the more impatient members of the Zanur started toward the stranger. De-me-Halmur stayed them with a wave of one slim, six-fingered hand. "Patience, my friends. Let us hear what this despoiler of etiquette has to say. Retribution can come later. We are no judges here."

The leader's words sparked the withered visitor's attention. He shrugged off the helping hands of his servants, much as he continued to push away the clutching hand of death. Though unsteady and shaking, he stood straight and by himself. "Good members of the Zanur, I beg forgiveness for this intrusion on the affairs of state. When one has little time left, one has no time at all for protocol. I have much to tell you."

De-Yarawut rose and pointed, hairless brows drawing together. "I know you. You reside in my district."

The elderly speaker tried to bow to the side, as etiquette required, and the effort nearly sent him sprawling. His servants rushed to help but he gestured them back.

"I am flattered by your remembrance, Zanural de-Yarawut. I am Bril de-Panltatol. A humble trader who works Upriver." The drama of the oldster's intrusion, his unforgivable breach of tradition, was beginning to fade. And he was known. No surprises were here.

Legends sing of the wrongness of such thoughts.

"No excuse can be made for your interruption, de-Panltatol," de-me-Halmur said. "You know the penalties."

"Your most excessive indulgence, Moyt, but as I said and as you can see, little time is left to me."

De-me-Halmur had not become ruler of a great city-state without the occasional ostentatious display of compassion. "You must have bribed efficiently to obtain this entrance, oldster. You are to be admired for that. Say what you have come to say."

"Good members of the Zanur, I have for most of my life been a trader of fine woods and metals between our great city of Po Rabi and the Upriver. Hai, even as far as Kekkalong." Kekkalong was a very long way Upriver, and many of the Zanurals had never journeyed beyond the boundaries of the city. They listened to the rover with a little more respect.

"I am a good citizen and work hard for my city. So I listen well to any tale or rumor that suggests the opportunity to increase my wealth."

"As do we all," Zanural de-Parinti commented. "Get on with it."

"Among the many tales of the Upriver are those which speak of a dead place, home to spirits and ghosts and demons beyond counting, who guard such wealth as could not be counted in a thousand lifetimes by all the accountants of all the city-states that ring the Groalamasan itself."

"A wonderful story, I'm sure," another Zanural called from his council seat. "I too have heard such stories."

"It is well known," de-Panltatol continued, "that the nearer one travels to the source of such tales, the more vivid and impressive they become—or else they fade away entirely.

"This particular tale is told over and over again in a hundred towns and villages of the North. I have listened to it for more than fifty years. I resolved finally to pursue it to the last storyteller. Instead it drew me onward, pulling me ever farther north. Sometimes the tale smelled of truth, more often of village embroidery, but never did I lose track of it entirely.

"I went beyond maps and merchant trails, always up the Barshajagad, following the current of the Skar and in places abandoning it completely. I walked—I, Bril de-Panltatol—upon the surface of the frozen Guntali itself!"

Now the whispers of interest were submerged by ill-concealed laughter. The Guntali Plateau, from which arose all the great rivers of the world that drained into the single ocean that was the Groalamasan, was so high and cold and thin of air that no Mai could travel upon it. Yet the wrinkled old trader was laying claim to such a feat.

Like his fellow merchants and Zanural, de-me-Halmur refused to countenance the possibility, but neither did he laugh. He had not become Moyt of Po Rabi by dismissing the most elaborate absurdities without careful dissection. "Let this one continue proving himself the fool, but let him not be convicted until he has finished his story."

"Up past even far Hochac I went," de-Panltatol was breathing harder now, "and my journey was but beginning. I lost servants and companions until I was obliged to travel on my own, because none would go farther in my company. All believed me mad, you see. I nearly perished many times. The rumors and the river led me ever onward."

[3]

"Onward to what?" another of the Zanural snorted derisively.

The oldster glanced sideways and seemed to draw strength from his scoffers. "To the source of all the tales and songs. To the land of the dead. To the part of the world where demons and monsters make their home. To the top of the world, good Zanural."

This time the laughter could not be contained. It did not appear to discourage the old trader.

"I found the City of the Dead. I, Bril de-Panltatol! And I came away with a piece of it." He frowned then, and wheezed painfully. "I don't remember that time very well. My mind was numbed by all I had endured. How I stayed alive I don't know, but I drove myself to make another boat. I made many boats, I think. It's hard to remember. I disguised what I had brought away beneath a bale of Salp skins and brought it all the way Downriver, all the way back to my home, to Po Rabi."

De-me-Halmur's wide black eyes flickered. "A most interesting and entertaining story, de-Panltatol, but all such tales of demon cities are entertaining. I hope you are a better trader than you are a storyteller." Polite laughter rose from the other members of the Zanur.

"Is that what you broke into our conference to tell us?" snapped another Zanural angrily. "If you can do no better than that, I promise you your age will not save you."

"There is only one thing I can add to what I have told you," the exhausted trader admitted. "For it I have ruined my mind and my self, so there is little for you to threaten me with. My triumph will be short-lived and I will not buy the seat on the Zanur that I longed for." A few insulted murmurs arose among the Zanural, loudest from those whose fortunes were smallest.

"So I will leave my tale to you, together with that one other thing, and let you judge, Zanural of the city, if I might have been thought equal in wealth to sit among you." He turned and blew on a small bone whistle that hung from a cord around his neck.

A dozen laborers entered in two columns of six. Between them they held ropes attached to a low dolly. Laughter gave way to curiosity and confusion among the members of the

Zanur. The dolly had six axles and fat rubbery wheels made from the treated sap of the arer tree.

From his place at the head of the long council table de-me-Halmur saw the pile of fine gray Salp pelts piled high on the dolly. They were valuable but not exceptionally so. Certainly they weren't heavy enough to require the use of a six-axle and twelve strong Mai to pull the load. He could see the way muscles strained against something massive but concealed. He stood slightly, unconscious of the movement, to have a better view.

The laborers halted and moved aside. With the aid of his servants Panltatol staggered to the dolly. Disdaining help, he reached out and shakily pulled the skins onto the floor. They'd been sewn together and came off as one.

There *was* something else on the dolly, as de-me-Halmur suspected, but the sight of it struck him speechless—a single metal bar reposed on the wooden platform. It was twisted and bent by some unknown force and was as thick as a large Mai's body. But that observation passed quickly. The Zanural were interested in its composition far more than its shape.

It had not been polished and it displayed long gashes and much pitting, evidence of exposure to powerful chemicals or energies. Its color was familiar.

"I did not actually enter the place of the dead." Panltatol's voice was weakening. "I was near, very near, when weather so terrible it cannot be imagined except in dreams finally forced me to retreat. This relic I found on the banks of the Skar, where the river had carried it. This alone I was able to bring back with me. Zanural of Po Rabi, this is my legacy."

Forgetting their dignity, abjuring protocol, they left their seats to examine the massive metal bar. Sensitive six-fingered hands caressed the smooth gray substance. The dull silvery sheen was a property of the metal itself.

It *looked* like sunit. It had the color of sunit. It felt like sunit. When three of the Zanural from northern Po Rabi tried to lift it and could not, they were positive it was sunit.

De-Changrit, who on the Zanur was second in power only to de-me-Halmur himself, removed a small ingot from the money belt that circled his waist. It was a *serl*, the largest denomination coined by any of the great city-states that lined the shores of the Groalamasan Ocean, newly minted in powerful Chienba. He placed it in one of the gouges cut in the flank of the bar and tried to calculate the worth of the twisted mass in his head. He was a superb businessmai and his estimate was very near the mark.

"Several million," he announced aloud. "At least." Having already made their own calculations, several of his associates nodded by way of confirmation.

De-Panltatol abruptly sat down on the edge of the dolly, leaning back against the bar for support. He ran one hand gently across the cold metal, lovingly, as if it were a woman reclining in his hammock. There was not a Mai among the Zanur who did not feel the same love for that bar. It represented a great and compact fortune.

When the murmurs and excited conversations began to die down it was Changrit who asked the question uppermost in all minds. "Is there more?"

His tone was respectful now, no longer sarcastic or accusing. Thus vindicated, Panltatol seemed to draw strength from some unknown source. They were no longer laughing at him.

"Honored sirs, I do not know. I found only this one piece, washed up on a rocky and wild shore. But the rumors that drove me to the top of the world always spoke of more in the City of the Dead."

Many signs were made by the Zanural, for they were as intensely superstitious as the common folk. Daily their lives were punctuated by the performance of rituals designed to ward off unfriendly deities and spirits, which all Mai knew ruled the affairs of each individual from birth to death. At the rear of the chamber a wide-eyed servant hastily dumped more incense in the ritual burner, in case the spirits in attendance that day were possessed of particularly large noses. The air of the chamber was immediately suffused with sweet fragrance.

"No actual City of the Dead exists," one of the Zanural ventured hesitantly. "It is not a real place."

De-me-Halmur used his hands eloquently. "No such solid piece of sunit as this exists, yet it sits there before us."

"More," Panltatol mumbled. "More in the City of the Dead."

"How much more?" asked Changrit with becoming avariciousness.

"They say . . . the rumors say . . . that the city itself is built of sunit." Dead silence greeted his declaration, appropriately. "I am sorry I did not go farther." A thin smile appeared on his withered face. His right arm lay like brown cloth against the cold metal. "I am so tired, honored ones. I must rest a while."

"Wait!" Changrit rushed forward. With his own arms he supported the oldster, a sign of the esteem in which Panltatol was suddenly held. "How do we find the City of the Dead? How could one retrace your travels?"

"Why, don't you know?" Panltatol whispered. "There is no City of the Dead. The journey cannot be made. But I made it. I, Bril de-Panltatol, went where it is impossible to go. But you can't follow, none of you." He said it with vehemence as he unexpectedly sat up without aid. "You can't follow because only an insane one could make such a journey. I am mad, you see, and you are not." A sudden thought made him blink with confusion.

"Very tired." He leaned back against Changrit again and closed his eyes. They would not open again.

Changrit gently lowered the thin body. "A true Mai. He sacrificed everything in hopes of improving his fortune. I honor him."

"We all honor him," de-me-Halmur said, "as we will honor his memory."

"What of the sunit?" Lust was apparent in the voice of the Zanural who voiced the common thought. All eyes were on the bar.

"You know the law," de-me-Halmur said sternly, if a trifle reluctantly. "I covet it as much as any of you, but it goes to his family and employees." He made a protective sign in case certain spirits were listening. "The law is clear."

Zanural de-Peyetmy was almost in tears. "Couldn't we bend the law just a little?"

"I am sworn to uphold it, and I will do so. Those who would bend the law ultimately find themselves strangled by it." Murmurs of assent sounded from around the table.

"Of course," de-me-Halmur went on, "there is the matter of a death tax." A few smiles appeared. "Also the fact that de-Panltatol undertook this journey without proper author-ization, and we still must deal with the matter of his rude intrusion into the Zanur Chamber." He studied the bar. "I would say that perhaps half should go into the city treasury."

"That still leaves a nice fortune." Changrit had retaken his seat on de-me-Halmur's left. "No family could be dis-appointed to receive such an inheritance. Now that the law has been dealt with, how are we to deal with this remarkable story?"

"A great journey," one of the other Zanural announced portentously. "One to be enshrined in memory and song. I myself will commission a song cycle to commemorate it."

"A thoughtful gesture," de-me-Halmur agreed, thankful for the Zanural's support. His proposal meant that de-me-Halmur would not have to pay for the requisite memorial. Other Zanural cursed themselves for not thinking to make the clever political move.

"Now who shall volunteer to help equip a new expedition to journey to the top of the world in search of this rumored City of the Dead?"

Suddenly every member of the council sought to shrink in his seat. One, bolder than the rest, said sharply, "I would not venture more than a thousand legats Upriver for all the sunit on Tslamaina."

"Nor would I," de-me-Halmur agreed. "De-Panltatol was quite right. None of us is mad. The very idea of setting foot on the Guntali Plateau is a concept only a disturbed mind could conceive. To attempt to retrace his wild path would be impossible." He gestured toward the bar and the body lying next to it. "We must be satisfied with this."

"Not necessarily." All eyes turned in surprise to Changrit. De-me-Halmur waited warily for any suggestion his rival might make. Each had much respect for the other, so much so that they never employed assassins. Such methods they left to cruder Mai while they dueled with words and gestures.

"It is true that any journey far up the Skar is daunting, let alone one to the top of the world. One might undertake such an expedition only to perish within sight of one's goal. It is more likely any travelers would end up staring at the inside of a Na's belly instead of the City of the Dead." Zanurals executed signs indicating anxiety.

"Or else they would find themselves deceived by the Tsla. We do not have the means for accomplishing such a journey, but there are those who do."

"I don't see them here," another Zanural called. Laughter punctuated his observation.

Changrit gave him a withering look until the laughter had subsided. "A good merchant knows his responsibility to the Zanur, to his city-state. He knows also his own limitations. I am quite aware of mine as you must be of yours.

"But there is something new come recently to Tslamaina. I speak of the visitors from the sky."

Uncertain mutterings were silenced by de-me-Halmur. "I've heard much of them. What is it you propose, Changrit?"

"I can propose nothing unless recent information I have received from my agents can be confirmed. Call for the ambassador to Losithi."

There followed a long delay, made palatable by a regal midday meal, while Ror de-Kelwhoang, ambassador to Losithi, was summoned from his offices in the Ministry. He arrived in due course, breathless and puzzled.

"For what reason have I been summoned in such haste, honored Zanural?"

There was much respect among the members for the skills of the elderly Kelwhoang, just as there was in the Zanur of Losithi. Po Rabi's main rival in trade and commerce, it lay several hundred legats to the southwest and controlled the western end of the Skatandah Delta, the great marshland formed by the emptying of the Skar River into the Groalamasan.

Midway between the two city-states but slightly nearer Losithi lay the station established by the strange visitors from the sky. Their science was much advanced and gain was to be made there for those who knew how to ferret it out. The visitors were carefully courted by diplomats from Losithi as well as Po Rabi.

"Tell the Zanur," Changrit instructed the ambassador, "what you told me several weeks ago concerning the visitors from the sky. The *new* visitors."

"New visitors?" De-me-Halmur frowned, as did several

[9]

other Zanural. "You mean that more of the large bug-creatures have arrived on Tslamaina?"

Kelwhoang looked toward his sponsor Changrit uncertainly, but received a gesture of openness by way of reply.

"All are friends here today, Kelwhoang. Speak freely."

The ambassador nodded. "There came upon us a day rainy and cold, which forced me to—"

De-me-Halmur interrupted him. "Our time is valuable, Kelwhoang. Spare us the poetry."

"Forgive me, Moyt. I was taken aback by this sight." He indicated the monstrous bar of sunit.

"Understandable. Your attention to potential profit marks you well in our sight. Still, make your tale concise."

Kelwhoang gestured in agreement. "Members of the Zanur. As you know, I make it my business during the long journey between our city and Losithi to take note of all of interest that transpires within the Delta. The visitors from the sky keep to their building-that-walks-the-water, but I have cultivated my acquaintance with them.

"Thus did I learn that five weeks ago allies from the sky arrived among them. I was astonished to learn that these newcomers look not like those who built the sky-station, but much like us." That bit of news prompted gasps of astonishment from the Zanurals.

"You mean," Guptinak asked, "that they are not as horrible to look upon as the large bug-things?"

"No," said Kelwhoang, gratified by the reaction his revelation had produced. "They are much like Mai, only taller, taller even than a Tsla but not so large as a Na. They have more body hair and their features are sharper and more pronounced, rougher and not as beautiful. They suffer from our climate much as does a Tsla, unlike their bug-thing friends who are quite comfortable in the Delta. One male and one female, similar enough to us that at a distance one could almost think them Mai.

"I did not meet them myself, only saw them conversing with the Moyt of the station, the one called," and he struggled with the difficult alien name, "Porlezmozmith. Later I was able to talk with her and she remarked on the similarity between us and the new visitors. Truly the resemblance is striking between us. These newcomers' faces have smaller eyes, larger ears that are great curved winged things visible even at a distance. Oh yes, they have but five digits on their hands and feet instead of the normal six, even as the bug-things have but four, though they have that extra pair of arms and legs. It may be that these new visitors are more akin to us than the Tsla or the Na, with whom we share our world."

"All fascinating," de-me-Halmur said, "but how does this profit us?"

"Tell them what the bug-thing told you his new guests have planned," Changrit prompted.

"Ah. I was told they brought with them a wondrous magical boat which walks upon the water more freely than the station the visitors first built. It does not depend on wind or muscle for power but carries its own energy inside it. I was told that it can travel at great speed *Up*river, against the current of the Skar."

More mutters of astonishment rose from the assembled members. "We've heard much of the wonders brought by the visitors from the sky," de-me-Halmur said. "I sense your thought, Changrit, but surely they would not sell us this amazing craft?"

"Never," the ambassador admitted. "I have been told many times by the Moyt Porlezmozmith that they can have only the briefest of contacts with us and that they are forbidden by their own laws to sell us any of the advanced tools and instruments they have brought with them."

"No profit in that," one of the Zanural grumbled. "Truly these visitors are alien."

"These newcomers who are like us," the ambassador continued, "are scholars, not merchants. They intend to make a study of the Barshajagad, the canyon which cradles our river Skar."

"Now that makes sense," de-me-Halmur commented. "There is always profit in good scholarship." He made a sign to invoke the spirit of knowledge and insight, but finally had to ask, "What is in your mind, Changrit?"

"These visitors from the sky still know little of our world. Beyond the Delta they are ignorant, for all their knowledge. They know nothing of the ways of the Skar, or of the Hotiek or the Aurang or any of the lesser tributaries. They know nothing of the peoples who inhabit the canyon. They will need guides."

"Ah!" De-me-Halmur's expression was fed by enlightenment. "Friendly locals to show them the way."

"Yes, to show them the way."

"And good friends that we are, it behooves us as the rulers of Po Rabi to find volunteers to assist them?"

"Every chance we can find," Changrit agreed firmly.

"How do we know that these strange creatures have any interest in traveling up the Skar farther than the town of Ibe?" a Zanural wondered aloud.

"We do not," Changrit admitted. "How does one divine the intentions of aliens? Yet if they are as similar in appearance to us as Ambassador de-Kelwhoang says, who is to say that their motivations are different?" He looked away from the table. "You've no idea how far they intend to go Upriver, Kelwhoang?"

"No. The bug-Moyt was not too clear. He did say a long journey. Certainly farther than Ibe."

"Then our course is clear, Zanural." De-me-Halmur leaned forward the better to emphasize his words and gestures. "We must do our utmost to ensure that these visitors make use of our good intentions and accept the aid that the people of Po Rabi will freely extend to them."

"Assuming they accept," said another member. "What if they do not travel to the region of our hopes? What if they reach Kekkalong and decide they have journeyed far enough?"

"Then perhaps," Changrit murmured quietly, "they might at that time be persuaded to loan us the use of their wondrous craft. I'm certain that the loquacious Ror de-Kelwhoang will employ all his admirable verbal talents to ensure that the immediate requirements of the Zanur are met."

"I shall do my best, of course." The ambassador performed an elaborate gesture designed to invoke the spirits of all the great diplomats of the past. He glanced sideways at the huge, gleaming mass of solid sunit.

"However, if I am to do my best, honored ones, it would help if you could explain to me the reasons behind my mission. Would I be remiss in assuming it has something to do

[12]

with the astonishing wealth that lies next to a dead Mai in the center of this chamber?"

"You would not," de-me-Halmur said. "Seat yourself."

Gesturing his thanks at the honor, de-Kelwhoang joined the table as Changrit related the events of the morning.

The subsequent discussion and laying out of plans lasted well into the evening. The heat of day was followed by the heat of night and still the Zanur sat in extended session. Bureaucrats and guards gossiped and wondered, but still the rulers of Po Rabi remained sequestered in their chamber.

It was only when they finally adjourned in the early hours of the morning that someone thoughtfully directed attendants to remove the stiffened corpse of that soon to be memorialized merchant–explorer Bril de-Panltatol. Great care had already been taken to ensure that a proper share of his legacy was safely transported to the city treasury.

Greater care and craft might make possible the seemingly impossible task of securing for the Zanur of Po Rabi the rest of his legacy.

〔 II 〕

Etienne Redowl was sick of measuring current flow. He was sick of taking samples from the river bottom. Recording the ebb and flow of sandbars and mudbanks no longer interested him, nor did watching the analyzer spit out graphs listing gravel composition mineral by mineral.

But there was nothing else for him to do at Steamer Station.

It seemed as if they'd been waiting for permission from the native authorities to begin their Upriver expedition since the beginning of time. Anyone who thought the bureaucracy of Commonwealth Science and Exploration difficult to penetrate should have to cope once in his life with the byzantine machinations of the Mai of Tslamaina. The station's location between the rival city-states of Po Rabi and Losithi only made it tougher to obtain the necessary clearances.

There was no pushing the matter, however. Where a Class Four-B world was involved, Commonwealth policy was strict. Porlezmozmith, the officer in charge of Steamer Station, was sympathetic to the Redowls' plight, but not to the point of challenging regulations. So the husband-wife team sat and sweated and waited.

Etienne paused on the ladder long enough to adjust the thermo-sense on his fishnet shirt and shorts. Minuscule cooling units woven into the material struggled to cool his skin. He checked his wrist telltale. A fairly mild afternoon, with the temperatures hovering around a hundred and twenty degrees and the humidity a mere ninety percent. He longed for the coolness of their quarters on the station platform above.

The thranx found the temperature a mite hot, but the humidity suited them just fine. That was why they'd been chosen to staff the only Commonwealth outpost. For them it was almost like home. For humans it was pure misery.

Survey should have named it misery, Etienne thought. Instead it had been named for its geology. That geology and the unique civilization it had produced were the reasons why Etienne and his wife Lyra had braved endless application forms and sweltering weather in order to be the first humanx scientists allowed to work beyond the boundaries of the outpost. Or such would be the case if the native authorities ever gave them the okay to travel Upriver. Until that happened they were stuck at the station. Months of waiting for permission to arrive, endless days spent battling the terrible heat and humidity had sapped his initial enthusiasm. Lyra was bearing up better beneath the day-to-day disappointment, but even she was starting to wilt.

He forced himself to see Tslamaina as it looked from high orbit. The refreshing, cooler image reminded him again why they'd come to the world its discoverers had named Horseye. Lyra had no room for flippancy in science and preferred Tslamaina, the native name, but the image certainly fitted.

Eons ago the planet had collided with a meteor of truly impressive dimensions. In addition to creating the vast circular basin that was now filled by the Groalamasan Ocean, the concussion had badly cracked the planet's surface. That surface, high above the single world-ocean, comprised the Guntali Plateau.

Water running off the Guntali for hundreds of millions of years patiently enlarged those surface cracks, eventually resulting in the most spectacular river canyons ever encountered. The combination of geological and climatological factors necessary to produce such awesome scenery had not been duplicated on any other of the explored worlds.

Of all the river canyons by far the greatest was the Barshajagad, which in the Mai language meant "Tongue-of-the-World." More than two thousand kilometers wide at the point where it finally emptied into the ocean, it reached northward from its delta some thirteen thousand kilometers to vanish in the cloud-shrouded north polar wastes. From the edge of the Guntali, a few hundred kilometers Upriver, to the surface of the slowly moving river Skar, the Barshajagad dropped approximately eight thousand meters in elevation. Where mountains rose from the plateau, the disparity was even greater.

So wide was the Barshajagad at its mouth, however, that a traveler on the surface of the river could not see where the gradually ascending slopes finally reached the plateau to east and west.

The result was an astonishing variety of life forms organized into ecological regions not by latitude but by elevation, as nature made use of the different temperature and moisture zones that climbed the canyon walls.

Three different intelligent mammalian races had appeared on Tslamaina, each confined to its own portion of the river canyons. The intensively competitive and primitively capitalistic Mai ruled the ocean and the river valleys. Above them in the more temperate zone between three thousand and fifty-five hundred meters were the Tsla. Clinging to the frozen rims of the canyons and freely roaming the Guntali were the carnivorous Na. Or so the locals claimed. None of them had ever seen a Na, and since Mai society was infused with a healthy respect for and belief in thousands of spirits, demons, and ghosts, Lyra Redowl, circumspect xenologist that she was, was reluctant to give instant recognition to the existence of this legendary third intelligent race.

Temperature and pressure and not national or tribal boundaries kept the races of Tslamaina separated. That made for a sociocultural situation every bit as unique as the local geology, as Lyra was fond of pointing out to her husband.

Their hope, the dream that had brought them across many

[16]

light-years, was to take a hydrofoil all the way up the Skar to its source, making a thorough study of the geology and the people of the planet as they advanced. But Tslamaina was a Class Four-B world. That meant they could only proceed with the natives' permission, and that permission still was not forthcoming, despite repeated anxious requests.

So Etienne had been confined to examination of the delta soils and the geology around the station which was, in a word, flat. Lyra was better off, able to visit with those fisherfolk who sometimes stopped at the station to chat and to attempt to steal anything not bolted down. Station personnel never ventured reprisals for the attempts. For one thing the attempts were always unsuccessful. For another, it was part of the local culture.

Six months had passed since the shuttle had deposited the Redowls at Steamer Station and Etienne was close to calling off the expedition. Only the knowledge that they would be the first to make an Upriver journey kept him from booking passage out on the next supply run.

It would help if Lyra would learn to keep her frustration to herself, but no, not her. She'd declaim long and loud to anyone within earshot. The thranx were too polite to tell her to shut up, and Etienne had tried many times and failed. After the first month he simply gave up and tuned her out. It wasn't hard. He had been doing it for twenty years. Eight or nine years ago the conflict might have ended in divorce, but now they had too much invested in each other. Convenience and familiarity balanced out a lot of bickering, though sometimes he wondered.

Something was itching sharply on the back of his neck. Holding onto the ladder with his right hand he reached up and back with his left, coming away with something soft and flexible. He eyed it with intense distaste.

It was as long as his hand and thick as his thumb, completely transparent except for the dark maroon color spreading slowly backward from the head. As he held it firmly it wiggled and twisted in search of the blood so recently discovered and quickly vanished.

The *dangui* was an elegant local bloodsucker related to the annelid worms but possessed of a cartilaginous backbone which when flexed allowed it to jump at its intended host.

[17]

It turned red as it filled up with blood. It looked like a glass leech and seemed to find human plasma perfectly palatable, much to Etienne's enduring disgust.

Forcing down the gorge rising in his throat he flung it as far away as he could, heard the faint *plop* when it hit the murky green water. He felt the back of his neck and his hand came away bloody. First stop inside the station would be for antibiotic spray.

The metal stilts on which Steamer Station rested carried a mild electric charge to discourage infestation by such local pests though they rarely troubled the thranx because of their tough exoskeletons. Etienne dealt in smooth, hard surfaces and clean stone and didn't care much for biology, particularly when it chose to get personal.

High thin clouds blocked out some of the ultraviolet, but Etienne was still grateful for his naturally dark coloring, a legacy of ancient Amerindians. A lighter-skinned human would quickly fry under Tslamaina's relentless sun. Though he'd been outside less than ten minutes, the sweat was pouring off him. The cooling meshwork shirt and shorts were all that kept him halfway comfortable.

Even the climate might be bearable if only they'd receive permission from the native authorities. The frustration of waiting was worse than any heat, he mused as he made his careful way up the ladder.

Behind him tall fat pseudopalms thrust enormous green fronds over the lazy water. Table tree roots exploded sideways from their trunks before dipping down into the mud. Nappers, tiny crustaceans with multihued shells, filled the air with their doglike barking.

Little relief beyond the shade it offered was available inside the station since the internal temperature was set to accommodate thranx and not humans. A hundred was certainly cooler than one-twenty, but the humidity was unchanged. Only when he entered the rooms reserved for less tolerant visitors did the humidity begin to drop. By the time he reached their quarters, station machinery had lowered the temperature forty-five degrees and sucked out more than half the humidity.

Lyra Redowl barely glanced up at him. She sprawled in a chair studying her clipboard viewer.

"Anything interesting?"

"Glass leech bit me."

"Bad?"

"I doubt it." He moved to a cabinet and removed a tiny spray can, dosed the back of his neck. "The Skar flows into the Groalamasan, the Groalamasan goes round and round and it comes out here." He gestured toward the lavatory.

She put her viewer aside, spoke coolly. "I don't blame you for being upset, Etienne. I'm as pissed off as you are. But there's nothing we can do except wait. Make an effort not to take it out on me, okay?"

"I'm not taking anything out on you," he said exasperatedly. "Why do you take everything I say so personally? Can I help it if this damn delay's got me running around like a monkey chewing his tail?"

"You have to work on your self-control. You'll end up with an ulcer."

"I keep control of myself!" He struggled to match his tone to his assertion. "I haven't got time to argue with you, Lyra."

"I agree." Her eyes moved back to the viewer.

He sighed, counted quietly to eight, then plopped down in one of the thin chairs. "What are you buried in now?"

"Varofski on multiple societal interactions."

"Haven't you read that already?"

"Twice. This is my third time around. What do you suggest I do? Squat here and watch thranx shadowplays on the tridee?"

"It would be a change, but I don't want to argue about it."

"You never do. That's why I'm always amazed how regularly you end up doing so." Suddenly she looked up at him and smiled. It was a little forced, but welcome nonetheless. "Listen to us, fighting like a couple of idiot children. Etienne, I'm just as frustrated as you are. What the hell is keeping those Moyts from giving us travel clearance?"

"Who knows." Rising from the chair, Etienne crossed to the kitchen area and thumbed the switch on the left side of the refrigeration unit. It dispensed fruit juice, heavily salted and sugared. The cooking facilities were nearby but rarely utilized. The Redowls preferred to take most of their meals cold; Tslamaina didn't encourage consumption of piping hot food.

Glass in hand he walked over to stand behind his wife's chair, rested a hand on her shoulder as he sipped at the icy liquid.

"Truce, Lyra?"

She reached up to pat his hand. "Truce. Can't we do something, Etienne?"

"Not a damn thing. You know the law. We're wholly dependent on the whims of the locals." She nodded, returned to her reading.

He never tired of looking at her. After twenty years he still found her physically alluring. Lately she looked even better than usual, having lost weight since their arrival. Tslamaina would sweat you down to skeleton size if you weren't careful.

"I don't understand the delay," she said. "I've talked to the local fisherfolk and traders and they just give me the local variations of a bemused shrug. From everything I've been able to learn both these city-states are hotbeds of new ideas and rapid development. You'd think one or the other would be eager to grant us permission to travel Upriver."

"I'm sure they would," Etienne agreed, "if we could promise them something solid in return. Unfortunately, the regulations protecting Class Four-B worlds prohibit any commerce with natives. No introduction of advanced technology allowed from external sources, and that's what they want to buy from us. The usual nasty cycle. The Moyts would like to grant us clearance for Upriver travel but they want payment in return. We can't pay them what they want because regulations forbid it. So here we sit, and sweat."

"Too true. How's your neck?"

He felt at the shallow bite. "Filthy little monsters. I don't mind dealing with something big and toothy, but I hate parasites."

"Let me give you another shot of antibio." She put down her viewer and reached for the spray. A cool dampness caressed his neck a second time.

"There," she said with satisfaction. "This is no place to pick up an infection, no matter how interesting. We've been lucky so far. Not that we've spent all that much time outside." She hesitated. "Etienne, I'm ready to start chewing the furniture again. We've got to get out of here—Tell you what. Why don't we check out the boat?"

He made a face. "We're going to wear it out before we get started, checking the systems so often."

"No, I mean *really* check it out." There was suppressed excitement in her voice. "Let's take it out for a run on the open sea. It's always cooler on the Groalamasan."

"Porlezmozmith will be miffed. She'll call us down for undue exposure of advanced technology to a presteam society."

"Crap. The local fisherfolk have seen us testing it lots of times."

Etienne grinned down at her. "Woman, you have a devilish sense of humor."

"It helps, when you spend your life trying to make sense of other people's cultures. Come on. It'll be fun. And a change."

Etienne was feeling better by the time they left their quarters. They threw together a cold lunch of native edibles. The consistency of the flat, crackerlike bread was unusual but the taste was delightful.

From their quarters it was a short walk down to Level Three, the lowest of the station, where the hydrofoil hung silent in its bay, a sleek delta-shape built of ultralight metals. A compact electric jet protruded from beneath the stern, looking like the mouthparts of a dragonfly nymph. The hydrofoil was an exquisite bit of engineering and despite its fragile appearance, could take a considerable pounding. Inside, the craft was spacious and efficient.

Ignoring the occasional stare of passing thranx maintenance workers, Etienne operated the bay controls. With a soft whirr the double doors parted, revealing the turgid mix of fresh and salt water that lay twenty meters below.

Bow and stern couplers lowered the hydrofoil toward the water. Lyra was already on board, stowing their lunch and running the autoprogram through diagnostic functions. Disdaining the ladders, Etienne wrapped arms and legs around one of the coupler cables and slid down to the boat. A touch on one switch sent the couplers upward, leaving the boat floating free on the water of the delta.

A plexalloy dome enclosed the cockpit where Lyra waited in the pilot's chair. The engine came to loud life as the photovoltaic coating of the boat worked to ensure that the fuel cells which supplied power were fully charged. The air conditioning greeted him with a blast of deliciously cold air.

Lyra nudged the accelerator and turned the wheel. They slid from the shade of the station and headed south. Soon they were clear of the last platform trees and high marsh grasses and out on the open ocean.

〖 III 〗

The steady trade breeze caught them, and the humidity on deck dropped quickly to a tolerable eighty percent while the temperature plunged to one-oh-five. Etienne took advantage of the much cooler weather to move out on deck. Occasionally he turned to smile and wave to Lyra, who remained inside the transparent dome handling the instruments.

Intakes mounted on the front of each foil sucked in water and fed it to the electric jet astern. The jet forced the water through twin high-pressure nozzles, sending the boat skimming over the surface at high speed. The hydrofoil had been designed to function as a river runner but could handle open ocean reasonably well as long as the waves didn't crest dangerously high.

Behind them the Skatandah Delta was a long line of green marking the horizon. Lyra sent them flying southwestward, toward the great city-state of Losithi. They were careful to stand well out to sea, clear of the heavy commerce that crowded the waters beyond the harbor.

A thousand kilometers and more to north and south, the

eight-thousand-meter-high cliffs of the Guntali Plateau probed the sky. From the Losithi–Po Rabi area, distance and planetary curvature made them invisible, though there were places where the cliffs dropped sheer to the sea, a sight unequaled on any other inhabited world. Only where rivers like the Skar had cut their way to the ocean were cultivation and urbanization possible.

Lyra's voice sounded through the intercom membrane built into the cockpit dome. "I've got something on the scanner, a few degrees to starboard. Want to run over and check it out?"

"Sure, I want to check it out. What Porlezmozmith doesn't know won't hurt her." He clung to the railing and watched the foils slit the surface of the sea.

Lyra smiled back at him as she angled the boat slightly to starboard. The moving dot on the scanner was soon within sight—a triple-decked trimaran, a big merchant cruiser and a fine example of Mai shipbuilding. Her three hulls rode low in the water, bursting with trade goods gathered from her journey around the circular sea. If she wasn't based in Losithi she would have just arrived from distant Ko Phisi and before that, Suphum. From here she would move on to Po Rabi on the other side of the Skatandah, thence around to Chienba and points east.

She was making good speed with the wind at her back. The trade winds moved eternally clockwise around the circumference of the Groalamasan. Only in the vicinity of the warm southern pole could a native captain test confused winds and sometimes shorten the homeward journey around the great ocean.

Gesturing and chattering, sailors were already lining the upper decks and scrambling into the rigging for a look at the strange alien vessel. More exciting to a Mai seaman than the hydrofoil's silhouette was the fact that it moved at impossible speed and *against* the wind, not to mention without sails. As Lyra raced the hydrofoil around the massive merchantman for a thorough look, Mai sailors and passengers rushed from deck to deck to keep them in view.

After recording the merchantman for their journal, the Redowls passed among a fleet of shallow-hull fishing boats reaping the rich harvest of life that thrived where salt water mixed with fresh.

As they slowed to thread more easily between the first islets and clusters of pseudopalms, one large craft suddenly moved toward them. Its occupants brandished eager expressions together with long gaffs, axes, and pikes. The Mai would gladly have slit the throats of the two humans in order to gain possession of the invaluable hydrofoil. Etienne experienced unscientific thoughts as Lyra nudged the accelerator and left the would-be pirates in their wake.

"Nasty little bastards," he muttered as he stared astern.

"That's not being very understanding of a primitive culture, Etienne," Lyra said disapprovingly.

"All right, so they're primitive nasty little bastards."

"Avaricious, not vicious," she insisted. "You must try to view them in light of their society's laws. A typically primitive plutocratic culture where personal wealth signifies an individual's social standing. You can't let your own viewpoint affect your observations."

"Like hell I can't. Porlezmozmith feels the same way about the Mai."

"She's an administrator, a bureaucrat, a byte-pusher who knows nothing of xenology and cares less."

"All I said was that some of their ingrained habits could stand some modification."

"Environment dictates their actions, not personal choice."

"What environment?" He made a sweeping gesture toward the nearing line of high trees. "This is a warm, lush land. How do you go from that to a highly combative society?"

"They sublimate most of a natural aggressive drive in competition for commerce and trade. Isn't that better than organized war between the city-states?"

"It's healthier, sure, but from the standpoint of what's civilized there's something to be said for slugging it out with your neighbor toe to toe instead of trying to steal him blind."

"Their attempts at thievery are governed by a strict code of rules, Etienne, which is more than you can say for war."

"Leave me to the structure of the planetary crust, not Mai society. It's cleaner."

"You mean simpler, don't you? There are so few variables

in geology. It makes it easy for you, but I don't envy you. There's no personality, no joy in studying the daily activities of a rock."

"Oh no? Let me tell you..."

It went on in that vein for another few minutes before Lyra finally ended it, as she always did. So many of their discussions lately seemed to end that way.

"Well if you're going to act like that then I'm just not going to talk about it anymore." And she turned her gaze resolutely away from him, directing her attention to the scanner.

He fumed silently all the way back to the station.

A services officer was waiting for them in the boat bay. Etienne shinnied up a cable, prepared to send down the couplers. The officer moved to stand next to him.

"Excuse me." Her symbospeech was rough and unpolished, a good sign that Horseye might be her first off-world post. She clung with tru and foothands to a nearby pillar and her four legs were spread wide. Her whole body shied away from the open bay.

That was understandable. Thranx were good floaters but poor swimmers and their breathing spicules were located on the B-thorax below the neck. A standing thranx could drown in shallow water while still being able to see and hear clearly. That was the only reason why Tslamaina was not a popular duty station among the thranx. The climate was perfect but much of the terrain threatening.

So Etienne didn't ask why the officer was clinging to the pillar for dear life, understood why nothing more was said until the hydrofoil had been drawn up into the bay and the double doors closed beneath it.

"What is it?" he finally inquired as Lyra moved to join them. She adjusted her halter top, did not look at him. Her expression was frosty.

"An ambassador from Po Rabi is due to arrive shortly," the officer announced. "Word has come ahead via courier boat. You have been granted permission to travel Upriver through the Delta along those branches of the Skar controlled by the Moyt of Po Rabi."

Etienne let out a whoop and did a back flip, much to the interest of the thranx working in the bay area. Such a gymnastic feat was beyond them. Lyra stood and smiled at the officer. The argument that had accompanied them back to the station was completely forgotten.

"It's about time," she murmured. "Did the courier say anything about the long delay we've suffered, why or for what reason?"

"Nothing additional was mentioned," the officer said, adding a brief gesture of negativity coupled with third-degree empathy.

"I'll bet I know what finally happened," Etienne declared. "Steamer Station's actually situated a little closer to Losithi than it is to Po Rabi. They must have decided that it was time to forget about hard bargaining and grant clearance before we struck some sort of deal with the Losithians."

"I am sorry to dump dirt on your theory," the thranx said apologetically, "but it would appear they still insist on some kind of token payment."

"But we've been through that a hundred times," Lyra pointed out. "They want advanced technology and we're not allowed to give it to them. Don't tell me they've decided to accept our nontech trade goods?"

"No. Commander Porlezmozmith has devised a method of satisfying them without contravening any of the regulations governing commerce with Class Four-B natives.

"Many areas of high ground do not benefit from seasonal floods of the Skar and so do not receive deposits of fresh silt or yield the crops they otherwise might. The commander has reviewed this with representatives of Po Rabi and they understand the implications quite well.

"Salvenkovdew, who is in charge of the station's chemistry section, has agreed to rig equipment to produce high-quality natural fertilizers for such highland fields. Under current regulations this type of fertilizer does not qualify as a high-tech commodity, so it can be traded to the natives, and the Po Rabians have agreed to accept it as payment."

"Good old Porlez!" Etienne exclaimed. "She's been working on our problem all along and never breathed a word of it."

"Probably didn't want to get our hopes up," Lyra said. "I hope the form of payment isn't to be taken as a comment on the value of our expedition."

"Who cares? We're on our way at last! Thanks," he told the officer. Twin antennae dipped and bobbed by way of gracious reply. "When's this ambassador supposed to get here?"

"The courier could not be certain. Perhaps tomorrow, perhaps several days from tomorrow. I am much gladdened for you both."

"Thanks again. We've been ready to leave for months, though I suppose we can find a few last-minute things to take care of."

"If you will excuse me." The thranx officer released her iron grip on the support pillar and slowly backed clear of the closed bay doors. She looked much happier after she had moved well away from the potential gap.

Deep in conversation, Etienne and Lyra returned to their quarters. Working smoothly they began packing a motile with personal belongings and other last-minute items. They were going to be away from civilization for a long time and there would be no returning for a forgotten chip or bit of clothing.

At least they could consume native foods. That left a lot of room on board for other equipment, extra medical supplies, and tridee cubes.

Stowed in one of the bottom compartments was their cold-weather gear, untouched since its arrival on Tslamaina. They would need the suits when they entered the north polar latitudes. After the relentless heat of the lower Barshajagad, both looked forward to some cheerful freezing.

Two days passed before the ambassador's ship appeared. His retinue was as modest in size and appearance as the vessel which bore them. Ror de-Kelwhoang looked disappointed when he was informed he could not bring any of his escort onto the station, but accepted the determination with diplomatic grace.

In its own modest way the ambassador's official craft was impressive enough. Hired rowers held their double-bladed oars at attention as the ambassador debarked, though they were unable to keep their eyes from wandering toward the strange alien castle that stood high above the water on massive metal legs.

The meeting took place on a deck that encircled the station's lower levels. Etienne and Lyra waited in their briefs and tops. Tslamaina was no place for formal wear.

The ambassador wore little more than the curious humans. His cache du sex was opaque, as was the custom, and his upper garment of silver and copper-colored threads concealed little despite covering him from neck to ankles. It made for a very flashy nonexistent costume. As Lyra had explained, the composition of the material as well as the intricate weave told a knowledgeable onlooker much about the wearer's status, as well as the time of year and what holiday it might be. A good Mai tailor could make much out of little.

Lyra found such details of native life fascinating. Etienne bore her enthusiasm stoically. He was interested in minerals, not millinery.

The Mai ambassador spread his arms wide and turned a slow circle. The movement was fluid but slow, reflective of his advanced age. Porlezmozmith, who had met him before, performed the formal introduction. Her Mai was competent but could not match that of the Redowls; that was due to the thranx larynx, not a lack of linguistic talent.

"Ror de-Kelwhoang, our visitors who would travel your lands, Etienne and Lyra Redowl."

"It is our pleasure to greet you," Lyra added. "We look forward with endless delight to exploring your magnificent country. We are endlessly grateful for the permission to do so granted by your Zanur on behalf of your most powerful and respected city-state."

The ambassador acknowledged the elegant tribute, which Lyra had rehearsed unto boredom, with a slight gesture signifying acceptance. His soft, perceptive eyes seemed fixed on Lyra. That was understandable. She stood eye to eye with the ambassador, which made her tall for a Mai female but not a grotesque scarecrow of a giant like her husband. It was the first time the ambassador had set eyes on the new aliens and he was evidently entranced by the similarities. Etienne had to stifle his amusement at the ambassador's unabashed preoccupation. By Mai standards Lyra's proportions were nothing short of awesome.

"It is with delight that I bring greetings and good wishes from Najoke de-me-Halmur, Moyt of Po Rabi. It has been decided after much careful discussion and agreement on a contract of exchange for certain materials to permit you free passage throughout all the vast territories controlled by our city-state."

"I'm glad everything's worked out," Etienne replied. His Mai was more colloquial than Lyra's, but the ambassador didn't seem to mind the informality of the alien's speech.

"What route will you be taking?"

Etienne smiled disingenuously. He and Lyra had debated the possibility of treachery by the locals and had decided it would be better to appear a little impolite and conceal the exact details of their itinerary.

"We're not certain. Here and there—we travel where our thirst for knowledge draws us."

Experienced diplomat that he was, de-Kelwhoang did not react to the probable evasion. "I envy you your freedom. Alas, my work rarely allows me to vary from a designated course. I have been told of the marvelous devices you possess which enable you to find your way at night and in bad weather as clearly as in cloudless daytime. Nevertheless, we would be remiss in our duty and it would be an offense to our honor if you were come to distress attempting to work your way into the main channel of the great Skar." Etienne was immediately on guard.

"It is also necessary that you carry more than signed documents, which can be forged, to prove that you travel under the protection of all Po Rabi. That way the ignorant bandits and suspicious villagers you may encounter, many of whom have not mastered the art of reading, will allow you to pass freely through their lands."

The ambassador turned and called over the railing toward his boat. A moment later two Mai appeared at the top of the stairs. Their fishnet attire was plain and their attitude deferential.

Etienne's first thought was that they constituted some formal part of the ambassador's entourage, but such was not the case.

"These will be your guides as well as your guarantors of safe passage," de-Kelwhoang announced. He bade each in turn step forward and make gestures of obeisance before the humans.

The male's name was Homat, the female's Irquit. No honorific "de" prefix, Etienne noted. Both wore simple face makeup and had their long hair bound back in single braids in contrast to the ambassador's elegant but thin coiffure. After bending and turning, both extended their hands outward toward the Redowls, palms upward.

After a moment's hesitation Lyra reached out and pressed her own palms to each proffered pair, palm down. The much longer Mai fingers extended well up against her wrist. Each of the six fingers ended in a soft fleshy pad. There were no nails, no residual claws.

Then she stepped back and drew her husband and Porlezmozmith aside, spoke in symbospeech. "What's your opinion, Commander? I don't really want these two along, but I don't want to offend this ambassador either, especially since we're not yet on our way."

"You are the xenologist, Lyra. But it would be bad diplomacy to refuse this offer of aid. They come to you as official representatives of their city. They do not look threatening to me and may indeed prove useful on your journey. Your mastery of Mai customs is far from complete."

"If it was we wouldn't be disappearing Upriver for a few months. Etienne, what's your opinion?"

"If it was up to me I'd rather not have them along, but as Porlez says, this is in the nature of an official presentation and I don't see how we can decline. I'm sure they're being sent along to learn everything they can about us for their Zanur, but I don't see much harm in that. They'll have to stay out on the stern deck anyway, away from any sensitive controls. The air conditioning in the main cabins would kill them in a few hours, or at least make them damn uncomfortable."

"All right then, they can come along. As you point out, Porlez, they may be of real help. If they cause trouble we can hold the Po Rabian Zanur directly responsible. Instruments aside, it'll be nice to have along a couple of locals who are familiar with the territory. Maybe they know how to cook. It would be nice when we enter colder climes to be able to enjoy a real hot meal instead of what the exciter oven throws up at us."

"I guess it's settled then," Etienne said, and couldn't resist adding, "Nice of you to ask for my opinion. Porlez, can you add anything?"

An inflexible thranx face cannot look thoughtful, but the station commander somehow managed to convey that feeling nonetheless.

"Just remember that when you pass above communicator range you're entirely on your own. We have no aircar here and it would be hard for me to muster a rescue party to come out after you under the best of circumstances. We do not care for travel by boat, as you are aware."

"We're aware of the dangers, as we were before we accepted this opportunity," Lyra reminded her. "We're looking forward to our independence and we're quite used to being on our own in difficult country."

"I know, I know," Porlezmozmith said. "I did not mean to sound as if I were chiding you. Once you pass out of communicator range I am no longer responsible for your safety, but I feel concern nonetheless."

Etienne was touched. Such compassion was a widespread thranx attribute and one of those characteristics that had deeply endeared them to humankind, but it still had the power to surprise.

"All the more reason then," he replied, "to have native help with us that we can count on. We'll have ample time to establish the reliability of our guests before we've gone beyond communicator range." He nodded toward the two slightly nervous guides.

"It would seem you are aware of what awaits you," said the commander. "I can think of nothing else to add." They all turned their attention back to the waiting ambassador.

For his part, Ror de-Kelwhoang had listened with interest to the harsh alien babble, which contrasted sharply with the rapid-fire sibilant singsong phrases of his own tongue.

"We thank the Zanur," Lyra said carefully, "for its kind thoughts and accept this offer of assistance with open hearts." Expressions of relief appeared simultaneously on the faces of de-Kelwhoang and the two guides. It would have gone hard on all if the offer had been refused.

Lyra couldn't resist adding to her knowledge of Mai customs. "Etienne and I are mated in the sight of the Ocean and the Oceans of all worlds. What of you?"

"We are not mated," Irquit replied, instantly establishing herself as senior of the pair. "Neither to each other nor others. The Zanur feels," and she made a deferential gesture toward the ambassador, "that in light of the many dangers that may lie in wait for us Upriver, it would be best if those with no family ties were honored by the opportunity to assist you."

"How encouraging," Etienne said dryly.

"I'm curious," Lyra persisted, "did you two volunteer for this, or were you 'honored' by choice of the Zanur?"

"Both apply." De-Kelwhoang stepped in gracefully. "Not all are qualified to serve as guides on such a momentous journey. Both these two have traveled far past the Skatandah. They have knowledge of its currents and its winds as well as many of the peoples you will encounter. I assure you that we have gone to great lengths to provide the most competent helpers Po Rabi has to offer."

Not wanting to risk impugning the Zanur's motives, much less its methods, Lyra switched to more mundane matters. "Irquit, we have some storage space available on our boat. What will you need to bring with you?"

"Very little. Some simple kitchen utensils and a single change of clothing. We will eat your food or purchase our own along the way. The Zanur has provided us with money. We can also cook for you, if you wish." Etienne looked pleased. "Both Homat and I are accomplished foragers."

Foraging was a word with many meanings in the Mai language, Lyra knew, referring to the ability to bargain sharply, scavenge efficiently, or steal without getting caught.

"We also," Homat said, speaking for the first time, "brought no weapons with us, having been told that should we meet hostile peoples you would manage our defense. We did not wish to bring killing instruments with us."

"Very thoughtful of you." Clearly Irquit is in charge of the little company, Lyra thought. But there was a natural shyness about Homat she found appealing. "That's all settled, then. If you would like to come help us with our loading—"

"No thank you," Irquit said hastily. "If you do not object we would much prefer to remain outside." She was staring with wide Mai eyes at the imposing alien structure. "If we are not to depart until tomorrow we can sleep outside, here, on mats."

"Are you afraid?" Etienne asked thoughtlessly.

Lyra shot him an angry glance, snapped in terranglo, "Don't you have any empathy for alien psychology? Can't you see they're trying to cover their fear gracefully?"

"I only thought that since these two are going to spend the next several months exploring strange country on a strange craft, they ought to start getting used to strangeness as soon as possible."

"They are not afraid," the ambassador said. He was picking his words with unusual care, Lyra thought. "There is something else."

"What something else?" Lyra asked, still upset over her husband's lack of sensitivity.

Ror de-Kelwhoang looked uncomfortable. "I would rather not say."

"Don't worry. We're scientists, here to study and learn about your ways and your world. We're just as interested in what you dislike as in what you like."

De-Kelwhoang did not look in Porlezmozmith's direction. "It is a question of appearances, you see. We place much value on appearance. There is truth in appearances. It is only that we have certain evil spirits cast in the form of ..."

"There is no need for apology." Porlezmozmith knew where the ambassador's desperate circumlocutions were heading. "We are used to shape prejudice." She spoke to the two guides. "Remain by yourselves outside, if it is your wish."

Strange, Etienne thought. How could the Mai fear the thranx simply because of their shape? Lyra would have told him to read his history.

"We do not mean to give offense," de-Kelwhoang said quickly.

"None taken," the commander assured him. "This is something we are used to dealing with. I and my assistants will withdraw. It was a delight to meet you, Ambassador. You and your fellows are welcome anytime at Steamer Station. As are those," she couldn't help adding undiplomatically but with ill-concealed enjoyment, "of great Losithi."

The ambassador stiffened at the mention of Po Rabi's rival but, good tactician that he was, retained his composure.

"Thank you."

Porlezmozmith and the rest of the thranx contingent departed, leaving the Redowls alone on the deck with the Mai.

"We wish you much delight and good fortune in your studies," de-Kelwhoang said earnestly. He did not look at the two guides. "We of Po Rabi hold scholarship in high regard, unlike the rulers of certain other city-states. We hope you may see your way clear to sharing your knowledge with us after you return."

"That is our intention," Lyra told him. "This is your world and we are guests upon it, and we are thankful for your assistance." She performed a gesture indicating great appreciation.

Reassured, de-Kelwhoang turned and walked slowly down the stairway ramp. Waiting hands helped him back into the boat. On command the oarsmen dipped their paddles and pushed away from the support pillar where they had tied up. The Redowls watched for a while as the boat turned eastward. Then their attention shifted to their unexpected guests. Homat and Irquit waited patiently, their small bundles of cooking utensils and personal effects looking humble indeed.

"You're sure you want to sleep out here?"

"Please, de-Lyra," said Irquit, "we would feel more comfortable and would be out of everyone's way." She ventured the Mai smile, a thin parting of the lips that barely revealed the small fine teeth beyond. The corners of the mouth did not turn up.

"As you prefer."

"When are we to leave? We have heard so much of your wondrous boat and are most anxious to begin this great adventure with you."

Homat smiled too but said nothing. Not the loquacious type, Etienne decided. Not that it mattered. The two Mai weren't coming along to provide casual conversation.

"Tomorrow morning," he informed them. "We're almost ready and it'll take just a few minutes to put our boat in the water."

Irquit looked puzzled. "It is not in the water now?"

"No. It waits suspended by," he tried to shape his thicker

[35]

lips and less bulbous cheeks to form the correct expression, "you'll see tomorrow. Showing is better than talking."

"Yes, better than talking," Irquit agreed. She looked nervously toward the dark building beyond, abode of grotesque bug-things. "We will be left alone out here?"

"Yes." Lyra assured her. "Though our friends are used to a life beneath the ground and have a more flexible work–sleep cycle than we do, they still prefer to sleep during the hours of darkness. No one will disturb you out here and you won't be in the way."

Irquit smiled again. "I am much delighted that we are going with you."

"And we are much delighted to have you along," Lyra replied. "We'll see you again in the morning."

"Come morning." The two females exchanged the palm-to-palm caress a second time, though Lyra was convinced she'd never be able to compensate properly for the lack of a sixth digit.

[IV]

The sun was barely aloft as the hydrofoil was lowered into the calm water beneath the station. The readout that indicated air temperature clung desperately to the hundred-degree mark, and there was no chance it would drop any lower. The Mai stood at the base of the loading ramp which had been dropped to the boat's stern deck, looking chilled and uncomfortable.

Afire with excitement that had been lost during months of waiting, the Redowls ignored them. When the last supplies had been taken aboard and stowed, they thought to offer moral assistance to their suddenly reluctant passengers.

Homat and Irquit boarded warily, eyes darting anxiously about in search of sails and oars. When Etienne tested the engine, both dashed for the rail and clung tightly to the unyielding metal.

Lyra wiped morning sweat from beneath her sun visor and tried to comfort them. "It's all right, it's only our engine. The device that moves the boat. It's loud, but harmless. The spirits within are fully contained."

"There are no sails," Irquit observed cautiously.

"Or oarsmen," Homat added.

"No, there aren't. We move by taking water in at the front of our craft and pushing it out the back much faster than we take it in."

"What pushes the water?" Irquit asked, slowly releasing her grasp on the railing; it was undignified. Homat continued to hang on tightly.

"Our engine. It would take a long time to explain. Maybe once we're on our way I'll try." She left Irquit with a reassuring smile and descended the ladder to the upper cabin.

"De-Lyra, I am fearful!" Irquit gave Homat a disapproving look, but Lyra paused and eyed him pityingly.

"All right then, come on inside. But you won't like it."

Homat followed her, Irquit tagging along because she didn't want to miss anything. Once below, the truth of Lyra's words became immediately apparent. At a cabin temperature of eighty degrees, both Mai found themselves shivering.

Etienne greeted them in the transparent bubble of the cockpit, left explanations to Lyra. Though she used simple terms and kept her science as basic as possible, it soon became clear that such concepts as electricity and light-emitting diodes were beyond the comprehension of their guests.

Before long Homat confessed, "I think I would rather be fearful than frozen," and he led the retreat back toward the stern.

Once outside he hopped around for a few minutes until his system warmed, then busied himself arranging personal effects on the deck. The Mai would sleep where they cooked, away from the terrible arctic climate their hosts appeared to favor.

Reassurances and explanations notwithstanding, it took Lyra another hour of quiet coaxing to convince them that the boat wasn't going to devour them if they let loose of the rail when Etienne raced the engine and sent the hydrofoil leaping forward. She showed them how the boat lifted clear of the surface on its twin metal blades, explained how that enabled them to move Upriver at seventy kilometers an hour.

As time passed and the smoothness and exhilaration of the ride overcame initial fears, both Mai not only relaxed but began to enjoy the journey, though from time to time

Homat made signs designed to keep them from striking a submerged log or drifting helplessly toward the clouds.

Villages crowded the shores of tiny tree-covered islets. Astonished children barely had time to shout before the hydrofoil had raced past their disbelieving elders. The boat's scanner picked out fishing craft ahead, enabling Etienne to steer safely around them long before they came into view.

Larger islands appeared as they moved farther Upriver. There the water had receded from the floods sufficient to permit planting of grains and other foodstuffs. Some villagers were engaged in crude but effective aquaculture, from the raising of crustaceans to the gathering of waterfowl. All looked askance at the spirit boat that roared past their homes and scattered birds and amphibians in its wake.

There seemed no end to the villages. According to the initial satellite surveys, the Skatandah Delta was the most densely populated section of Tslamaina, which was why it had been chosen as the site of the first Commonwealth outpost.

As they traveled toward the equator the temperature intensified, if that was possible, and no occasional sea breeze battled the humidity. Despite months of acclimatization, the Redowls spent the majority of their time sequestered in the air-conditioned interior of their craft. Merely to step out on deck risked a shock to the system. Homat and Irquit were right at home on the stern deck, however, and readily exchanged muted comments about the fragility of the human system.

Homat made a game of trying to outguess the scanner, sitting on the bow and staring at the water in search of submerged rocks or other obstacles. He always lost, but the acuity of his eyesight impressed both Etienne and Lyra.

By analyzing the current and the debris the water carried, the hydrofoil's computer could make a decision on which branch to take, but it was still nice to have Irquit confirm the choice. Without the computer or their guides they could have spent years wandering through the Skatandah in a futile attempt to locate the main course of the Skar.

As the days slid past in superheated study, the Redowls found themselves more and more grateful for the presence of their two passengers. Having completely overcome their fear of the boat, the Mai had revealed themselves as efficient, helpful, and good company. Lyra derived an added benefit from being able to study their reactions to new discoveries, additional information on Mai society which she regularly entered into her scientific log.

They also turned out to be excellent cooks as well as sharp bargainers at the villages where they stopped to purchase supplies, and except for periodic raids on the salt tablet and vitamin stores, the humans' stock of packaged food remained nearly untouched.

Irquit and Homat didn't try to hide their delight. Not only were they enjoying themselves, but Lyra knew they must be anticipating the honors that would come their way after they returned home. Their careers were made. She was pleased for both of them.

It was clear that those Mai fortunate enough to make their homes in the delta were more content than their urbanized relations. Government control so far from Po Rabi was lax, food was abundant, and there was little to inspire conflict. The social setup would change, Lyra suspected, once they left the lush Skatandah region behind and emerged into the main channel of the Skar. Farming above the delta would require more effort and extensive irrigation. Competition would be tough, as it was within the city-state boundaries.

The heat, the friendliness of the villagers, the lazy days passed in discussion and study produced in the Redowls a feeling of inner security. It was left to Homat to remind them that they were traveling on an alien world and not Earth's relatively benign waters.

Etienne had gone over the side and was leaning back against one of the curving support struts that ran from hydrofoil to hull, trailing one leg in the cool water and letting the spray from the foil wash over him. They were traveling fast enough to alleviate concern about glass leeches and he was completely relaxed beneath the refreshing spray.

He gave Homat a curious glance as the Mai started to descend alongside him, carrying a metal prod. Now that he'd overcome his initial fear of the strange vessel, the shy native clambered nimbly over it while displaying an agility Etienne could only envy.

It was the prod that caught his eye. "What's that for?"

Homat gestured with the metal. Etienne wiped spray from his face and looked behind him.

Attached to the foil just beneath the glassy surface of the water and slowly creeping toward Etienne's feet was a thin dark shape, three meters long and as thick as his arm.

"Sandrush," Homat said curtly as he worked his way around the strut until he was holding on behind Etienne.

"Poisonous? Parasite?"

"No. Inhaler."

"What does it inhale? Blood?"

"Inhale you." Etienne watched with interest as the Mai used the prod to pry open the creature's wide round mouth. The teeth were small and curved inward. The jaw dislocated itself and Homat spread the gape wider still. As they watched the sandrush began to fill helplessly with river water until it had swollen to four times its normal size. The dull green membrane was evidently capable of expanding to hold prey larger than itself, and the meaning of Homat's words became ghoulishly clear.

Eventually the pressure of the water proved too much for the powerful suckers that lined the sandrush's ventral side. It relinquished its grip and fell away astern. Etienne was suitably impressed.

"If it gets a hold of you, very bad," Homat explained unnecessarily. "It won't let go unless it dies and sandrush is very hard to kill. Swallow you whole." He turned to climb back up toward the lower deck.

Etienne wondered at the flexibility that would allow an animal to expand so far beyond its normal size even as he thoughtfully removed his legs from the water. He wondered what other charming native fauna lurked just beneath the surface of the river, following the boat hungrily.

Since there was little here for him to study he did most of the piloting, leaving Lyra free to record her impressions of village life and culture within the Skatandah. While the communities there differed little from those clustered around Steamer Station she continued to take her usual copious notes. Even the tiniest change in social structure or clothing or fishing methods was occasion for excitement.

Gradually the marshlands and islands of the delta began to fade behind them. Fewer platform trees and pseudopalms were seen, more open water and less land. An unknowing observer might have concluded that the Redowls had taken a wrong turn and were heading once more out into the open ocean.

But the water they skimmed over was now almost entirely fresh. They had entered the main body of the Skar, a river large enough to make the Amazon or Nile or any of the other known rivers of the Commonwealth look like a meandering creek. From the center of the river it was impossible to tell you weren't traveling on a freshwater sea, because there was no sign of land to starboard or port. Beyond invisible banks the cliffs that marked the edge of the Guntali rose unseen toward a cloud-flecked sky.

Etienne eased the hydrofoil to starboard until the shoreline hove into view. Thereafter they were able to cruise on autopilot, allowing Lyra to concentrate on her note-taking and leaving Etienne free to stare through the telescope mounted atop the observation mast. Numerous villages dotted the bank. Farther inland he saw farming communities and small commercial centers. At the extreme range of the scope's resolving power he could discern the first gentle slopes, evidence that they really were traveling up a river canyon.

While the temperature crept toward the hundred thirty mark in early afternoon, the humidity fell slightly. It required an effort to remain outside the boat's air-conditioned interior for longer than half an hour. Lyra spent much of her time outside chatting with the owners of the small trading boats that pulled alongside whenever they stopped. While she dictated notes, Homat and Irquit bargained for provisions. Irquit did most of the trading while Homat attended to the cooking, having mastered the electric oven the Redowls insisted he use instead of the wood-burning stove he had brought on board.

They were then a thousand kilometers north of Steamer Station and the mouth of the delta, cruising the smooth back of the river Skar at a steady ninety kph. They had barely begun their journey.

Everywhere the Mai citizenry was friendly and open, though more primitive than those of the advanced societies of the city-states that ringed the great world ocean. All was not peaceful and pastoral along the river, however. The presence of village stockades and other fortifications hinted at sporadic conflict, and there were those who were less than overawed by the peculiar visitors' advanced technology.

"Hon, I think you'd better have a look at this." Etienne kept his gaze on the scanner as he took the boat off autopilot.

"What is it?" Lyra's voice sounded over the intercom in the cockpit.

"Ships ahead, lots of 'em. Fishing boats by the computer image."

"What's notable about that? I'm busy, Etienne."

"Lyra, there are at least a hundred boats. That's not usual, is it?"

"No, it's not." The intercom went quiet for a moment and when she spoke again her tone was thoughtful instead of impatient. "Are you sure?"

"I'm quite capable of following the readouts," he said sarcastically. "It isn't normal, is it, for a fishing fleet to attain that size?"

"Not from what we've seen thus far, no, but maybe it's normal up here."

"Why don't you ask Irquit?"

A sigh whispered at him from the grid as she put her beloved work aside. "I suppose I'd better."

Irquit sat on the open rear deck of the hydrofoil, cleaning vegetables for the next meal. Purple and maroon predominated, but that didn't detract from the tastiness, Lyra knew. Homat peeled tubers by hand.

"Irquit, my husband says that there are at least a hundred fishing boats in the river ahead of us." Neither of the Mai expressed surprise at this calm revelation, having already become familiar with much of the hydrofoil's instrumentation. They called the cockpit scanner the iron eye.

Irquit looked uncertain. "That is more than I have ever heard of fishing the river. There are never so many grouped together down by Po Rabi. Is de-Etienne certain they are just fishermen?"

"We can't tell that through the iron eye. What could they be doing except fishing?"

"It could be a war fleet," Homat suggested tentatively.

"Out to attack one of the villages? This doesn't seem to be a poor area."

"It is sometimes simpler," said Homat with innocent wisdom, "to take rather than to work, no matter how easy the work may be."

She could have argued the point but it was not the time to engage in idle sociological speculation. "Tell that to my husband, Homat."

He made a sign of acknowledgment and worked his way around the boat until he was standing outside the transparent dome of the cockpit. He could see Etienne clearly. Condensation was banished from the clear acrylic by the silent efforts of special air circulators. He leaned toward the speaking membrane.

"De-Etienne, I fear the many vessels you say lie ahead of us."

"Is there any way you can tell what they're up to by looking at them?"

"Yes. If they have their gill nets out I think they're just fishing and not ready for war. Gill nets cost too much to risk in a fight."

Etienne considered. "Better tell Lyra to come forward, then. The iron eye can't distinguish something as wispy as nets. We'll need somebody to make visual confirmation."

"I'm already here, Etienne." The membrane picked up his wife's voice before she stepped into view. Irquit was with her. "You don't have to tell me my job."

"I wasn't telling you your job," he snapped, "I just— never mind. We'll be on top of them in a minute." He examined the crowded screen. "I'll have to slow down or we're liable to run over somebody."

"We've never run into more than four or five boats fishing together before. Too much competition," Lyra murmured. "It doesn't fit the established pattern." Masted wooden shapes were appearing on the horizon ahead.

The roar of the electric jet dropped to a rumble and the hydrofoil's speed dropped radically until the hull once more broke water. As they began to pass among the component vessels, the fishing fleet was even more impressive up close than it had appeared on the scanner.

The craft that plied the warm waters of the Skatandah

Delta rarely required the muscles of more than three or four fishermen. These great bargelike vessels each boasted two dozen crew or more. They lay across the Skar in three rows, blocking a decent part of the river's considerable breadth, and were roped together.

To Etienne's relief they clearly saw the huge gill nets strung between the ships. Since they didn't drift with the current they must utilize heavy anchors to hold them in place. Women and children manned the nets and lines alongside the men.

Every tenth barge was a vast floating platform nearly as big as some of the ocean-going trimarans they'd encountered out in the Groalamasan. The reason for their extraordinary size, as well as for the number of fishing craft, soon became apparent. It had to do with the size of the catch.

Some twenty vessels were swinging close together, bumping sides and full of organized confusion as their crews strained at nets and lines. The water between began to froth and bubble, was finally broken by the emergence of an immense rainbow-hued head. More glowing color breached the surface and the fisherfolk redoubled their efforts to haul in their whale-sized catch.

"Arwawl!" Homat exclaimed excitedly. "I've tasted its dried flesh but never seen one before. They run only in the main river and come nowhere near Po Rabi's shallows."

The chanting of the fishermen was a steady, triumphant chorus now as they hauled in the huge interlocked nets. As they did so ten ships passed to port of the immense barge, ten to starboard. The barge crew lent its muscle to the task and long gaffs, attached to winches, were brought into use. Slowly the arwawl was hauled onto the deck, bending the stern beneath the surface of the river for long moments before the silvery tonnage could be better distributed.

The single catch was enough to feed many villages, Etienne mused, but the fleet apparently wasn't satisfied. Still other nets were out, trailing from the less fortunate boats. He admired the fisherfolk's persistence.

It was left to Irquit, less mesmerized by the efficiency of the fleet, to sound a warning. She moved closer to Lyra, who was intent on recording the fishing with her instruments.

Irquit performed a diminutive half bow. "Forgive me for troubling you, de-Lyra, but I think we are in danger."

"What?" Lyra strained to refocus her attention. "What's that, Irquit?"

The Mai stepped to the railing and pointed over the bow. "I have been watching those four ships." Lyra raised her gaze, saw nothing unusual about the quartet of fishing craft dead ahead.

"What about them? They are fishing, like their companions."

"Not like their companions," Irquit argued. "They are moving toward us. They should be anchored in place, holding their nets against the flow of the Skar. They are drifting downstream."

"Maybe they're trying to reposition themselves in a better spot. Fishermen move all the time."

"I'm sure they are moving to a better spot, but not to catch fish, I think."

Lyra frowned. "What makes you think so?"

"Two drift to our left, two to the right. Their nets lie between. If we continue on this course they will soon ensnare us."

"I'm sure it's not intentional," Lyra replied, but inwardly she wasn't so sure. The boats were very close now and the big gill nets lay concealed by the rolling water. "We'll warn them clear."

"The nets of the Upriver fisherfolk are wondrous strong, de-Lyra," Irquit said anxiously. "I don't know that even your spirit boat could escape from them. There is something more. See how busy the crews are?"

Lyra squinted, peered through her recorder's telephoto for a closer look. "I see. Isn't that normal?"

"I am no fisherwoman, but I have visited this part of the Skar before. To travel downstream is simple. One simply raises the anchors and drifts with the current. Never have I seen so much activity surrounding so easy a task. When one works that hard at something that simple, one usually has something to hide."

Lyra thought a moment, leaned over to call toward the cockpit. "Irquit thinks the four fishing boats coming Downriver toward us might be trying to ensnare us in their nets."

Etienne wished the hydrofoil's scanner could provide more detail. "What's your opinion, Lyra?"

"I don't know what to think, but I don't want to take any unnecessary chances. I'd like to find out so that we'll have a better idea what to expect in case the same situation reoccurs in the future. Let's do our guesswork now."

He nodded. "We'll let them play all their cards, then. Tell Irquit not to worry. I can handle it."

"Handle?" Irquit was trying to divide her attention between the stocky human female and the suspiciously active fishing boats dead ahead. "What does de-Etienne mean 'handle?'" The boats were near enough now for the *otolk* wood floats to stand out clearly against the water.

"He means he's ready to deal with any hostile moves."

"But you must move away, move to avoid them while there is still time! I know that the spirit boat can move quickly to the side, and..."

"Have a calming, Irquit. Etienne knows what he's doing. Everything's under control."

A gentle shudder ran through the hydrofoil's hull as the bow made contact with the heavy nets and two of the oblong floats. As they continued Upriver, pushing the net with their bow, the four fishing boats were drawn toward each other...and the hydrofoil was caught between them.

Explosive roars of triumph sounded from all four Mai vessels and all pretense vanished. It was suddenly clear that they were interested in tougher quarry than fish. Gaffs gave way to long pikes and spears, and the chanting that accompanied the appearance of these weapons was very different from that which had provided a quaint backdrop to the landing of the *arwawl*.

Homat began to moan and rock from side to side. "Doomed we are. These river primitives will show us no mercy!"

Irquit merely looked resigned. "I warned you, de-Lyra."

"And you were right," the xenologist replied calmly as she turned again toward the cockpit bubble. "We've established their real intentions, Etienne. I've made my recordings." She paused as something whizzed past overhead. "Let's not hang around. They have bows."

"Don't you want to observe native weaponry in action?" She ducked as a wood-and-bone shaft splintered against the deck. "Don't get funny, honey. If you want to linger, we can switch places first."

"Never mind." He grinned at her as he gunned the engine. The jet nozzle pivoted a hundred and eighty degrees until it was facing toward the bow.

"Hold tight," Lyra warned the two morose Mai. They barely had time to reach for handholds before the hydrofoil shot backward in full reverse. Suddenly nothing kept the four fishing boats apart. The nets fell limp into the river.

The chanting subsided as the would-be pirates watched their quarry vanish astern at sixty kph. Then crews rushed to the oars as all four crews realized there was nothing to stop their momentum. Frantic yells and curses replaced the warlike chanting of a moment earlier.

Etienne slowed and reversed direction once more, watching with interest as the four fishing boats, still linked together by their nets and lines, slewed inexorably toward each other. Loud snapping sounds filled the air as hastily manned oars were splintered against colliding hulls. Curses were drowned by shouts of confusion and conflicting orders as nets became tangled with rudders and broken oars.

Keeping well beyond arrow range, he edged the hydrofoil easily around their would-be captors, toward the center of the river. A few of the unhappy fisherfolk, unable to attack with their short bows, settled for bombarding the spirit boat with ferocious insults. Homat stifled his laughter at their plight long enough to translate those couched in the local dialect or too complex for Lyra to understand. She patiently entered them all into her journal under a subheading drolly labeled MAI INVECTIVE—LOCAL VARIANTS AND DIALECTS. All grist for the xenological mill.

Etienne half-expected some of the other fisherfolk to aid their brethren in the attack, but he was pleasantly disappointed. Instead of joining in, the Mai who'd stood to the side to watch were lining the sides of their own vessels and cheering the spirit boat's escape.

"That's not the reaction I expected," he shouted toward the speaker membrane. "Irquit, what's going on? They don't seem angry at our escape."

"Why should they be? They chose not to participate in the attack on us. So they do not share in its failure. They admire the successful, no matter where they come from. So they applaud our escape." Irquit leaned over the railing to peer astern. The four badly entangled fishing boats continued their steady drift Downriver.

"By the time they get themselves separated, de-Etienne, they will have a long hard row Upriver to return to their homes. That will give them time to think anew about trying to capture a spirit boat. I hope not many were hurt. There is much confusion."

"And I hope half fall overboard and drown." Homat spat over the side. "Let the river eat them. May they stew in their own urine! We meant them no harm and still they would have slain us!"

Lyra paused in her note-taking. "It's difficult for poor people to turn down the chance to acquire great wealth, Homat. I'm not defending their actions, understand, but I can empathize with their feelings." She had to use four connected nouns to make the idea of empathy comprehensible to the Mai guide. "Do you think we'll be subject to more such attacks?"

Irquit made a gesture of uncertainty. "Who can predict? As you say, de-Lyra, your spirit boat represents power and wealth to all who set eyes upon it. Your property will be coveted from the Skatandah to the region of ice." Another thin smile. "Clearly any who try will have much difficulty in taking it."

"We can take care of ourselves," Lyra assured her.

"That is proven. I will not dance with worry next time. None can threaten the spirit boat."

"Oh, we're not omnipotent," Lyra corrected her, "but we're far from defenseless. If necessary we can do more than just dodge gill nets."

"Yes. I have seen the weapons that rest in the holders alongside the round tiller de-Etienne steers the spirit boat with."

"Those are only for use in dire emergency," Lyra said firmly. "We carry them to defend us against dangerous animals, not intelligent peoples. My Zanur would be very upset with us if we used them against your people."

[49]

"My people are the people of Po Rabi," Irquit replied, indicating with gentle bloodthirstiness that it wouldn't bother her in the least if it became necessary to shoot a few riverfolk. Lyra sighed inwardly. Once upon a time, back in the tribal days, her ancestors had felt similarly. A few throwbacks still did.

The kilometers slid beneath the hydrofoil's keel by the hundreds, the Skar still running wide and slow, the distant walls of the Barshajagad still rendered invisible by haze and distance. Lyra began to enjoy the bargaining for supplies that took place whenever they pulled in to shore.

"You can learn a lot by watching Homat and Irquit," she told Etienne on more than one occasion.

He would nod politely, but the methodology of native barter didn't intrigue him. Instead, he spent the trading time sequestered atop the observation mast with one eye glued to the telescope, studying the nearing lower slopes of the canyon with their irrigated fields and elaborate terraces.

As a precaution, they spent each night well out in the middle of the Skar. The hydrofoil's autoalarms would alert them to the presence of any potential danger.

Occasionally, Etienne would vary the routine by climbing the mast to turn the telescope skyward, quizzing himself by trying to identify the strange constellations overhead. On this particular early morning there was no rain and few clouds. The humidity was lower than usual and the temperature had plunged into the nineties. He was very surprised to see Homat's wide-eyed hairless face appear outside the transparent scope enclosure. The guide looked nervous, and not from the height.

Etienne unfastened the plastic to admit the edgy Mai.

"Something wrong, Homat?" he inquired solicitously.

"I—I must talk with you, de-Etienne."

"Must be important to bring you up here from beneath a warm blanket."

"It is, very important."

"Just a second." Etienne swung the telescope aside on its gimbaled mount to make more room, thoughtfully shut off the blower that was pouring refrigerated air into the enclosure.

As soon as the temperature had warmed, Homat entered and sealed the entrance behind him. In the cramped space atop the mast Etienne was more conscious than ever of his bulk compared to that of the diminutive native.

"What is it?" Beyond Homat he could see two of Tslamaina's four moons gleaming on the river. The other two would appear within the hour, he knew.

"For a long time I have meant to do this, but I did not know how to do it and have not had a chance to do it."

"Do what?"

"Warn you, de-Etienne. You and de-Lyra are in great danger."

Etienne leaned back in the narrow swivel chair and smiled at the native's concern. He swung one leg idly back and forth.

"We're in constant danger, yes. The fisherfolk we just ran into Downriver demonstrated that."

"No, no!" Homat whispered intently. "Not that. The danger of which I speak is nearer and more insidious."

Etienne studied the guide's face closely. "Homat, what is it you're so frightened of?"

"I am not bold by nature," he explained anxiously. "I have traveled as widely as I have not because I desired to but because I was ordered to ao so by those who employed me.

"Now I have found that I cannot go on without telling what I know, de-Etienne. Something within pushes me to make confession. All my life I have been a small person, one who scrapes and nods and follows the orders of others. You and de-Lyra have treated me most fair, better than I have ever been treated by any other employers. I have come to like you very much. For the first time in my life, someone makes me feel important. It is a feeling I want to keep."

"Why shouldn't you?" Etienne found himself taken aback by the unexpectedly emotional confession.

"Because of Irquit."

"Irquit? What can she do to you?"

Homat's wide eyes darted nervously around the plastic enclosure. "Are you sure no one can hear what we say?"

"Of course I'm sure. The intercom's not on and we're high above the rest of the boat. Homat, explain yourself.

Why are you so afraid of Irquit all of a sudden? I hadn't noticed that she's been treating you badly. She's been very helpful."

"That is her task. To be helpful until..." he hesitated. "Mai-with-Hair, remember that what I am about to tell you is worth my life—Irquit is the direct representative of the Zanur of Po Rabi."

Etienne was beginning to lose patience with his visitor. His viewing time was slipping away and he wanted to get in some sleep before sunrise.

"We already know that, Homat. You are, too."

"No! I am a hired guide. She is responsible only to the Zanur itself. Tell me, de-Etienne, have you not remarked on her intense interest in your spirit boat and its functions?"

"Naturally. Do you think we're only attuned to technology? My wife is particularly sensitive to the actions of," he almost said primitive peoples, but quickly changed it to "other individuals. Irquit's interest is only natural. Lyra ought to know. She's studied guests on other worlds beyond this one."

"I know what that means, de-Etienne," Homat replied somberly. "Tell me: on those other worlds did she ever encounter any assassins?"

[V]

Etienne's smile vanished and he sat up straighter in his chair. His impatience was replaced by sudden interest.

"Would you mind explaining what you mean, Homat?"

The guide shifted nervously. "Your wonderful craft makes use of many impossible-to-understand spirits, de-Etienne, but it seems to me not so difficult to command them."

"Operation is highly simplified for users not technically oriented, yes."

"Simple enough for Irquit to operate?"

"Maybe, if she were to stick to basic go—stop type directions. What about it?"

Homat gestured forward, past the moonlit bow. "Tomorrow we are to stop at the village of Changrit to restock our larder. Changrit has an alliance with Po Rabi."

"I didn't think Po Rabi's influence extended this far north," Etienne told him.

"Changrit is independent. It is a trade alliance only, but that is enough when much is at stake. Long before Ambassador de-Kelwhoang delivered us to you to serve as your guides, river riders were sent racing north to Changrit. An

[53]

understanding was achieved with the Moyt of Changrit." He brushed absently at the single knot of long hair that trailed from the top of his head.

"The ambush is to take place at night, while you are anchored out in the Skar and less on guard. Your spirit boat is to be taken so that its secrets and treasures may be shared by Changrit and Po Rabi." He hesitated only for a moment. "You and your mate, of course, will not survive."

"I see," Etienne said quietly. "Suppose Irquit proves unable, despite her studies, to operate the boat?"

"All is planned for. In that event it is to be loaded upon a barge and shipped Downriver."

"I don't see any problem, Homat. We just won't stop near Changrit for supplies. Even if they're lying in wait for us out in the river we can simply run past them."

"It may not be so easy, de-Etienne. Even now word is relayed along the riverbank marking our progress. The fighters of Changrit will be ready to challenge you no matter when you try to pass their city."

"I'm curious. How did the Zanur plan to explain our disappearance, in the event our friends back at Steamer Station learned of it?"

"You have been watched and studied. Not all who sought to talk with your mate while you waited to travel were simple fisherfolk. Changrit was chosen because it is the northernmost city with which Po Rabi has an alliance and it was believed to lie beyond range of your talk-through-air spirits."

"That's right enough."

"There is no reason why your friends should connect your disappearance to Po Rabi or any other city. For all they will know you perished when your boat sank in the Skar, as many boats do."

"And what if our friends come looking for us and find our boat in the possession of the Zanur, or the Moyt of Changrit?"

"Then it is to be said that you were swamped by an arwawl, that this was seen from shore, and that your boat was towed to safety but not in time to save its crew. I am not privy to all the details, as Irquit is."

"But they had to tell you this much so that you could help at the critical moment."

"Yes." Homat dropped his gaze, unwilling to meet his benefactor's eyes. "My ancestors are ashamed."

"All right, you've told me about the proposed attack. That doesn't make Irquit an assassin."

"She will become one only if it proves necessary," Homat explained. "She is there to make certain the attack does not fail. When it comes she will pretend surprise and will appear to aid you, but if it looks like the attack may fail, she is to choose a moment when you are not on guard to push you overboard or put a knife in your back. Have you not noticed her skill on things bigger than vegetables." He looked away.

"I just thought she was a deft cook," he muttered.

"Deft indeed, de-Etienne. I have seen her demonstrate her skill on things bigger than vegetables." He looked away. "I was to help in all this, of course."

"Of course," Etienne said dryly. He reached out and pushed a button. A tired moan came from the grid.

"What is it? I was just getting into a really decent dream."

"Would you come up here a minute, hon? I'm observing something I think you'd find intriguing."

"Come on, Etienne. Maybe tomorrow night."

"It may be less visible tomorrow night. I wish you'd come up *now*. Our position tomorrow will be radically different."

"All right, all right," she snapped back at him. "This better be good."

He waited in the enclosure with the nervous Homat until a sleepy-eyed Lyra had ascended the mast to join them. There was very little room to move around with three of them atop the platform.

"What now?" She was still blinking sleep from her eyes, but her expression turned to one of confusion when she noticed Homat.

"Where's Irquit?" Etienne asked her.

"Irquit? What's she got to do with?...On the stern deck, I would imagine, blissful in the arms of the local representative of Morpheus. What the hell's going on up here?"

"Homat has something to tell you."

Lyra listened quietly as the guide repeated the tale he had told Etienne. She considered quietly for several long moments once he'd finished.

"We could turn back. We're scientists, not soldiers-of-fortune and not hard-contact explorers. We're not prepared to deal with large-scale local antagonism. If this town is linked by treaty and duplicity to Po Rabi, we can apply for clearance and protection with the Zanur of Losithi."

Etienne looked doubtful. "Wouldn't work. Word will reach Po Rabi and they'll know we found them out. That could put them into open conflict with Losithi. We don't want to be responsible for starting a major local war. Besides which there's no guarantee we'd fare any better with the Zanur of Losithi than we already have with Po Rabi. Better the devil you know, et cetera."

"They are as envious of your technology as is the Zanur of Po Rabi," Homat agreed.

"Then there's the distance we've already come. Returning and retracing our steps would take at least a month, even if we were lucky enough to obtain immediate permission from Losithi. We've passed the equator and we're above the worst of the climate. Not that this oven has suddenly become comfortable, but it's bound to improve.

"I've no desire to retrace our steps, restudy what we've already thoroughly recorded, and I'm sure you don't either, Lyra. And there's always the chance that Losithi could arrange a similar kind of ambush when we resumed our journey, and they'd be better prepared for us than these Changritites are likely to be. The geology's finally starting to get interesting, Lyra. I don't want to go back to taking mud samples for an additional two months. Despite Homat's fears I don't imagine we'll have any trouble passing through whatever barrier of nets and ropes the locals can erect."

"I know that," Lyra agreed. "It's not that. I just don't want to harm any natives. You know what a resident commissioner would have to say about that."

"There's no resident commissioner on Tslamaina. Not advanced enough yet. No one's going to know anything, and even if we were found out we'd just tell them that we had to defend ourselves, which is likely to be the truth."

Lyra turned her attention to Homat. "What happens once we're safely past Changrit? What about the next town? Could it be in alliance with Po Rabi too?"

Homat spoke with conviction. "No. Changrit is the only far north city allied with Po Rabi. Beyond Changrit much is unknown and all are independent of the city-states that line the Groalamasan. And Changrit was chosen because it alone can muster enough strength for such an attack."

"Everything you've told us makes sense," she murmured. "It's what you haven't told us that worries me."

"I do not understand your words, de-Lyra."

"Why are you so eager to betray your own city?"

"I have told you that I have come to like you, and that you have given me a sense of self-importance and true worth that I have never felt before."

"That's not good enough." For emphasis she added a powerful Mai gesture of disbelief. "You could have kept silent and fulfilled the dictates of your masters. If we had succumbed to this trap you would have enjoyed much honor in Po Rabi, and if we had escaped you would still be safe. Why risk the one by throwing in so openly with us when you'd have been safe both ways by keeping quiet? I'm glad that you 'like' us, but I've studied Mai society for too many months now to believe that you're doing this out of the goodness of your heart."

Homat looked uncertain, turned to Etienne for guidance.

"You'd better tell us the truth, Homat."

"Don't you believe me, de-Etienne?"

"Yes, I do, but my wife's a born skeptic. Unlike intelligent beings, rocks and minerals aren't intentionally deceptive. You're going to have to convince her to convince me."

Homat nodded. When he spoke again much of the nervousness and all of the soft deference had vanished from his voice.

"I told the truth about coming to like you, and about not wishing to be a party to such a vile deception. But de-Lyra suspects me rightly. I have another reason for confessing this now.

"It is true I would risk nothing by keeping my silence, but also would I gain nothing. Po Rabi is my home, but I have traveled widely and have come to think of the world as my home. There are many great city-states where one may make a fine life. In Po Rabi I have little chance to rise above my station. True, if the attack on your spirit boat were to succeed I would return home to a fine reward, but in you off-worlders I see the chance to do much better. With the

[57]

knowledge I can gain from you I can make myself valuable beyond mere 'rewards.' Thus far only Losithi and Po Rabi have dealt with your hard-shelled friends. Suphum would welcome my knowledge and make me a member of their Zanur, as would Tolm and many others. I could not hope to rise so high in Po Rabi on the results of my labors as an assassin.

"I have provided you with information which may save your lives as well as your expedition. In return for this information and for my loyalty, I expect suitable recompense."

Lyra looked satisfied. "*Now* I believe you, Homat." She added to Etienne in terranglo. "Typical power–wealth decision. Very Mai. The fact that we're not of his race doesn't enter into the equation. Business takes precedence over vague feelings of loyalty to home and kind." She switched back to her very fluent Mai.

"You are a more complex person than you've led us to believe, Homat. You're a very effective deceiver." This last was, in Mai, a compliment, and Homat looked quite pleased with himself.

"All of us carry deceptions. They are worth little. Truth is all that can be sold. I am only a simple one seeking to lift himself from the depths in which he was born."

"Having deceived us this long, how can we be certain you won't try to strike your own bargain with some village Moyt?"

"If you do not return safely to your Steamer Station, I gain nothing from helping you now. I do not wish to take the spirit boat. I believe I have more to gain by helping you."

"A straightforward enough commercial decision, Etienne—devoid of sentimentality. I'd rather rely on that than on his fondness for us. Having made his confession and his choice, it's now in his best interests to see to our continued health and safety."

"Delightful so," Homat agreed. "Then you believe me about Irquit and the attack?"

"We'll find out for certain tomorrow," Etienne told him. He turned his attention to the telescope. "Now if you don't mind, Homat, I still have some observations of the sky I want to make and Lyra needs her beauty sleep."

Homat gaped at him. "But you are to be attacked! You must make preparations to defend yourselves."

"Maybe we won't have to fight, Homat."

"We'd better not," Lyra murmured uneasily. "Self-defense or no, if word ever got back to our sponsors that we'd engaged in a running battle with Class Four-B natives we'd never get another grant in our lives."

"Don't be so damned concerned for the welfare of the charming, considerate locals. What are you worried about? Is Homat going to appear before the Research Advisory Board to announce that we knew about the attack in advance?" After months of fighting with his wife, Etienne was more than ready to fight something else, and to hell with the regulations.

Besides, Po Rabi's deception grated on him. He remembered the ambassador's politeness, the warm feelings of contentment and achievement they'd felt just before setting out Upriver. If Homat's confession proved true, that meant all those kind words of help and assistance and talk of mutual sharing of knowledge was so much dung.

Maybe Changrit was the last city in league with Po Rabi, and maybe it wasn't. It wouldn't hurt to send a lesson not only to the Zanur of Po Rabi but to any other Mai who coveted the spirit boat, that the peaceful human visitors weren't to be trifled with. Yes, they all but owed it to the Mai to show what scholars could do when aroused. In so doing they might quickly discourage all future such assaults, thereby saving lives.

"It still bothers me to have to fight," Lyra said softly.

"I understand." He was quite willing to be understanding now that he'd made up his mind how to handle the Changritites. "But if it comes to that, it's self-defense. Anyway, by fighting we're only adhering to local custom. Remember how the rest of the fishing fleet cheered us on our way? Maybe some timorous board member would disapprove, but not the rest of the Mai."

She spoke in terranglo again while Homat looked on blankly, desperately wishing he could comprehend the alien babble.

"We could just use repellers."

"Dangerous if they managed to get a net or two on us.

[59]

You know how unstable the boat is on repellers. That's a last resort. Besides, if we don't invite some kind of reaction, we'll only have Homat's word about Irquit. What if she's no assassin, merely a guide? What if their orders are only to stand aside and let the Changritites do all the dirty work? Maybe he's just trying to shut her out of the bit of business he's working with us. By watching her reactions we'll have final proof of his words. If she doesn't make any threatening moves, once past Changrit we'll have a new problem to deal with."

Lyra sighed, shook her head sadly. "This is going to complicate the hell out of my notes."

"If that's all we have to worry about as we pass Changrit," he countered, "we'll be well off. Besides, think of the potential opportunities for studying the behavior of the Mai in battle."

She responded with a rude noise which even Homat could understand.

The following night on the Skar was equally cloudless and clear. As the sun began to shrink behind the distant ramparts of the canyon wall, Etienne peered through the cockpit bubble at an anxious Irquit. He nodded to himself as he studied her expression. Point one to Homat.

The guide was talking to Lyra, who stood watching the western shore.

"We are almost all out of meat, de-Lyra. I thought we were to stop here at Changrit." She gestured with a six-fingered hand toward the dots of light which marked the riverbank. "We will soon be past the harbor."

"We're not stopping tonight, Irquit," Lyra replied. "We have ample supplies of our own foodstuffs down in the hold. Maybe we'll stop in a couple of days. It's such a beautiful night, Etienne thinks we should enjoy the weather. I agree."

"But Changrit is such a wonderful place!" Irquit protested. "There is so much to see, so much for you to put into your records, de-Lyra."

"Oh, that's okay. I'm sure we'll find other places to stop that are just as interesting. We can stop and study there."

"None are so grand on this part of the Skar as is Changrit."

Irquit was glancing nervously past Lyra, apparently studying the river ahead.

"Something wrong?" Lyra asked innocently.

"No, no. I only wanted so much for you to see so powerful and beautiful a city. I felt that . . ."

Etienne tuned the pleading voice out and concentrated on the scanner by his right hand. He knew what Irquit was looking for, out there atop the dark water. The green screen was filled with bright shapes of many sizes strung out in three parallel lines across the Skar. It must have taken the Changritites weeks to gather the enormous flotilla.

He lost speed as he studied the scanner, looking for the place where the boats were spread thinnest.

There were more boats ahead than he'd expected, and the danger was greater. Some of his initial enthusiasm for a fight evaporated. The capture was no game to the local Mai, and despite superior technology there was something still to be said for commanding overwhelming numbers. He made certain the repellers were functioning, just in case they had to employ them.

Pick your way through, he suddenly decided, and take care not to get entangled in those damn nets and heavy wooden floats. Above all, don't let any of the locals on board. Surely they wouldn't have any *real* difficulty breaking through.

Irquit was failing at not looking Upriver. She knew about the ambush. That much of Homat's story was obviously accurate.

"Please, de-Lyra, it would be so much better to make port at Changrit tonight. I can shop very cheaply at first light and we can—"

"Go astern, Irquit," Lyra ordered her sharply. "We're not tired or hungry, we don't need to stop for supplies, and we're going on tonight."

The guide started to object again, then thought better of it and followed the rail sternward. Etienne wondered what she'd tell Homat, whom she still thought of as a partner in deception, and how well Homat would hide his true feelings.

Then he made out a dim irregular shape off to port, through the transparency of the cockpit bubble, and he no longer could spare the time to worry about the Mai already on board. None of the four moons were aloft yet and the river ran clear and unslivered beneath the hydrofoil's keel.

A half dozen tiny objects appeared suddenly on the scanner, heading for the hydrofoil. "Spears, Lyra!"

She dropped to her belly on the foredeck, behind the metal dome over the heavy-duty fishing equipment. A couple of sharp points whanged off the bubble and he flinched involuntarily. They did no damage to the tough plastalloy.

Large shapes hove into view, lying where the scanner had predicted their presence. Etienne turned off the sensitive audio pickups. They weren't necessary. He could hear the shouting and excited hailing of the boat's crews quite clearly in the still night air.

Arrows and warcries followed the first volley of spears, then something long and heavy flew over the bow and clung there as Etienne turned sharply to port to avoid a small fishing barge filled with gesticulating, wide-eyed bowmen. Arrows splintered or glanced off the clear cockpit bubble, but the larger affront remained. It was a heavy fishing net attached to huge bolts which had evidently been fired by several catapults or large crossbows operating in unison. Several such nets, flung one atop the other, could seriously obscure his vision. He could still run on instruments, but not if the thick mesh was entangled in the engine nozzle.

Putting the hydrofoil on autopilot and entering evasive orders, he took his pistol from its charging socket near the pilot wheel and headed for the stern. Lyra met him halfway through the cabin.

"Who's driving?" she asked curtly.

"Multiple K."

"Not good enough. Too many boats." She eyed the weapon in his right hand. "I came down so I wouldn't have to do that."

"It's to burn that net, not Irquit."

"What net?"

"You'll see when you take over." He pushed past her, slipping the safety off the asynaptic pistol.

He was halfway to the foredeck when something buzzed him like an apoplectic wasp. The fast-moving, elegantly agile hydrofoil made it difficult for the Mai marksmen to aim but occasionally an arrow or spear would *spang* against the hull or whistle past overhead. Despite their inaccuracy, the sheer volume of primitive projectiles made moving around out on deck dangerous.

Dropping flat and utilizing the slight inward curve of the metal gunwale for protection, he crawled toward the bow. Once alongside the cockpit bubble he rose and carefully began burning away the net that covered the plastalloy.

The bow section was aerodynamic so there were few projections for the nets to catch onto, and he had half of the net cleared away before a sudden burning made him glance down at his left arm. A small stream of blood dripped from where a passing arrow had dug. Etienne made a mental note to ask Homat if the Upriver inhabitants ever used poisoned barbs in their fishing. He turned back to the work at hand.

Lyra appeared to be fully occupied with the task of steering them through their assailants while causing as little damage as possible. She was darting rapidly from side to side, working with unexpected animation. He frowned, leaned close to the bubble. Yes, she was very active, and so was the second figure she was grappling with.

The hydrofoil lurched abruptly to starboard and nearly threw him overboard. Only his grasp on the remaining Mai net kept him from a fatal dunking. As he struggled to his feet he identified the second figure in the cockpit: Irquit.

But that was impossible. Because of Homat's warning they made doubly sure to lock the cabin door every time either of them entered or left. Irquit should have been stuck outside, on the stern deck where she slept with Homat.

Lyra was heavier than the Mai and probably a good deal stronger, but if Homat was to be believed Irquit was a trained killer. Lyra's experience ran to more genteel pursuits. From what he could see, his wife was having a hard time fending off a wicked-looking blade. He shouted at her, aware as he did so how useless his words were.

Without Lyra at the instruments and with the autopilot turned off, the hydrofoil was beginning to slow. That was a safety override, designed to keep a boat with a disabled crew from running into the shore. As the whine of the jet faded, Etienne saw shapes begin to close in on them. They'd run past most of the Changrit armada, but were still near enough to be overtaken by determined oarsmen. He could hear them chanting in the dark as they strained to overhaul the spirit boat.

If they were allowed on board, asynapts wouldn't be enough to cope with the sheer weight of numbers. His first thought was to get back inside. He could lock any boarders out, and with their primitive weapons they couldn't break in, but they could certainly disable the engine or clog the water scoops.

Bowmen were close now and suddenly found themselves presented with a relatively stable target. They kept him pinned down by the fishing dome, unable to move through the shower of arrows.

Suddenly he saw a third shape inside the cockpit. For a moment he despaired. If Homat had lied to them, if he'd been a willing ally of Irquit's and of the Zanur all along—he screamed Lyra's name.

But if that were the case, then why the trembling expiation last night up on the telescope platform? As Etienne watched he saw Homat edge carefully around the pinwheeling combatants, climb up into the pilot's seat, put both six-fingered hands on the wheel and nudge the accelerator.

Again he found himself thrown to the deck, only this time it was due to the hydrofoil's sudden leap forward. Shouts of dismay and anger reached him from the two fishing boats that were almost within boarding range. Two Mai actually made the jump and landed aboard.

The asynapt flashed twice in the darkness. There was a brief bright blue flash where each charge struck flesh, the smell of ozone in the air, and a single splash as the first victim tumbled overboard. The second fell near Etienne's sweaty face, curved knife locked in a stilled grip.

Etienne scrambled erect and ran to the nearest entryway. When Irquit saw the other human enter the cabin she broke free and rushed astern, trailing curses in her wake. He just missed her in the main corridor, collided with Lyra instead. It was a timely collision, since his impact knocked her aside and clear of the knife that whistled past them.

He fired wildly and seared a section of ceiling, as a funny, high moan sounded from the direction of the cockpit. Homat fell away from the wheel as Lyra moved to help him.

Another pair of fishing nets clung to the boat, and Etienne

pushed a few tangles aside as he cautiously emerged on deck. Irquit was unarmed, however, except for her mouth. She snarled something that Etienne translated crudely as "Death to the Faceless One!" Whether the curse was aimed at Homat or himself he had no way of knowing and likely never would know, because their former guide and cook threw herself over the side and instantly vanished astern. No doubt her Changritite allies would fish her out of the river and send her on her way Downriver toward Po Rabi.

Etienne was gratified that they'd put their trust in Homat. Certainly he had burned his bridges behind him. There was no way the Mai could ever show his face in Po Rabi again.

If he didn't live, though, it wouldn't make any difference. Etienne remembered that surprised moan as Irquit's knife sailed past his ear. With the Changrit flotilla rapidly falling astern, he turned and hurried back into the cool interior of the hydrofoil.

The pilot's seat was unoccupied and he slid behind the wheel, made a fast check of the instruments. The scanner showed only a few small logs floating to starboard, in contrast to the thick cluster of shiplike shapes behind them. In a minute or two those distant threats would slip off the screen altogether.

Homat was lying on the floor moaning. Lyra had pulled the knife out and was working to stanch the bleeding. The weapon lay near her right leg, a very large blade to have struck so small a humanoid. A couple of centimeters to the left, and they'd have found themselves continuing their journey without either of their guides. Lyra had removed her halter and bound it over the hole. The halter's air-conditioning system was still operating full blast, and he thought to ask why when it occurred to him that the cold would promote coagulation. On rare occasions it struck him that he'd married a woman of more than average intelligence.

With the flow of blood slowed she disappeared astern, to return a moment later with a handful of vials and spray cans.

"I don't know how well this is going to work on you, Homat. It wasn't designed to be used on a Mai, but it's all we have and I don't know what else to try. Can you understand me?"

He nodded slowly, his small sharp teeth grinding together in pain.

"You're fully mammalian and from what I've been able to learn your physiology's close enough to ours so that—"

"Screw the biology lecture, Lyra!" her husband snapped.

She glanced sharply up at him, but this time only nodded. Her unvoiced admission of his rightness gave him no pleasure. He was too worried about Homat.

The freeze spray on top of the effect produced by her halter's cooler stopped the rest of bleeding. Homat gasped at the chill and tried not to look at the intimidating alien machines they were using on his body. Then she took a small curved device that cupped the curve of her palm, adjusted it carefully, and held it over the wound as she removed the bloodied halter. As she passed the device over his shoulder and upper chest it hissed softly. A faint bright yellow light poured from its underside.

Homat writhed in pain, but when she pulled her hand away and snapped off the surgiseal he could see that the cut had been closed completely, and sterilized in the bargain. There would be a permanent scar, but Lyra was no surgeon and there hadn't been time to consult the computer.

"Any poison?"

"No, de-Lyra," Homat whispered at her, staring at his chest in amazement. "A clean knife for a clean death." Etienne received this information with relief. His arm had ceased bleeding and now he could stop worrying about his own wound.

"You'll be all right now," Lyra assured their guide. "Just take it easy for a few days and try not to use that arm too much." He was shivering steadily and it occurred to her it wasn't from shock.

"He'll freeze in here, Etienne." The cabin thermometer registered a temperature of eighty degrees. "We've got to get him back out on deck."

"Go ahead, we're well clear now. I'll help you." He allowed the autopilot to resume control of the boat and moved to lift Homat in his arms. The slim Mai was a light burden and once he had been placed on his sleeping mat, Etienne turned back to the stern gangway. It didn't take long to discover how Irquit had made her way inside to attack Lyra. A small wad of *sikreg* gum, a local product Irquit employed to help thicken her stews and soups, had been jammed between the center seal and the door, preventing the lock from functioning.

Thoughtful of Irquit, to have made such a study of how the doorways operated. Undoubtedly she'd been studying hard ever since they'd departed Steamer Station. It was their own damned fault, Etienne told himself. They were going to have to cease thinking of the Mai as ignorant primitives.

The thought made him frown as he turned to stare at Homat. Their remaining guide was sitting up now, propped against the low bar of the railing that ran around the top of the gunwale. The Mai had operated their boat!

"That was very quick thinking of you, Homat. Taking control of the boat while Lyra was fighting with Irquit. Another couple of minutes and the Changritites might have overwhelmed us."

"Yes, I was standing here watching them close on us, de-Etienne, and I thought to wonder what was wrong. I saw the door there by your hand swinging open, and with heart in hand crept inside despite the cold to see what was the matter, for I knew we should not be slowing.

"I have watched for a long time now, through the round glass, as you and de-Lyra ran the spirit boat. While I still have no idea what controls the spirits that make it go, it is not hard to see how you control those spirits. I told you that Irquit thought she could do it, so I saw no reason why I also could not do so.

"You turn the wheel to change direction and push the little button to increase the speed."

Etienne relaxed a little. "Put that way it doesn't sound terribly complex, does it? How are you feeling?"

"Your wondrous tools have delighted my side. Much better, all thanks from my ancestors and me to you."

Etienne nodded. "Did you hear what your former companion said as she took her leave of us?"

"No." He gave a shaky Mai smile. "I can imagine it was not very polite."

"Not very. Enough to insure that you'd better never go within a dozen legats of Po Rabi again."

"I had already committed myself to that. Did you not believe me?"

Etienne looked uncomfortable. "It is hard on a strange world to know what to believe and what not to believe, Homat. Forgive me if I seem insensitive."

"Do not feel so, de-Etienne. They say that the people of Suphum do not pause for midday rest but work straight through 'til sundown. That is also hard to believe. Truly is the Everything filled with wonders. I do not regret my decision, though I might have had I died under Irquit's knife, may her flesh rot in the river. I do not need a home, now that I have you and de-Lyra as my friends and protectors."

"Don't worry, Homat. You'll have your reward when we get back to Steamer Station." Lyra was adjusting a clean halter top. "I don't care what the regulations say. We'll slip you something that should make you wealthy for life."

In true Mai fashion Homat instantly pointed to the interior of the boat. "That machine you used to heal me. Could I have one of those?"

Lyra laughed. She hadn't laughed like that in a long time, Etienne thought, surprised at how sharply it pierced him.

"The surgiseal would wear out before very long and you wouldn't be able to have it fixed, Homat. There's nothing worse than a magician whose magic unexpectedly deserts him. Don't worry, we'll find you something suitable that will last."

"I am not worried," Homat replied calmly. He moved his arm gingerly. "Truly a delightful instrument, though."

"Hadn't you better check the autopilot, Etienne?"

"We're okay. We're back out in the middle of the river and the scanner will sound if there's anything ahead it can't deal with. Maybe we ought to start thinking about replenishing our stores. Irquit was right about our being low." He looked down at Homat. "You're *positive* Po Rabi's influence doesn't extend any farther Upriver than Changrit?"

Homat sighed. Sometimes you had to tell this peculiar folk the same thing several times before they believed you.

"The next major trading town beyond Changrit is Kekkalong, de-Etienne. I have never been there but I know it thrives independent of any ocean-city's rule. It lies some three thousand legats north of Changrit."

Lyra did some fast mental calculating. "Five hundred kilometers. We can hold off that long. Since it's a major port, maybe we can tie up there for a couple of days, take a rest. I can do some intensive research. I'm certainly not going to have the chance to do any work in Changrit."

"A most delightful major port," Homat agreed. "Not as big as Po Rabi or Losithi, but nearly as large as Changrit. Beyond Kekkalong all is unknown country, unknown to me and to any living trader of Po Rabi. None have journeyed so far Upriver from the Groalamasan."

"Then you'll be the first," Etienne said. He turned apologetically to his wife. "Two of them got on board. I had to use the asynapt on them. There was no time to shoot to incapacitate, Lyra."

To his surprise she didn't bawl him out. Perhaps Irquit's assault had made her a tad less protective of the people she had come to study.

"Only two? That's not bad. Probably not enough to start a blood feud with the Changritites."

"That's good, because when we return we might have to deal with the same situation all over again."

"Our return's a long ways away yet, Etienne. We'll worry about it months from now. By that time the Changritites may have grown bored with watching the river and sent Irquit on her way. At least we won't have to watch for any on-board threats." She glanced down at Homat, who was rubbing his miraculously healed shoulder.

"I apologize for doubting your story, Homat."

"No, no, no reason to apologize, de-Lyra. I would have doubted you if in your place. Doubt is healthy."

She stared out into the damp night. Occasionally a light from a house on shore would flash dimly in the distance, like a star. All was calm and quiet.

"I'm beginning to think that it is," she murmured softly.

[VI]

Kekkalong turned out to be all that Homat had promised. A natural harbor had been scooped from the shore of the Skar by powerful currents. As they entered, small fishing boats and pleasure craft clustered like whirligig beetles in the hydrofoil's wake.

As was the style in the great oceanic cities, half the buildings were contructed below the surface, the other half above. There was the expected profusion of tall, thin towers. Unlike the structures of ancient human cities, which they superficially resembled, these narrow cylinders reached deep into the earth. Some served to convey cool water to the surface while others allowed hot air to rise from the town's subterranean levels. The Mai flourished in a brutally hot climate, but they enjoyed a cool breeze as much as a human, even if their idea of a cool breeze was a gust of damp air at ninety degrees.

The townsfolk were friendly and did their best to restrain their curiosity about their tall, hairy visitors. As Kekkalong was ruled not by a single Moyt but by a coalition of merchants, there was something of a respite from the overpowering urge to compete that drove the inhabitants of the southern cities. Lyra took notes as fast as she could address her recorder.

With the loss of Irquit, Homat's bargaining abilities were brought to the fore, and he proved himself an adequate replacement. As soon as he overcame his ingrained shyness he proved quite adroit at dickering for supplies in the marketplace.

They were walking through the central market, buying samples of the local carvings for their stock of primitive specimens, when Lyra called to her husband. As usual he'd left the trading to her and Homat, being more interested in the stones that had been used to pave the street.

"What is it? Lyra, did you know that some of this might have been quarried out of a pegmatite dike?"

"Sure I did," she replied sardonically, "but I'll try to forget it for now. Come over and listen to something."

She stood before a very old Mai. Trying to muster some interest, Etienne observed that the wrinkles on the Mai face formed whorls with age instead of lines.

"Only two hundred legats up the Skar," the oldster declaimed, "lies the place where it is joined by the great Aurang."

"He says," Lyra told him, usurping the old one's tale, "that the Tsla have a major town not far up the Aurang."

Etienne eyed her uncertainly. "How far is not far?" She gave him a figure in legats and he converted the native measurement in his head. "Between eight and nine hundred kilometers. That's a hell of a 'not far.' Our itinerary calls for us to follow the Skar to its origin, mapping and taking notes along the way. Nothing was said about making any major detours."

"It would give us the chance to study a wholly new race, Etienne, examine an entirely different culture. We have to make contact with the Tsla sooner or later."

"I thought the plan was 'later.'"

"But it's such a wonderful opportunity! I'm told the Tsla build very few centers and that this Turput is one of the main ones."

"It would still mean a radical change in our plans," he argued. "Lyra, not a day's gone by since we set down on this world that you haven't been able to wallow in your work, whereas I'm still waiting to reach the point where the Bar-shajagad narrows enough for me to do some serious research and studies in *my* specialty."

"If we go to this Turput, you'll have that chance, Etienne. They can't live in the river valley." She exchanged some rapid-fire chatter with the oldster. "His description of Tur-put's location fits what we've learned about their ecological niche. Turput's at least three thousand meters above the Skar. Apparently the Aurang hasn't cut nearly as deep a canyon. You should be able to dive into your studies sooner if we visit Turput than if we avoid it."

He considered carefully. "I know that we're supposed to make detailed studies of the Tsla as well as the Mai, but the plan was to do that during our return journey, after we'd attained the other major objectives."

"Etienne, my primary interest in coming here is to see how several entirely different cultures coexist side by side in separate habitation zones. To do this I need to observe how the Tsla live and react to the Mai."

"Can't it wait until we're on our way back?"

"We *owe* ourselves the detour. At three thousand meters above sea level the temperature will drop at least forty de-grees from what it is here on the Skar, with a corresponding fall in humidity. For the first time since touchdown we can slip into real clothes and dispense with air conditioning. Doesn't that interest you?"

He had to admit that it did, but there were other factors she hadn't mentioned, possibly by design.

"From what this old one said, Lyra, Turput lies only eight hundred kilometers upstream from where the Aurang enters the Skar, right?" She nodded. "Okay. That means climbing three thousand meters up the canyonside over a short dis-tance. Too steep a slope for the boat to navigate and too far to run on repellers."

Lyra pointed to the old trader. "Ossanj says there's a decent-size town at the confluence of the two rivers, called Aib. He says we might hire them to watch the hydrofoil as well as find porters to ferry supplies up to Turput."

"Really? Does he happen to have any relatives in Chan-grit?"

"Etienne!" She sighed with exasperation. "We're far beyond Changrit's influence. You know that."

"Maybe so. Pardon me if I seem excessively cautious. It's just that we haven't done so well where local help's been involved."

"Come on! You know we can take enough precautions to insure the safety of the boat."

"Granted that we can, I'm still not sure I'm ready for a three-thousand-meter hike. That's going to make hash of our itinerary."

"Our itinerary's not graven in stone, Etienne. If the weather's bad when we come back down the river we might not be able to make the climb at all. We can't pass on the chance. The weather's favorable *now*. Surely we can hire some kind of local transport so we don't have to make the entire climb on foot." She turned back to the trader. "Tell him about Turput, Ossanj."

"A most delighted wondrous place," declared the oldster. "Mysterious are the workings of the Tsla." He made a gesture to protect himself from any interested spirits. "Their fields climb the sides of mountains. They grow there delighted fruits and vegetables that wither here by the river."

"How do you know all this, Ossanj? I thought the lands of the Tsla too cold for your people to tolerate."

"With much clothing to keep warm, we can visit there for short times."

"And we'll be comfortable, Etienne," Lyra added encouragingly. "Doesn't that sound inviting?"

"Not as inviting as continuing Upriver."

"But that's just my point. Here's a chance for you to see some real topography."

"Lyra, I'm sick of river valley, you know that. But we ought to stick to our itinerary."

She drew away from him. "I see," she said coldly. "Fine. You continue Upriver with Homat. I'll take enough of the trade goods to tide me over until you return and I'll go up to Turput myself. Meet you on the way back."

He sighed. "Lyra, you know that's no good. What about the cultures Upriver from here? Am I supposed to do your fieldwork as well as my own?"

She shrugged. "Okay, then take a month or two and go

where you wish, study what you want, and come back for me. But I'm going to Turput tomorrow, Etienne, while I have the opportunity and while the weather's good."

"Damn you," he said quietly. "You know the dangers in splitting up. You get your way, as usual. I'll come with you. But I won't like it and you'll have to listen to me bitch about it all the way up the canyon."

"I'll suffer it." She smiled triumphantly at him. "Consider it serendipity instead of an enforced detour. Many important discoveries are made because of serendipity."

"Bullshit. You've just decided that you want to go *now*."

That prompted a glare that chilled the air in the market-place. She didn't speak to him for the rest of the afternoon.

Homat would have voted for staying on the river. Though he had eaten the produce the Tsla traded with the river dwellers and had heard much of their marvelous accomplishments, he'd never seen one and didn't care if he ever did. He thought that de-Etienne should have argued more powerfully with his mate, and if that had failed, given her orders. But it would seem that male–female relationships among the off-worlders were very different from those among the Mai. He spent a whole morning making signs and attempting to propitiate the proper spirits before they set off Upriver once again.

It wasn't long before the hydrofoil's instrumentation warned them of the approaching confluence of the Skar and the Aurang. Ahead, the Skar executed a sharp bend westward while the Aurang flowed into the main river from out of the north. Given the Aurang's immense flow and orientation, anyone not knowing which was which would have proceeded up the tributary, thinking it the Skar.

Making landfall on the eastern shore of the river just above the town of Aib, they dispatched Homat to inquire about the availability of transportation and porters. Despite the high rate of pay offered, engaging help turned out to be difficult.

"They are reluctant to leave their homes to travel to the land of the Tsla," Homat explained.

"Why is that?" Lyra inquired. "I thought that trade went on daily between Tsla and Mai, and has since ancient times."

"That is truth," Homat agreed. Behind them, fisherfolk

[74]

and farmers gathered curiously around the anchored hydrofoil, engaging in the usual futile hunt for sails and oars. "But that does not mean that the Mai are anxious to go up there." He held up something oval that resembled a cross between a grapefruit and a sick lime.

"This is a *gououn*. It cannot grow below the level of Turput." He bit into the shiny-skinned fruit with gusto and spit out several purple seeds. "This and much else can be grown by the Tsla alone. This makes many Mai fearful of them. And there are other things." He made hasty protective signs.

"The Tsla trade with the Mai, but they also trade with the Na of the Guntali."

"Then they're *not* rumors," said Lyra with excitement.

"Oh no, very real, de-Lyra. Too real." He shuddered. "Skins of strange creatures they bring down from the Guntali, and much *serash*." Etienne knew *serash* to be the word for the local equivalent of ivory.

"We Mai never see the Na, for we would freeze in moments in their lands. Their air is difficult to breathe and we would grow dizzy with fear.

"But some will come for hire. There are always some who will come, if the pay is sufficient," he said with assurance. "I wish muchly though, my *des*, that you did not have to leave the spirit boat behind." He looked at the curious to make sure they weren't being overheard.

"Aib is little better than a large village. The Oyts of such towns have few morals. Better to have left it behind in Kekkalong."

Etienne made the Mai movement for negation, glanced sourly at his wife. "We're already taking too much time out of our schedule for this side trip, Homat. Leaving the boat at Kekkalong would've cost us several weeks of overland travel. Don't worry though. The spirit boat will be quite safe until we return."

Homat looked doubtful, still watching the crowd. "I cannot dissuade you, friends from across the ocean of night, but I do not think this a wise decision. Even the porters I have hired have come down to us from Upriver and not from Aib. I fear treachery."

"Relax. We'll have our weapons with us. No one's going

to bother the boat in our absence. You'll see." He indicated the fishing dock where they'd tied up. "Has not the Oyt of Aib promised us that he'll keep the dock sealed off and all the curious away? None will be permitted to come near and he's said he'll utilize his personal guard to insure that. We're paying him a handsome amount to see to it that any locals stay clear."

"The sum is not so handsome as the spirit boat itself," Homat grumbled. "As for the guard he will post here, would that it had come from Kekkalong. Still, if you are satisfied, Homat is satisfied." There was no satisfaction in his tone, however. He found it a struggle to understand these peculiar creatures. In many ways they were unimaginably sophisticated and in others, childishly naive.

"We know what we're doing, Homat."

"Could you not at least take it a safe distance up the Aurang?"

"And dock it in the middle of the river, exposed to unknown currents and high winds?" Lyra asked. "It's safer here. Besides, anyone who wanted to find it could do so just as easily a few dozen legats up the Aurang. We'll worry about our property, Homat, and you worry about the cooking and the guiding."

"As you say, de-Lyra."

In truth, he greatly enjoyed giving orders to the half dozen porters. It was the first time in his life he'd been able to exercise any power over his fellow Mai. Power gave rise to wealth, to new knowledge and capabilities. Power was the measure of an adult. He enjoyed himself so much he managed to forget his fears about the safety of the spirit boat.

The Oyt of Aib, a bucolic youth named Gwattwe who fancied himself something of a dandy, personally saw them safely on their way. He had his own spirit doctor cast a spell for their healthy return.

From Aib they would ride on lowagons northward until they encountered the Aurang's southerly flow, then turn northeast following the trading trail into the highlands.

"May you return in delighted safety," Gwattwe told them. "As one who has traded often with the Tsla, I would go with you myself to serve as guide and interpreter, but a village Oyt must watch over his people."

"We understand," Lyra assured him. "We know that you'll take good care of our property."

"Have I not sworn the oath?" Gwattwe looked injured. "Have I not given promise upon my mate and children and most of all, my fortune? Not to mention that I do not receive the second half of payment until you return."

I trust *that*, Etienne thought as he listened to the Mai's speech, more than any other assurance. Among the Mai, money was as blood.

As they turned to enter the waiting lowagons a bored-looking chorus of small children launched into an irritatingly atonal chant of farewell. They kept it up until the little line of porter-driven lowagons had moved beyond the first bend in the road, then scattered before the blows their chorus master dispensed impartially.

Gwattwe watched the strange visitors depart, then turned glittering eyes to the dock where the hydrofoil bobbed lazily at anchor, tethered to the landing by two wondrously strong metal cables.

"What do you think on all this, wise Enaromeka?"

The spirit doctor eyed the alien craft thoughtfully. "Give them six days before taking possession, Gwattwe."

"My purse itches feverishly. I don't know that I can wait six days."

"Better caution than confrontation. I do not think they suspect, but it would be awkward if they were to double back along the road to see what we were doing. Patience. We shall be masters of all the Skar. Even the oceanic states will do us homage ... *if* we can make the spirit boat obey us."

"Even if we cannot," Gwattwe said, "we can make the hairy ones pay a huge ransom for its safe return. If they refuse, surely there are many items of great value within the craft that can be removed and sold. These are no wizards, no gods come among us, Enaromeka. Lightning does not fly from their fingers, no matter what the Downriver rumor-mongers would have us believe, and the rocks do not shake beneath their tread. They are like unto the Mai, save for their size and hairiness, and they have fewer fingers and toes to drive them through life. If cut, I am sure they would bleed, and if they bleed, they will die. I understand them, and I think with care we can come to understand their spirit boat.

"Besides," he added with a smile, "they will be gone long to the city of the Tsla and long returning. We will have ample time to study and experiment with their vessel."

"It shall be a legendary triumph for you, Gwattwe," the spirit doctor declaimed with becoming unctuousness.

"And for you also, my good friend and advisor, for to you falls the honor of extracting the secrets of the spirit boat."

Enaromeka suddenly felt ill. "What? To me?"

"Are you not the smartest of the Aib?"

"The cleverest, but you, great Oyt, are the smartest."

"Your flattery is unnecessary. I know when I am beyond my depth."

Enaromeka looked resigned. "It will truly be a delightful great honor. I will enlist the aid of my most precocious students. In time, we will learn all that can be learned."

They observed and measured, discussed and debated for six long days. By that time Gwattwe was trembling with impatience to step aboard and claim possession of the spirit boat for Aib and his family line. Word filtered through the town that the day of Taking had arrived and many of the villagers put aside their daily chores to gather on shore above the dock. All wished to partake of their community's triumph, for all would benefit by the successful "repossession," as the town adjudicator had described it in a moment of florid rationalization.

The power and wealth that accrued to Aib would be shared by all, and the name of Aib known all along the river.

Enaromeka made certain everyone heard him clearly. "I claim the honor of being the first aboard." Gwattwe responded with a gesture of deference. This was as rehearsed and part payment to the spirit doctor for his services.

The gunwale was bumping gently against the wooden dock as he stepped gingerly over the side onto the exposed rear deck. Nothing happened. Enaromeka turned a slow circle, looking quite pleased with himself until a voice rumbled in perfect if slightly stiff Mai:

"Visitor, you do not belong on this boat. No permission for visitation has been granted. You have twenty *anats* in

which to vacate this boat or you will suffer dire consequences. You have been warned."

Enaromeka stood as if paralyzed, while Gwattwe blinked
and tried to see through the transparent bubble enclosing
the cockpit. The warriors arranged nearby forgot their po-
sitions as they searched the windows for the invisible speaker.
So did Enaromeka's assistants.

There was no sign of life within the boat. Nothing moved
beyond the transparencies and the boat itself continued to
bob on the breath of the current.

Enaromeka overcame his initial panic and moved cautiously to where he could look down into the boat. "I see
no one."

"Nor do I," Gwattwe said from the dock.

"I will go inside and look." Enaromeka reached for the
door handle and pulled. "I can't move it."

"That is to be expected," said Gwattwe. "It is not to be
anticipated that they would trust us enough to leave their
vessel unlocked. Would a long knife help?"

Enaromeka put his face to the window that comprised the
upper half of the doorway. "It is strong. Little lights inside
are blinking on and off, like the fires of hunting parties up
the side of the canyon. Perhaps the lights have something
to do with the lock. Fire spirits. Give me a *zhaloo*."

From within the ranks of warriors a heavy spiked club
was passed forward. One of the spirit doctor's students
handed it across to Enaromeka.

"Five *anats*," the voice announced dangerously. "Leave
this boat *now*."

"I know what it is," Enaromeka declared suddenly, unwilling to abandon his moment of glory to an unseen specter.
"A spirit voice locked within the boat, left here to frighten
us." He spoke boldly. "I, Enaromeka, am not frightened by
spirits. I will learn the secrets of this craft despite all the
voices that shout at me. I am not afraid of voices!"

Taking careful aim with the club, he brought it down over
the transparency covering the blinking lights. A brilliant explosion of light momentarily blinded the watching crowd and
there was much screaming. Women and children fled for the
safety of boulders and sun shelters. Several of the warriors
lined up in stately procession along the dock broke formation

to sample the cool waters of the Skar. Gwattwe had enough presence of mind to note their names and former rank.

When his sight had recovered somewhat from the effects of the unexpected flash, he turned back to the spirit boat. It still rode easily on its lines. Curled up on the rear deck was the object that an instant earlier had been his spirit doctor. Smoke rose from the skull and sides of the fetal shape while the leather sandals burned ferociously.

One of Enaromeka's students jumped onto the boat. Gwattwe held his breath but nothing happened to the scholar as he beat at the fire consuming his instructor's feet. With great presence of mind, the student yelled instructions. There was movement among the onlookers. A bucket was located, filled with river, and carefully handed over.

As the student dumped the water on Enaromeka's corpse, a solemn voice intoned, "Visitor, you do not belong on this boat. No permission for visitation has been granted. You have twenty *anats* in which to vacate this boat or you will suffer dire consequences. You have been warned."

"I'm not leaving!" the student announced, making a sign to ward off the most dangerous of unknown spirits. Reaching down, he picked up the ineffectual *zhaloo*, hefted it angrily as he moved toward the doorway that had defeated his instructor.

Gwattwe was not as surprised by the light this time. The student was barefoot, and the water in which he stood did not protect him from the fire spirits. His departure from existence was much more spectacular than Enaromeka's. Swallowed by the burst of energy, he gave a tremendous convulsive twitch and leaped or was thrown over the side of the craft.

Two warriors reluctantly doffed their armor and dove into the river to pull him ashore. Gwattwe examined the student's body with much interest. It was broken and distorted, though differently from Enaromeka's. The soles of his feet had been carbonized and black streaks ran up both legs. The smell of burnt flesh was strong in the morning air.

But there had been no fire, only a burst of light and a loud crackling sound. Pungiram, one of the elders of Aib, had come down onto the dock.

"It would appear, my Oyt Gwattwe, that the hairy strangers are not so dumb as they first seemed."

"So it would appear." Gwattwe showed no distress at having been abruptly deprived of the services of his spirit doctor. He eyed the boat with more interest than ever. "In this first test of trust and friendship, they have come out ahead. But I am persistent, old one. There must be some way to drive the protecting spirit out of this boat so that we can take possession of it."

Pungiram decided to speak up. "You will not find many ready to do battle with unknown spirits, especially spirits that slay as efficiently as do those guarding this boat."

"I am not afraid of spirits," Gwattwe said as he hastened to shield himself with a couple of quickly executed signs, "that are of this world, but it is a new thing to try to deal with a spirit that comes from beyond. However, I am not so sure that we are dealing with a spirit here. This boat is a thing of metal and other strange substances. It is not a proper spirit house."

"Do we have any idea what other spirits consider a proper abode?"

"Perhaps we may learn. I will not give up and walk back to my house." His gaze rose, turned to the trade road which had swallowed up the tall hairy ones. "A long way to Turput, a long way back. We have much time left to us."

The surviving students had clustered around the Oyt. He frowned at them. "What ails you?"

"We must do something about the Teacher." The speaker gestured toward Enaromeka's blackened body. "He must be given a proper burial."

"He must have his wood and his journey to the sea," another insisted.

"I agree," Gwattwe said. "Which of you will honor him by being the first to step onto the spirit boat to remove the body?"

Rapid glances were passed among the scholars. They decided it would be best to discuss the matter in depth before making any firm decisions. They drifted away toward the town, arguing vociferously among themselves.

His peace and quiet restored, Gwattwe again considered the object of his dreams. He had never been to any of the wondrous city-states that traders told of, had traveled only a short distance Downriver. But he'd visited Kekkalong and had admired its wealth. The spirit boat was no more than another new thing to be studied and understood, as he had come to understand power and wealth. He would make a massive effort to be patient. He would have to be or he would quickly run out of advisors.

He would make a speech praising brave Enaromeka. Then everyone would go back to work. Tomorrow he would consider the problem anew. That was all that was required; careful thought and sufficient tomorrows.

But he would have to cajole as well as order his advisors. The odor of a colleague's burning flesh was a powerful deterrent to curiosity.

〖 VII 〗

"De-Etienne, de-Etienne, we must stop and rest!"

Etienne halted, staring ahead to where the trading road climbed still another of the endless vertical walls in a series of laboriously cut switchbacks. The roar of the Aurang cataract was a constant buzz in his ears, even though it was out of sight far off to their left.

"We're nearly there, Homat. I don't want to spend another night on the road. Tell them no."

"It does not matter, de-Etienne." Homat gestured at the line of heavily laden porters behind them. "They say they will go not a step farther until they are given time to put on their warmest clothing."

Etienne made a face as he checked his wrist instrumentation. The air temperature was eighty-four and holding. Despite that, several of the porters made no attempt to hide their discomfort, and two were shivering. For his part, Homat was manfully trying to hide the chills that wracked his own body.

"Very well, but tell them to be quick about it. I want to reach Turput before dark."

"We should, we should, de-Etienne," Homat said gratefully. He turned and relayed the information to the porters. They responded with a babble of thanks, dropping their packs with fine disregard for the contents in their rush to help one another on with heavy coats and hats.

Lyra watched with interest. It was strange to see a Mai clad in long-sleeved and long-legged attire. The cold-climate gear was made of double layered cottonlike fiber stuffed with some puffy plant material.

"In the land of the blind the one-eyed man is king," Lyra murmured.

"I don't see how that relates to our present situation," Etienne commented.

"In the land of the bald, the hirsute man is king."

"That's a lousy analogy."

"You never did have much of a sense of humor." She turned away from him.

The distant Skar was now only a faint silver thread lying against the western horizon. A considerable walk indeed. The fact that the air at three thousand meters was almost Earth-normal was a great comfort. Down on the Skar, they'd been forced to breathe mud. Or so their lungs had persistently told them.

The thinner air did not seem to have troubled the porters, but the drop in temperature had been affecting their performance for several days. Bundled up in their heavy clothing, they looked much more comfortable.

Etienne had to admit that he was enjoying himself. The multicolored strata they passed as they made the ascent were an unending source of wonderment. Tslamaina was an ancient world, and its entire history lay exposed within the canyon walls. He wished only that he could see across the canyon, but at the confluence of the Aurang and the Skar it was still well over a thousand kilometers wide.

At least the road had been wide and clear, with no rough places, and they'd encountered few of the vertical walls with their leg-straining switchbacks. Wind and water had turned the steep walls here to a manageable slope.

For the first time he could see the edge of the Guntali Plateau, revealed in the distance from time to time when the high clouds cleared. The uneven rocky rim rose another three thousand meters higher than Turput, sharply defining the original surface of the planet.

At this altitude the *strepanong*, *dorril*, and *malming* became more than distant circling dots, their enormous soaring shapes resolving into living creatures with five- to eight-meter wingspans. The great scavengers rode the superheated air that rose from the floor of the Barshajagad and rarely scoured below the two-thousand-meter line. This according to the porters, who were nonetheless terrified of them.

They'd climbed past the last Mai village days ago and since then had seen only an occasional solitary hunting party swathed in heavy clothing. Etienne was enjoying the comparative silence.

"Billions of years," he murmured. "That's how long it took the rivers to cut those canyons."

Lyra turned from her study of the porter's cold weather gear to grin knowingly at him. "Then you're glad we made the detour?"

He was still unwilling to grant her the small triumph. "Certainly it's more interesting than the section of the Barshajagad we left, but I'd still prefer that we'd kept to our original itinerary."

"Can't give in gracefully, can you? You can't ever let me win. Why can't you admit when you're wrong?"

"I will, when I am wrong."

"Sure. You're the stubbornest man I've ever met, Etienne."

"Then why did you marry me?"

"Always the same question. Always testing, never content. One of these days I'm going to..." she turned and walked away, mumbling to herself. She always stopped before finishing that sentence, for which he was grateful. Or at least, it used to be that he was grateful. Ten years now she'd put off finishing that sentence.

Homat hurried up alongside him as they resumed their climb. "The porters pass on their gratefulness. They are still cold but it leaves their bones."

"Should be warm enough," Etienne snapped, unaware of the sharpness of his tone. "Took them damn near an hour to change clothes."

"They are not used to such cold, de-Etienne." Homat

tugged at the rim of his own hood, trying to cover as much of his bald pate as possible. "Nor am I. They dressed as rapidly as they could." He tried to see into Etienne's eyes. "Truly, you and de-Lyra are not cold?"

The geologist wore modified lederhosen and a heavier shirt over his mesh briefs. "Not only that, Homat, I'm still on the warm side."

Homat considered this. "Our bodies do not appear so very different, de-Etienne, and while you and de-Lyra have more fur, much of you still is bare skin, as are our bodies. I would not think that you would still be warm here."

"Different environments induce difference adaptations, Homat."

"Truly," Homat confessed.

"If you're through lording it over the natives," Lyra said in terranglo from her position farther up the road, "maybe we can make a little progress before nightfall?"

"I wasn't 'lording it,'" he shot back angrily, "I was just explaining to Homat that—" but she'd already turned away from him to resume her climb. When she did that it made him mad enough to spit wood. Short of grabbing her and forcing her to listen to him, however, there was little he could do, and he didn't want to engage in a shouting match in front of the porters. So he swallowed his anger, convinced it would go straight to the ulcer he was building in his gut, the painful cavity that had his wife's name written all over it.

It was early evening when they finally crested the last ridge overlooking Turput. Neither of them knew what to expect. A smaller version of Kekkalong, perhaps. They were pleasantly surprised.

Neat narrow streets paved with gray flagstone ran down to the fast moving Aurang and continued on the far shore. Both banks were lined with wooden water wheels that turned steadily in the swift current. Instead of the blocky Mai architecture they'd come to associate with civilization on Tslamaina, they saw buildings designed with flowerlike domes and elegant arches. Graceful winding walls connected the main structures, and fluted slate tiles drained rainwater from the roofs. Small observation towers bloomed amid the larger edifices. Excepting the towers, nothing rose higher than three floors.

Above the town the Aurang split into a series of gentle cataracts where dim figures worked with long fish sweeps. Terraces heavy with fruit bushes stepped toward heaven. At the far end of the formation Etienne identified as a hanging valley, a wide waterfall crashed into the riverbed.

Most magical of all were the sounds made by the profusion of bells and wind chimes that inhabited every house and shop, dangled from windows and rafters and projecting beams. The tinkling and clanging and bonging were audible even above the rush of the Aurang. There were bells of metal and ceramic, of glass and clay and wood, bone bells and stone chimes.

"Isn't it magnificent, Etienne?" Behind Lyra Homat made an impolite noise while Etienne elected to reserve judgment. Alien beauty could be deceptive.

"Very aesthetic appearance," he grudgingly admitted. But he found it hard to resist the multicolored town after the bland whites and yellows of Mai communities. It seemed as if every building in Turput was painted a different color. The town, like the air above it, was alive with rainbows.

They started down the ridge. As they neared the town they saw one could enter from any direction without encountering an obstruction. There was a single small gate, an afterthought of wooden logs and planks. One could walk around it as easily as through it. It also offered them their first Tsla.

Lyra and Etienne were not familiar with Tsla characteristics and so could not tell how old he was, but both scientists received an impression of age. In height he stood midway between Etienne's and Lyra's. The resemblance between Tsla and human, and for that matter between Tsla and Mai, ended there.

His toga-and-cape attire could not conceal the fact that he was covered everywhere save on the forearms and forelegs with a short, soft brown fur. The head rested on a neck that was curved forward, giving a false impression of age. Ears were short round stubs set atop the head. The six fingers were shorter and stubbier than those of Mai or human while the eyes displayed a dewy luster.

Most prominent of all the facial features was the quartermeter long flexible snout like that of the terran tapir. It bobbed and dipped with an independent life of its own, no doubt conveying subtleties of expression discernible only to another Tsla. Twin nostrils were visible through the fur at the tip.

It strained Etienne's laboriously memorized Tsla to translate the Tsla's greeting. "I am Sau, Keeper of the Gate of Hospitality." To Etienne's relief the Tsla switched to fluent Mai. "Word of thy coming has preceded thee. You are the visitors said to come from another world."

Lyra nodded sagely. Her affinity for languages reached far beyond Etienne's, and she wasn't hesitant about trying the local dialect. "We are they, Keeper. Your gate must be of hospitality, for it protects nothing but air."

"A conceit." The Tsla spread both hands to the air, showing bare skin up to the elbow. "Most visitors seem to expect a gate, so one was made. Higher towns than Turput have need of real gates. We do not."

The language of the Tsla was slow and languorous, a startling contrast to the fast-paced singsong of the Mai. Etienne found himself impatient for the Keeper to continue.

"Thee are welcome here. We hope that thy visit will honor us."

Polite, open, with none of the double meanings the Mai attached to such phrases of greeting. Despite his initial reservations Etienne found himself developing a fondness for the Tsla. There was a graciousness about this creature no Mai had displayed, not even the obsequious Ambassador Ror de-Kelwhoang of Po Rabi.

"Follow me and I will take you to a place of rest. Thy friends," he added with a barely perceptible hint of distaste as he indicated the porters, "are also welcome."

"Most generous of thee," Lyra replied properly as the Tsla turned to lead them into the town.

Their escort kept up a fair pace, moving with deliberation so as not to tire the visitors. Instead of lifting each foot and then setting it ahead and down, the Tsla moved with a gait more shuffle and slide. The cape covering the creature's broad back was dark brown split by a single yellow stripe running down the middle. This simple motif was present on the toga as well. Etienne found himself unexpectedly pleased by the sight of another intelligent creature with hair. Baldness was the norm not only among the Mai but the thranx as well.

After they entered the town, each Tsla they encountered marked their passage by duplicating the Keeper's raising of hands, as if they were caressing the air. The Mai muttered among themselves and packed into a tight knot behind the humans. Etienne wondered at their paranoia, which was typically Mai. There was no suggestion of treachery here.

Clusters of Tsla children followed a polite distance behind, wiggling curious stubs of snouts as they took the scent of the peculiar strangers. Before too long the Keeper halted outside a long barnlike building with a gently curving roof. It resembled a broken olla set on its side against the earth.

"This is the Trade Place," one of the porters said. "I was here once before, though I did not stay long."

The Keeper beckoned them to enter. Inside it was dark and cool. Off to the right they found a row of interconnected chambers with skylights set into the curving ceiling. The glass was well-fashioned, with few bubbles. It was a good twenty degrees warmer in the room than it had been out in the hallway.

"For thy friends," the Keeper announced, "and for thee as well if you so desire."

"No, thanks." Etienne watched the Mai pile joyfully into the big room and stand with their faces turned up to the sunlight. They divested themselves of their burdens without being told. "I think we'd prefer the type of room you use yourselves."

"As thee wish." The Keeper took them back out into the hall and led them farther into the building to a smaller room full of the aroma of fresh incense.

"If this suits thee, I must leave now."

"It suits," Etienne said.

Lyra was running a hand over the near wall. "Look at this, Etienne. The entire inside wall is glazed, like a big pot!"

He let his fingers touch the slick surface. "Watertight and cool in summer, reflects the heat of a fire in winter." The single skylight did not trap the heat as did those in the porters' room. A window at eyelevel allowed a view outside to the paved street.

After a time a second Tsla joined them. He was taller than the Keeper and stood a little straighter while still displaying the curved upper spine. He wore a similar toga and cape arrangement, but this one was black with two gold stripes dividing it.

"I am Tyl. I have the honor to be thy host and guide during thy visit to Turput." He made no secret of his own curiosity regarding the strangers. "Anything thee wish thee have but to ask and if it can be provided it will."

"We can't stay long," Etienne replied, chosing to ignore his wife's radiant expression. She was in xenosociological heaven. "We left our boat down on the Skar and we have to return there soon."

"Never mind that now. Tyl, we want to see everything we can. It's true we have little time, but I want to learn as much as possible about thy people and their customs, their way of life. That is my job."

"Worthy scholarship," said Tyl. He had an unexpectedly deep voice that came rolling out in breathy, rounded syllables from beneath the flexible snout. "If thy time is constrained thee must listen close as well as look. Tomorrow, if arrangements can be made, I will take thee to the temple of Moraung Motau."

"Maybe we'd like to see something else first."

"Etienne! Don't be impolite. You've been too long among the Mai. I swear, you're starting to act like a riverfront merchant."

He was too tired to bicker with her, simply turned away and examined the wall while she continued to converse with Tyl.

"If thee prefer," their host said, "there is a little time left to the day. We could begin now."

"Not on your—thy—life." Etienne headed for a padded bench that obviously was designed to serve as a couch or bed or both. "I'm worn out."

"Well I'm not," Lyra snapped. "You may show me around if thee wish, Tyl."

"My greatest honor."

Etienne thought of a suitably sarcastic rejoinder but found

it hard to find a reason for spiting the Tsla's courtesy. He said nothing as they departed. The sound of chimes and bells was like a sedative and the couch-bed surprisingly comfortable. Before he knew it he was sound asleep.

Light from a candle set in a glass dish on a high shelf awakened him. No doubt it had been lit carefully while he slept by some conscientious servitor.

"Wake up, I said."

He rolled over, found himself staring up at his wife's excited face. He rubbed tiredly at his heavy eyes. "What is it?"

"Etienne, Tyl took me through half the town, by torchlight. The system of government these people have developed is unique to sentients in this technological classification! These Tsla are a xenological wonder. Do you know that the spiritual administrators—and they're not priests, more the equivalent of primitive psychoanalysts—actually hold half the seats of government?"

"That's interesting." He began to roll over but she put a hand out to restrain him. He looked irritatedly back over his shoulder.

"Etienne, *listen* to me! This social structure is unprecedented. This is a presteam civilization, yet the people are socially advanced enough to pay extraordinary attention to something as sophisticated as mental health. They don't define it quite like that, of course, but it comes out the same. They may be the stablest primitive alien society yet encountered, and they do this without holding any unwarranted illusions about themselves.

"No wonder the Mai fear and suspect them! The Tsla are so much better balanced. The Tsla have come to terms with the health of their minds earlier than most peoples do with the condition of their bodies. Even Martinson's work on Alaspin is proof of it. This discovery, Etienne, it's worth all the trouble of making the expedition." She stood and began to pace the room.

"The Tsla are special, unique. There's more than a chip monograph here, there's an entire volume."

"I'm thrilled for you." He let out a helpless yawn. "Do keep in mind that we have half a river left to explore."

She started to comment, changed her mind in midthought.

"You're exhausted, Etienne. We'll discuss this in the morning."

"You should be exhausted too."

"I know, but I can't hold back the enthusiasm. I'm running on adrenalin, Etienne, and I have to share this with someone. Who else if not you?" She hesitated and added in an odd tone of voice, "Tyl would be interested."

"Tyl strikes me as a good listener." Etienne pulled the light blanket up around his neck.

"He is, and a good talker as well. From all I was able to discern he's regarded very well by his fellow Tsla. I watched him perform his evening *prann*. Beneath all those robes and cloaks they wear, some of these people are very impressive physical specimens, Etienne. Much more impressive than the Mai."

"Makes sense. The climate up here's less benign and working steep terraces requires more strength than tending to a floodplain."

"Yes. Much more in the way of physical strength," she murmured.

"I'm glad you had such a profitable evening. Now if you don't mind, I really was enjoying my sleep."

"Sorry. Inconsiderate of me." She tiptoed backward from the room. "I'll leave you now, Etienne, and I'll try not to wake you when I return. I have to find Tyl."

"Sure," he mumbled, already half-conscious again, "go find Tyl."

He felt much refreshed the next morning. The sun was shining brightly through the skylight and window and a basin of clear cold water was waiting for him by the foot of his bed. It was the best night's sleep he'd had since leaving Steamer Station.

He splashed water off his face, dried himself with his shirt, and looked around.

"Lyra?" The other couch-bed was empty. He raised his voice a little. "Lyra!"

She entered through the arched doorway a moment later, already fully dressed and wide awake. He frowned at her.

"Didn't you get any sleep?"

"Sure did. Slept like Lazarus, got up at dawn. This is such

a wonderful place, Etienne. I know it's an unprofessional thing to say, but there's no comparing these people to the Mai, Homat being an exception. From what Tyl tells me there's next to no crime among the Tsla. We can leave our possessions anywhere in town without fear they'll be stolen. That's another byproduct of their concern for mental health. They've learned to cope with their baser instincts not only better than the Mai, but better than many people I know."

"That's quite a judgment to make on the basis of half a night's conversation with one native. Isn't it an unwritten rule that all primitive cultures have their hidden eccentricities? I'm sure the Tsla's will appear in due course." He hunted for his lederhosen.

"Maybe so, but I haven't seen any evidence of it yet and I've been looking. Hurry up. Tyl's waiting for us."

"Waiting for us? Why?"

She didn't try to mute her exasperation. "To guide us to the temple of Moraung Motau, remember?"

"Sorry. Still full of sleep. What about something to eat?"

"That's waiting too. I've already sampled the local cooking. It's blander than the Mai's but perfectly palatable. Don't worry about Homat and the others. They've already eaten and they're stretched out under their skylights, soaking up the ultraviolet."

The meal that was brought to their room was simple but ample. Tyl joined them, watching while they ate and sharing their enjoyment if not their table.

Etienne muttered a terse thank you, asked, "How far is it to this temple?"

"A day's journey. We will spend the night near there."

Etienne searched his memory, was unable to conjure up the sight of any large structures at the far end of the valley and told Tyl so.

"You did not miss seeing it, friend Etienne. I perhaps should have said it lies a day's ride from Turput. We will not use our own feet."

"Lowagons?" Etienne inquired, thankful for his feet.

"No. Those are tools of the Mai. We will ride *lekkas*. When thee are ready, I will take thee."

In the stable area behind the hospitality building they encountered their first *lekka*, a furry thin-legged creature

[93]

with an incongruously rotund body and a double tail that switched nervously from side to side. Blunt furry faces turned to glance curiously at the bearers of strange new smells. They waited with placid expressions and chewed their cuds as Tsla handlers attached reins to the base of high, forward-curving ears. The forelegs were longer than the hind, an unusual arrangement for an animal built to run. Etienne thought of hyenas and giraffes, though the *lekka* was bulkier than either.

In consequence, there was no pommel on the woven cloth saddles. Instead, each boasted a high backrest designed to keep the rider from sliding backward down the sloping spine. It was heavily padded. There were no stirrups. The handlers brought stepstools to assist in mounting.

The reins were simple and straightforward and both Redowls were mounted in minutes. Tyl turned his own steed, spoke comfortingly.

"One thing to be careful of. The *lekka* stands quietly, but they love to run. So be prepared." A stableyard gate was swung open ahead and he swung his *lekka* around.

As their guide shouted an indecipherable Tsla word, Etienne's mount made a sudden rush for the gap, reaching out with those long forelegs and nearly throwing its rider feet over head despite the saddle's solid backbrace. As it was he almost kicked himself in the mouth. Lyra's deep, vibrant laugh didn't make him feel any better. He threw her a murderous look which she ignored as she smoothly followed Tyl out the gate.

Etienne brought up the rear, furious at his own clumsiness and determined to master his animal. Before too long his hips adjusted to the odd reaching gallop and he was speeding up the wide dirt road as comfortably as Lyra.

The track ran parallel to the river. The Aurang here was some six kilometers wide, a mighty torrent but only a trickle compared to the Skar. At the far end of the hanging valley the river fell to earth in a broad waterfall, sparkling and most impressive. It was a good hundred meters high and reminded him of the great waterfalls trideed on the tropical thranx worlds that they some day hoped to visit.

He nudged his mount nearer Lyra and Tyl, called across to their guide.

"It is called the Visautik," Tyl informed him. "We will reach it by midday."

Etienne was studying the sheer wall that seemed to mark the end of the valley. "Then what?"

"There is a trail not visible from here, a trading road that climbs a rockfall on this side of the Visautik. It rises to the next valley. Many legats beyond lies the temple of Moraung Motau. And the Cuparaggai."

"What's that?" Lyra asked, simultaneously noting that the Tsla used the same unit to measure distance as did the Mai.

There was no way of telling if their guide smiled, since his mouth was hidden by the weaving proboscis, but Tyl nonetheless managed to convey a feeling of anticipation as well as delighted amusement as he said, "Thee will see."

〚 VIII 〛

They heard the Cuparaggai long before they saw it, and felt it before they heard it. It announced itself as a buzzing in the ears, a vibration in the bones. Its roar drowned out the rush of Visautik Falls before they crested the canyon wall.

The temple valley was not as large as the one in which Turput lay, and it appeared narrower and smaller still because of the height of the walls that enclosed it. Jewellike fields filled the valley, nourished by the Aurang's flow. At the far end of the valley lay the still unseen source of steady thunder, marked only by sunlit mist.

They paused atop the ridge and had an interesting lunch that consisted of some kind of local rolled meat and thick, sweet breadsticks. Then they remounted and rode on. Several hours later Tyl paused and extracted a handful of small round cottony pads.

Lyra examined the pair he handed to her. "What are these for?"

Tyl pointed to the small shapes atop his head, then pushed one of the pads inside.

"Oh!" Lyra hadn't noticed that they now had to shout in order to be heard over the nearing roar, but she was made aware of it as soon as she inserted the pads and silence returned.

Despite these precautions they were quite unprepared for the sight that greeted them when they turned a sharp bend in the canyon.

Several kilometers ahead, sheer rock walls met to form a vertical defile no more than four kilometers wide. For the first time since they'd left the Skar, Etienne forgot his irritation with Lyra. He was enveloped by wonder.

"How high?" she shouted at him, leaning close so that he could hear her through his earplugs. He'd already taken a sighting with the instrumentation on his wrist.

"Twenty-five hundred meters!" Only the fact that the spray did not rise half as high as the falls themselves enabled them to see the cliff where the Aurang River flowed over the edge of the Guntali Plateau. It was a frightening, magnificent drop and the result was a cascade of unmatched proportions, fittingly located on a world of geological superlatives.

It seemed impossible that the stone at the base of that torrent could withstand the impact of so much water falling from such a height without turning to powder. Just as it seemed impossible for the ancient multistorey edifice that clung to the cliff face just to the right of the waterfall to remain in place without having been shaken to pieces hundreds of years ago.

Tyl pointed. "Moraung Motau."

"How old?" Lyra shouted as they raced toward it.

"A thousand years, two thousand, who can say?" Tyl spurred his *lekka* on.

Hundreds of windows threw back the sun from the rambling, rock-climbing structure, which appeared more than large enough to shelter the whole population of Turput. Huge bas-reliefs covered the facade with writhing figures and decorative motifs. Only the fact that the building had been hewn from the raw stone of the cliff face enabled it to withstand the steady vibration produced by the immense waterfall nearby.

Several thousand years, Tyl had said, and Etienne had

no reason to doubt the Tsla's veracity. He had shown himself to be truthful in everything else.

As they drew near he saw that the thick green lines that covered the lower part of the cliff on both sides of the Cuparaggài were not sculpted and painted decorations but enormous vines, unlike anything they had observed growing on Tslamaina before. Tsla toiled among them, tending to roots and leaves. They wore longer capes of some shiny material which kept them from being soaked by the omnipresent spray.

Tyl reined in his *lekka* and the two humans slowed accordingly.

"Aren't we going any farther?" Lyra asked, shouting to make herself heard over the Cuparaggai's thunder. "Aren't we going inside the temple?"

Tyl gestured negatively and looked apologetic. "I am sorry, but it is not permitted. Thee are not initiates. Nor could thee stand it for very long. The monks who live and work at Moraung Motau are attuned to the old books and ancient ways. They are also quite deaf. It has always been so."

He led them through the gate of a nearby farm. Etienne could not tell if the stop had been prearranged, but the farmer and his two mates were as cordial and relaxed as if they'd known their guests for years.

There they stayed and spent the remainder of the day talking, or rather, everyone listened politely and attempted to answer Lyra's unending questions. She inquired about division of labor in the valley, family structure, monkish ritual, about trading procedure and education and what the Tsla expected of an afterlife until the poor farmer and his mates were exhausted. Eventually Tyl intervened.

"Much of what thee request of this family they can not provide for reasons of ignorance, inhibition, custom, or uncertainty. Nor can I. There is one who might sate thy endless curiosity."

"Then that's who I want to meet."

"Mii-an is Chief Consoler and First Scholar of Turput. His time he gives of but sparingly, for he is old and tired. But I believe he will consent to share himself with thee."

"That would be wonderful." Lyra put a hand on her husband's arm. "Wouldn't that be wonderful, Etienne?"

"Wonderful. You won't mind if I don't tag along?"

She looked shocked. "Etienne, this is a special opportunity. How can you?..." She caught herself, coughed. "You'd rather look at the rocks, wouldn't you?"

"That's right. I'd rather look at the rocks. You go ahead and sit at the feet of this Consoler." He glanced past her, to Tyl. "Provided it's no imposition."

"Friend Etienne, the sharing of knowledge is never an imposition, just like the sharing of self. It gives pleasure."

On their way back down to Turput, Etienne let his *lekka* fall behind Tyl's so that he could talk to his wife without shouting.

"Lyra, don't you think you're starting to view these people with something less than scientific detachment? Of all people, you ought to know better than to idealize a primitive race, no matter how superficially attractive their philosophy may seem."

"It's not superficial. You put too high a premium on technology, Etienne. There are other definitions of advancement, other kinds of higher knowledge."

He found himself growing angry. "Come on now, Lyra. The Tsla are nice enough, and they *seem* content within themselves, but that's hardly reason enough to go overboard about them. I never thought I'd see you romanticizing a bunch of elephant-nosed aborigines."

"I would not use the word 'aborigine' to describe them," she replied coldly. "They have advanced far beyond that stage. As for 'romanticizing' them, I don't consider you qualified to use the word."

Her whole attitude struck him as so absurd that the put-down missed its intended effect. "This is supposed to be a scientific expedition," he told her, "and we've been more than a little occupied with business. I'm sorry if I haven't found much time for romance, but I'm not used to strumming guitars beneath four moons, let alone one. Besides which it's a two-way street. A little encouragement on a second party's part might be in order."

She bridled at that. "I've given you ample opportunity."

"You don't say? How exactly do you define ample opportunity, and how does that have anything to do with encouragement? They're two different things, you know."

"If you don't know," she snapped, "I certainly can't tell

you." She spurred her *lekka* forward until she was cantering alongside their guide.

Etienne watched as the pair of them began an animated discussion of some obscure aspect of Tsla behavior. Infatuated, he told himself. A good scientist like Lyra, infatuated with a bunch of furry primitives. It was hard to believe.

Well, she'd get over it soon enough. Everything about Tsla culture was new to her, each bit of information a surprise and contrast to what they'd learned about the Mai. As soon as she worked it out of her system they'd head back down into the Barshajagad and life would return to normal. Let her rhapsodize about her work. He had plenty of his own to do for a change. If she tried to draw him into her discussions all he had to do was start talking enthusiastically about the amount of pyroxine in the local metamorphics and she'd leave him alone quickly enough.

True to his word as always, Tyl succeeded in obtaining permission for Lyra to have an audience with the Chief Consoler. From then on Etienne saw very little of his wife save at mealtimes. He lost himself in his own field studies, making as complete a record of the canyon of the Aurang and its formations as possible, estimating the age of various strata and returning several times to marvel at the power and majesty of Cuparaggai Falls.

It was only several weeks later, during one of their increasingly infrequent meetings in their room, that he remarked again on the amount of time she was spending among their hosts, and it was not something she said that prompted his comments: it was her appearance.

"Where did you get that outfit?" He stared at her and tried to withhold his laughter.

Lyra executed a slow pirouette for him. The brilliantly striped free-flowing gown and cape swirled loosely around her.

"Tyl gave it to me. Mii-an ordered it. It seems that he thinks very highly of me. We've been exchanging information, you see. He teaches me, I teach him. Mii-an lives for the sharing of knowledge."

"Glad the two of you are getting along so well. But really, Lyra—native dress?"

"What's wrong with it? It keeps off the wind, it's as warm

during the night as my long sleeves and cooler during the day. Eminently practical. They had to modify the shoulder area for me. We don't have that curvature of the upper spine, and my arms are longer, but it's such a tentlike garment little work was necessary. Mii-an insisted."

"Nice of the old boy. What enlightening discoveries have you made?"

"Everything I've learned to date only confirms what I originally suspected. The Tsla are the most sociologically advanced race of their class yet discovered. They have no standing army, no police force, and all citizens bear arms on the rare occasions when it's necessary."

"No crime at all, in a society this primitive?"

"There you go with your preconceived notions of what's primitive, Etienne. There's some crime, naturally. It's handled by the Consolers and Advisors. They treat the culprit like a patient, not a criminal. Cure and not punishment. According to the First Scholar there is perfection in everyone."

"You included, naturally."

"Me included." The sarcasm went right past her. "You included. The Mai and the Na included." Then she said something which made him sit up and take notice. "Etienne, I believe the Tsla may be mildly telepathic."

"Now that *would* be a discovery worth shouting about. There are no known telepathic races, only mutant individuals. What makes you think so?"

"Their remarkable perceptivity. They seem to have an instinctive grasp of what I'm going to say before I say it."

His initial excitement faded. "What makes you think it's anything more than that?"

She suddenly looked uncomfortable. "For one thing, Tyl has commented on more than one occasion that he doesn't believe you and I are getting along too well."

The sharp laugh that filled the room was wholly spontaneous.

"And you're basing your assumption on evidence like that? You don't have to be a telepathic native to see that you and I aren't exactly acting like the ideal couple. I'm sure you've shared that knowledge with this Mii-an also and he passed it on to Tyl."

"You just don't want to consider the possibility, do you?"

"Possibility? Show me some real evidence for telepathic ability and I'll consider the possibility. I'm starting to worry about you, Lyra."

"Save yourself the trouble." She turned to leave. "I should have known better than to confide in you."

"Lyra..." She hesitated. "Lyra, we've only been here a few weeks. The Tsla aren't natural wonders any more than they're living examples of Rousseau's natural man. They're simply a nicer group of folks than the Mai. For all we know they may make mass sacrifices every six months."

"I don't understand your hostility. Why this sudden antipathy toward the Tsla? They've been perfect hosts."

"There's no antipathy and what I'm saying has nothing to do with the Tsla. All I'm saying is that no conscientious researcher should jump to conclusions, much less make value judgments about an entire race on the basis of a few weeks spent among one group of villagers."

"I can agree with that, Etienne. A lot more study is needed to confirm my findings. There are several volumes to be composed. I haven't even had time to examine how the Tsla's position as middlemen between the Mai and the Na has affected their outlook on life and their social development."

"I'm sure someone will resolve all the loose xenological ends neatly some day." She said nothing and a sudden thought changed his tone. "Lyra, are you trying to tell me something?"

"Yes. I'm not ready to go Upriver again yet, Etienne. My work here is barely under way."

"When will you be ready to go Upriver again, my love?"

"Maybe in a couple of months. Certainly no sooner."

"That takes us into local winter. That wouldn't cause us any problems here, but up near the arctic circle the Skar may freeze solid. The hydrofoil's not equipped for ice skimming, Lyra. We can't wait two months."

She turned again, a swirl of brightly striped cottonlike folds. "I'm sorry, Etienne, but I can't abandon my work here. As you so aptly pointed out, I don't have sufficient evidence to support my numerous conclusions."

"Where are you going?"

"Evening meditation. I've been invited to watch and to participate if I desire. I'd ask you along but you wouldn't find a bunch of aborigines sitting around attempting to get in touch with their inner selves very interesting, would you?"

And she was gone. He stared after her for a long minute.

"Well, damn!" He would have kicked his bed if it hadn't been constructed of solid rock. He settled instead for slamming one fist into an open palm until the latter was sore.

Of one thing he was certain. No matter how vital Lyra considered her work here, they had to return to the Skar. That was the agreement. Similar agreements had kept their marriage together for twenty years and he was damned if he was going to alter that relationship because of a sudden infatuation on her part for a race of pseudolamaistic anteaters with soulful eyes.

She didn't come to the room that night. It wasn't the first time she'd stayed away all night, but it was the first time he'd lain awake long enough to notice it. It was very early the next morning when he strode purposefully down the hall toward the porters' quarters.

Like his companions, Homat lay asleep beneath a half dozen heavy woven blankets. Etienne estimated the room temperature at seventy degrees. He nudged the Mai hard.

"What is it, de-Etienne?" Homat inquired as he tried to clear his vision.

"Get up. Get everyone up. We're leaving."

"Leaving, de-Etienne? I thought—you did not say, and it is very early."

"There's been a sudden change of plans. You'll find out that we humans have a tendency to do things on the spur of the moment."

"I understand that, de-Etienne, but—"

"I'll be in the courtyard if you need me. Tell them to hurry it up." He left a very puzzled Mai behind him.

Evidently meditation was over, or else someone had roused his wife from her contemplation. She stormed out into the open courtyard, ignoring the strained singing of several lizardlike *puouts* on the main gate. Etienne didn't look up from his work. He was checking the supplies several somber Tsla were providing.

"Etienne, this is childish. You know how I hate it when you turn childish."

"Yes, I know, and you hate ultimatums even worse."

"That's because ultimatums are the worst manifestation of childishness. I thought everything had been settled last night."

"Settled to your satisfaction. Not to mine. I'm leaving." He tugged brutally on a backpack's straps.

She sighed deeply. "I told you that my work here is just getting under way, that I'm only beginning to make some real progress in understanding this culture, these people."

"Fine. I understand that." He moved to check another pack. Homat and the rest of the porters began filing sleepily out of the hospitality building, shivering in the early morning cold. Few Tsla were about this early and the sun was just peeking over the eastern wall of the canyon.

"You stay here, Lyra. You don't have to come down with me. If all goes as intended I'll be back in six months to pick you up. Stay and meditate like mad."

"You can't go north alone," she argued. "Two is the absolute minimum authorized for an expedition like this."

"Then from this point on the expedition advances without authorization, I guess. Homat's learned enough to assist me. Haven't you, Homat?"

The Mai guide's gaze shifted warily from one tall alien to the other and he found reason to work on the pack farthest away from them both.

Etienne started toward another bundle and Lyra rushed to confront him, blocking his path. "Stop it, Etienne. Stop it right now. I'm not in the mood for a fight."

"Why not?" he asked sarcastically. "Did I upset your morning devotions? And as long as we're on the subject of childish acts, how would you define someone who forgets eight years of higher education and goes native despite twenty years of arduous fieldwork that consistently proves such activities are counterproductive to good research?"

"I've explained before that the Tsla are a unique race deserving of special study. Sometimes to obtain the best results it's necessary to bend the rules."

"Not as far as I'm concerned it isn't." He waved expansively at the surrounding buildings. "But you go ahead. Stay and have yourself a deliriously good time. Bury yourself in native customs and habits. Inhale primitive wisdom, join the local religion, become a Tsla nun if they have such institutions—I don't care. I never put restraints on you, Lyra, despite all your talk of ultimatums.

"As for me, I intend to locate the source of the river Skar and study its history and geology from there to the morass of the Skatandah. Halfway along that journey of discovery I will make it a point to stop back here and pick you up."

"Etienne."

"What?" He stepped around her and bent to the pack with a will.

"Etienne, you know I can't let you go without me."

"Why not? What about your carefully timed research program?"

"We're a team, Etienne. We complement each other. Neither of us does our best work solitaire."

"We'll just have to adapt somehow, won't we?"

"No," said a new voice. Etienne frowned, looked toward the hallway. He and Lyra had been arguing in Tsla, using the local language out of habit.

The Chief Consoler and First Scholar of Turput stood in the portal. It was the first time Etienne had seen him and the Tsla's advanced age manifested itself in the streaks of silver that dominated his face, the wrinkled flesh of exposed forearms. Tyl stood at his right shoulder to lend support should it be needed. Mii-an leaned on a twisted cane.

"I was told of the disturbance," he said in a surprisingly strong voice.

"No disturbance," Etienne muttered, inspecting the packs. "Just a friendly domestic conversation, that's all."

"We do not mean to intrude," Tyl said. "It would give me much unhappiness if I thought that we—"

"Oh for heaven's sake." Etienne turned sharply to confront the newcomers. "Must you people always be so damned *polite*?"

"We're sorry," said Mii-an. "It is our nature."

Etienne threw up his hands.

"Such a disturbance cannot be allowed," Mii-an said.

"What do you mean it can't be allowed?" Etienne asked him.

"Discord among guests is not to be tolerated."

"Really? And what do you propose as a solution?"

Mii-an shambled across the paving to stand close to Lyra. He took her left hand in some strange alien grip Etienne hadn't observed in use before.

"Thee must go with thy mate. If thy duality is to be the price of thy studies, I cannot allow thee to continue. When all is resolved, return to study with us another time."

"But it was already settled," she protested. "I was to remain here and continue my research, learn your ways and—"

The Chief Consoler raised a six-fingered hand. "We will miss thee, for thou has a thirst for learning that all but matches our own. If thee could bring thy mate's work here all would be simplified, but mountains are difficult to move. It is more sensible for thee to accompany him. Besides, thee may still continue thy studies, for some of thy work can go with thee, a boon for which we would be most thankful."

"I don't understand, Mii-an." Etienne listened without looking. Apparently the First Scholar was taking his side and he was embarrassed by his early display of anger.

"Beyond the lands that lie Upriver from Turput are many that are unknown to thy Mai companions." He gestured to his right. "If thee will permit it, Tyl and four bearers will accompany thee. He has traveled extensively, knows many Upriver dialects and peoples. When you pass beyond his realm of knowledge, he will be there to see and to study for all Turput. And when not guiding thee he can continue to instruct you in our ways."

"You said you'd do that yourself."

"The instructor is not important. All that matters is the knowledge."

"It's not that simple." She glanced at Etienne, who carefully avoided her stare. "Looks like you win after all. I can argue with you but not with Tsla logic. That is, if you have no objection to Tyl joining us."

"I've no objection, but it's not entirely up to us." He rose from the pack he'd been inspecting so intently. "Homat?"

"You already have a guide, de-Etienne," he replied slowly.

"We do, and a fine one, but what the old Tsla says makes

good sense. Haven't you said that the river beyond this point is new to you?"

"Yes, yes." Homat was still reluctant to surrender any of his hard-won authority. "I see that you are right, de-Etienne. A Tsla who knows the way would be welcome." He tugged at the hood of his coat. "Anything would be welcomed that takes us quickly out of this cold country."

Etienne grinned. "I apologize. I guess I did kind of drag all of you out of a warm bed on your equivalent of an icy morning." He turned to the First Scholar. "We accept your kind offer. Tyl's been nothing but helpful since we got here and I see no reason not to share his company. How do you feel about this, Tyl? You haven't said anything."

"It is Mii-an's place to say, but I look forward to it. I will gain much knowledge. It is a unique opportunity for me."

"It's settled then, I expect." Lyra started for the hallway. "I'll go get ready. See what I mean about Tsla judgment, Etienne? They have enough sense to see that we're a team even when we don't."

He left the Mai to make final preparations and hurried to catch up with her. She was resigned to leaving, which was very different from being agreed.

"I'm sorry I had to force the issue like this, Lyra, but I was at my wits' end. I couldn't think of anything else."

"I accept that." She slowed and some of the hardness drained from her expression. "Maybe you're right, Etienne. Maybe I've gotten a little too close to my work here. The soul of a good working team is its ability to compromise. I'm compromising. Just remember, you owe me one."

"I promise, Lyra. On the way back you can spend as much time as you want. But we must make it to the turn-around point, the source of the Skar, before winter sets in up north. We've no idea what to expect, since the southern winters are moderated by the Groalamasan."

"So you keep telling me."

"What about this Tyl?" he asked, changing the subject. "You've been working with these people. He's a scholar. Do you think he's up to a difficult, dangerous journey? Physically, I mean. Mentally I know that he's ready."

"Don't worry about his stamina, Etienne. The Tsla are as adaptable as we are, not at all like the Mai. He'll be able to handle the heat down in the Barshajagad. We'll make space for him inside. There's plenty of room. He and his companions will manage."

"Companions?"

"You didn't hear the First Scholar's last words?" Etienne shook his head. "Mii-an doesn't want to send Tyl by himself. He wants to send him with four porters, to replace the Mai who will leave as soon as we reach the river."

"We don't need porters on the river."

"Mii-an has told me several times these past days that there will come a point where we'll have to leave the river, leave our boat."

"We can't leave the boat. You know that."

"I know it, yes, but Mii-an insists that without porters we'll have to turn back at a place somewhere a couple of thousand legats Upriver."

"It's true." They turned around, saw Homat standing behind them. "I listen and hear many things, de-Etienne. The Tsla speak of this after you have come inside." He eyed Lyra with great interest. "Why do they say such things?"

"Mii-an talks about a spot far Upriver where the Skar undergoes . . . he called it a dramatic change of personality. It's like the Tsla to ascribe such traits to inanimate objects, and he was very clear in his description of this place. It's called the Topapasirut."

Homat's extreme reaction was unexpected. His eyes went very wide as he executed a half dozen powerful signs designed to ward off dangerous spirits.

"It means," Lyra told her husband, "Cleansing Place of all the Waters."

"That doesn't sound very threatening."

"I agree, but Mii-an insists we can't pass beyond it with the boat. Hence his insistence that we accept porters."

"Another waterfall? Satellite topographics don't show any large waterfalls in the northern region of the Barshajagad, though admittedly pictures are less than perfect."

"No, not a waterfall. Something else."

"Five Tsla, Homat?"

"I dislike the presence of so many strangers on board the spirit boat, de-Etienne, but it seems we must tolerate all to gain the knowledge of one."

Etienne Redowl considered, said finally, "Tell the one called Mii-an we accept his generous offer, but that all the porters are to be under your command." The Mai seemed to grow several centimeters.

"They won't stand for that," Lyra argued.

"Won't they? Surely your high and mighty Tsla can take orders from a mere Mai. Don't tell me they'll *argue* about it."

"Tyl is an important scholar."

"I said that the four porters would act at Homat's direction, not Tyl. You'll just have to explain to Mii-an that Homat's been with us a long time, that he's familiar with our boat and its workings, and that he's our right arm. Or left, whichever they accord more weight to."

"Neither. They're physically as well as mentally ambidextrous."

"We need a chain of command. It's going to be crowded on the boat. As for letting them inside the cabin with us, I understand the need but are you sure we can trust them?"

"I trust Tyl completely, Etienne. And the porters will look on their work as the Buddhaistic equivalent of making a pilgrimage for merit. So they'll work their hardest to make sure the expedition's a success."

"Tell them to hurry themselves along then, Homat. We have a long way to go."

"To the river, de-Etienne, and to *real* weather! I will hurry them with delightment!"

【 IX 】

Compared to the long climb up from the shore of the Skar, the descent was as pleasurable as an afternoon stroll through the gardens of New Riviera. In addition, the loads had been distributed among twice as many porters, the Tsla shouldering their new burdens alongside but separate from their Mai counterparts.

The Tsla joked amiably among themselves, their evident good spirits proof enough of Lyra's claim that all were willing volunteers. Whenever Tyl moved among them they deferred to him as they would a superior, but without any of the bowing and scraping common among the Mai. The porters recognized and honored him as their mental and spiritual superior. He, in turn, did not use his position to lord it over his fellows.

There was something of a subtle hierarchy among the porters, however, as if each one knew his place without having to be reminded of it. At the bottom of the pecking order was one exceptionally large, powerful, and mentally slow individual named Yulour. He hardly spoke at all and was often the butt of gentle, nonmalicious humor on the part of his companions, to which he invariably responded with a smile. It took a while for Yulour's slowness to manifest itself beyond a doubt, at which point Etienne slipped back from the head of the party to take Tyl aside.

"Yulour?" Etienne wished he could see if Tyl was smiling, but that weaving flexible snout concealed the lower half of his expression. "He was orphaned in the mountains, his parents slain by some carnivore he could not well describe to us. Perhaps the terror of that moment stopped his mind from growing." Tyl made a gesture Etienne did not recognize.

"He was raised a part of Mii-an's extended family, but it did not help him *here*." Tyl tapped the side of his head. "For all that he is a goodly soul, with a kind heart, and his back is strong if his mind weak. He will gain much merit from this journey, perhaps even enough to admit him to the afterlife."

"It's not my specialty, more my wife's province, but I didn't know that the Tsla believed in an afterlife."

"Not all of us do. I do not know if Yulour does, so I try to believe for him. He appears content with his lot, unfair as life has been to him. There are many I know who envy him his unshakable contentment. On this journey of discovery he is my greatest responsibility—save for thee and thy mate, of course." There was no guile in those warm brown eyes.

"If he were to wander away from us he would never find his way back. Indeed, though he has lived there all his life, he could not find his way back to Turput from this spot. He would not have enough sense to follow the road." Tyl waited and when no more questions were forthcoming, fell back among his fellows.

Everything Lyra claimed for the Tsla was borne out by each new experience. They were a kind, likable people. So why did he persist in trying to find a reason for disliking them?

He knew the answer to that one. Lyra was not fond of the Tsla. She was absolutely infatuated with them. But was that the root of his problem? He pressed on with his internal argument. No, it was something else. There was one Tsla in particular, one she spent all her spare time with, one she looked up to and turned to with every new question: Tyl.

Now there was a bizarre thought, he told himself. No question about it, Tyl was an impressive specimen of mammalian life. It wasn't the first time Lyra had grown personally fond of some object of study.

Patrick O'Morion's space, I'm jealous of an alien aborigine, he told himself. The shock of realization so numbed him he nearly wandered off the road toward a hundred-meter drop. Lyra noticed the dazed look in his eyes.

"Etienne? Are you okay?"

"Sure. Yeah, I'm okay." He blinked, extended his stride until he once more assumed the lead. Lyra stared at his back, shook her head in puzzlement and hurried to catch up with him.

The Tsla brought up the rear. Tyl stood next to Yulour, dwarfed by the porter's bulk. "Yulour?"

"Yes, Learned One?"

"What is the sign made by crossing the Oo and the Strike?"

The porter's brow did not furrow. There was no point in straining his capacity over the mildly complex concept.

"I do not know, Learned One."

"That's all right, Yulour. It's not important. Tell me, what do you think of our new friends?"

Yulour looked over the heads of his companions, at the two humans. "They are very nice, Learned One, though they have so little fur. And when they talk among themselves it is strange talk, neither like ours nor the Mai's. But they are nice."

"Yes, they are. Thank thee for thy opinion, Yulour." The porter made a movement with his trunk.

Tyl rejoined the objects of his interest. "Your curiosity induced me to chat with Yulour, Etienne. I put to him a question simple enough for a cub to answer, and he could not. It was beyond his simple powers of reason. Yet it struck me that he may be happier than we. While he is free of intelligence, he is also free of the pains and travails higher thought brings. Ignorance, frustration, envy: he is subject to none of these."

"You make him out to be a perfect saint."

"Sometimes I wonder. He is so content, and still there are times I do not understand him."

"We have a saying among our people, Tyl." Etienne struggled to translate it into Tsla. "Better a lucky idiot than an unlucky genius."

"Ah, this strange concept of 'luck' again. Lyra mentioned it to me. We have no such concept. You must explain it to me further." Etienne made an attempt to do so as they plodded steadily downhill toward the ever widening streak of silver that was the Skar.

Days passed and the heat intensified, rising past ninety degrees. As it did so the Tsla began shedding their clothing, capes and togas vanishing into packs, not to be used again until the climate of the far north was encountered.

It was the first time Etienne had seen a Tsla without the familiar cape-and-toga attire. They appeared quite comfortable without it, as if clothing was employed for protection against the elements and possibly to signify social standing, but not because of some primitive nudity taboo.

Not that they were naked in the human sense, since soft brown fur covered everything except forearms and forelegs. The only surprise was the unexpected presence of a tail, a short stub five to six centimeters in length. It made them look animalistic, though several intelligent races retained tails. The AAnn, for example, considered the retention of a tail as a sign of intelligence, not vice versa.

In other respects the Tsla were very human, if one discounted the six-fingered hands, six-fingered toes, and myrmecophagous face. There was one other aspect of their anatomy that interested him. He fully intended to question Lyra about it as soon as he could be sure she wouldn't misinterpret his curiosity. Undoubtedly she would have found his uncertainty amusing.

By the time the temperature touched one hundred degrees the Mai were shedding their cold-climate attire, able for the first time in weeks to luxuriate in the stifling heat and humidity.

They reached the bank of the Skar and turned toward Aib. Etienne was looking forward to a cool shower on board the hydrofoil. As soon as they'd cleaned themselves up they'd hand over the second half of the agreed-upon payment to the local Oyt and make preparations for resuming their journey Upriver.

That evening they were confronted by the leader of their

[113]

Mai porters. So rapidly did he talk that even Lyra had trouble following his words. It was left for Homat to interpret.

"It has something to do with the season of sowing," he explained. "They are all late to help and are anxious to be on their way. There is also talk of local taxes. They come not from Aib itself but from the outlying farming district."

Lyra nodded knowingly. "I understand. They want to skip with their payment before the local authorities can demand a cut. Perfectly Mai."

The porters organized a hasty ceremony of departure, took their payment, and left in a rush. Only slightly discomfited by the heat, the Tsla assumed the second half of the divided burdens. Larger and stronger than the Mai, they had no difficulty with the full loads.

Two days later they were nearing the outskirts of Aib when Etienne's eyebrows drew together. "That's funny."

"What is funny, Etienne?" Tyl asked uncertainly.

Etienne ignored the question. Impolite, but he was concerned with something besides alien concepts of courtesy.

"I don't see the boat, Lyra."

She strained her eyes. "Neither do I. Your eyesight's better than mine, Etienne, but you're right. I don't see it. Surely that's the dock where we left it moored?"

"Has to be," he muttered. "See, there's the basaltic outcrop the local ruler used for a dais."

"Something is wrong?" Tyl asked. "I feared as much. These Mai," he said evenly, not caring whether Homat overheard him or not, "will steal anything left unguarded for half an *anat* and consider it moral."

"We made an arrangement," Etienne explained even as his pace quickened, "with the head of this town to watch our boat for us. We paid him half the set fee prior to our departure."

Forbearing to say, "I told you so," Homat instead chose to put the best possible light on the situation. "Perhaps the people of Aib are not responsible for the disappearance of the spirit boat."

"You rationalize hopefully, Homat. What do you really think?"

The Mai's gaze shifted rapidly from one alien to the other.

It was a look Etienne had become familiar with and he hastened to reassure their guide.

"You have nothing to fear from us, Homat. We are your friends."

"You recall, de-Etienne, how I warned you against this possibility?"

"All too clearly." They were almost running now. The dock was an empty gesture protruding into the river.

"I cannot see, de-Etienne, how the spirit boat could have vanished without the Aibites knowing. If they did not take it themselves, they surely did little to prevent its being taken. I thought you said that it could not be stolen, that it would protect itself."

"That's what we thought," Etienne replied grimly. "It looks like we were wrong." He looked toward the town. "Let's pay our good friend Gwattwe a visit, shall we?"

The modest residence of the Oyt of Aib was guarded by a brace of well-armed but obviously nervous warriors. The Oyt, one of them explained, was not at home.

"Then you've no objection to our entering to lay tribute at his table?" Lyra replied.

"I was told to admit no visitors." The soldier looked very unhappy.

Tyl spoke. "This refusal gains your master no grace, to flagrantly flout the laws of hospitality concerning weary travelers."

"In addition to which if you don't let us inside, we'll call on our otherworldly spirits to blow the place down." This was more bluff than promise, since an asynapt wouldn't do more than scorch the stone wall before them, but the guard didn't know that.

The guard looked askance at the pistol riding Etienne's hip, having already assumed it was some sort of weapon. He had no desire to personally discover its capabilities. "I will find out what best be done." He turned and vanished into the domicile, reappearing after a lapse of a few minutes. A curious, hesitant crowd had emerged from other nearby structures. They milled about well clear of the travelers, staring at the pair of aliens and the five Tsla.

"You are to be admitted," the guard informed them, "but only if you leave your spirit callers outside."

"Our spirits come with us," Lyra informed him in no-nonsense tones.

The guard sighed. "I was asked only to request it. Enter."

The stone and wood edifice was something more than a house and a good deal less than a palace, but was no doubt the best a small town like Aib could afford. Although the matter of their boat's whereabouts occupied most of his thoughts, Etienne still managed to note the mixture of envy and distaste with which the local Mai viewed the Tsla.

As Etienne had expected, Gwattwe had been there all along. Etienne thought he looked unwell, as if all the traditional bravado had been knocked out of him. Strange. If he intended to bargain for the missing hydrofoil he was beginning badly.

"Where is it?" he snapped at the Oyt, in no mood for protocol.

"I do not have to guess to what you refer," said the Oyt tiredly. "Your spirit boat is not here."

"You stole it," Etienne growled. "We trusted you, we left payment as security for that trust which you betrayed. You promised that our property would come to no harm."

"I lied," said Gwattwe.

Venerable mastery of diplomacy, Etienne mused sardonically. But this wasn't what he'd anticipated when they'd entered the town. Something was wrong here.

"Where have you hidden it?"

"We do not have your spirit boat." Gwattwe executed a most profound gesture of regret and helplessness. Tyl was watching him carefully.

"I believed you when you offered us assurances. Why should I believe you when you offer disclaimers?"

"It matters not whether you believe me. We do not have your boat. We did not steal it. Oh, we tried to." His expression turned sour. "Most assuredly we tried. Your spirits slew my advisor and several of his students, one at a time." He paused, but if he was expecting some word of contrition from Etienne he was going to have a long wait. He continued.

"We tried everything that we could think of, but we never had a glimpse of the spirits that watched over your vessel, nor of how they slew." He rose from his couch and balding houris rolled clear of his feet.

[116]

"Then where's our boat?"

"It pains me to have to tell you that it was stolen."

"But not by you?"

"Not by us. Why do you think it pains me?" Clearly Gwattwe of Aib was distressed only because another had succeeded where he had failed.

"When I lost my best advisors in matters spirit-wise I finally resolved to contact the renowned Davahassi, who is head advisor to Langai of Hochac."

Tyl leaned close to Etienne and spoke in Mai. "Hochac is a very bad place. It lies a few legats north of the place where the Aurang flows into the Skar. We rarely trade with them, for the people there are mean of spirit and sometimes prefer to kill for what they want rather than pay for it as many Mai are wont to do."

Etienne saw Homat stiffen, but the guide held his tongue. He would have to convince Tyl to be a little more circumspect in his comments concerning the Mai whenever Homat was around.

"It was hoped that Davahassi might solve the secret of your spirit boat as he has traveled widely and gained much knowledge. He came down by boat with Langai himself and a large escort of advisors. I was suspicious then but didn't know what else to do.

"They studied your spirit boat for many days and buried three advisors of their own in the river before Davahassi hit upon his plan. The secret, he announced, was to leave the spirits that protected your vessel in place and not to intrude on their privacy, for clearly the craft was their home and they defended it as such from any intruder. But that did not mean that the home itself could not be moved, provided the spirits within were left undisturbed.

"Therefore at his instructions Langai had a great wooden cage constructed. Many spells were then placed upon the spirit boat as the cage was placed around it and bound in place. It was then dragged from its home, the water, and placed on a platform whence it was transported to the center of Aib. It sat right there while we all celebrated." He pointed toward the town square outside the official residence.

"During the celebration our spirits were high. All would share in the profit from this action. We relaxed with our good 'friends.' Davahassi, may his entrails entice parasites, drugged our fine wine. When we awoke the next day it was found that Langai and his advisors had slipped the spirit boat back into the river. The wooden platform on which it had been placed apparently made a most delighted raft that they used to carry their booty homeward, like carrion eaters.

"We pursued, but too late, and Langai had stationed soldiers in the hills between here and Hochac. Certainly we could not have approached by water in time to intercept them." He concluded his tale of woe and lost opportunity with the Mai equivalent of a disgruntled shrug.

"You see, we did not steal your boat, but it was not for want of trying."

"How noble of you to say so."

"A wooden cage," Lyra murmured. "Wood's a rotten conductor. Once out of the water they'd be safe enough so long as they didn't make contact with the hull."

"'Left the spirits in peace,'" Etienne repeated. "That explains what happened. Nothing's wrong with the ship's defensive systems. They just avoided provoking them. I never thought the locals would have enough sense to move the whole boat without trying to get aboard and at the controls or contents." He turned back to Gwattwe.

"We'd like your help in recovering our property. You can compensate for your own attempted thievery and earn your fee by providing us with a troop of soldiers to help us assault Hochac."

"Would that such a thing were feasible," Gwattwe murmured. "I would do it for the chance at revenge alone, but Hochac is not Aib, hairy one. It is not much larger but it is far stronger. It would take many more soldiers than Aib could provide to overcome it, for Hochac is a walled town and heavily defended. Otherwise it could not withstand the attentions of its neighbors, whom it makes a practice of bullying and defrauding. The Hochacites are known for their love of battle. We of Aib are a peaceful folk."

"Sticky fingers and now sticky feet." A hand came down gently on his shoulder.

"Perhaps," Tyl whispered to him in Tsla so that Gwattwe could not understand, "it might be better for us just to go. The Hochacites may be expecting a big attack. If we approach with patience and caution, we may surprise them. But do not inform this one of our intentions. Like all his kind, he may yet find profit in selling such information to those who have already stolen from him. Feuds are like chaff to the Mai, and as permanent as their promises."

Etienne turned back to the waiting Oyt. "As we apparently have lost our craft and cannot recover it, we must return Downriver to the Groalamasan and our base in order to obtain another. You owe us for what we already have paid you."

"I do not deny that. Business is business," Gwattwe readily admitted.

"We will accept recompense in the form of a couple of riverworthy sailing craft so that we may safely return Downriver."

Gwattwe looked relieved, if not downright pleased. "That is fair," he said quickly. "The craft you wish will be provided. And may you have a safe journey Downriver."

Safe it would be, Etienne mused, but they had no intention of heading south.

Having no reason to ply the Skar, the Tsla were not very good sailors. But Homat felt right at home. With his help, both small boats managed to make their way slowly Upriver.

They anchored well out in the river away from the walled harbor of Hochac. Occasional fishing boats drifted past and their crews hailed the newcomers. Etienne and Lyra stayed out of sight belowdecks while Homat fielded the passing inquiries. The sight of the Tsla raised curious stares, but many of the drifting fisherfolk were from farther Upriver. Their questions were not threatening. Only a few of the curious called Hochac home port. To them the sight of Tsla on the river was unusual, but hardly cause for alarm.

Langai of Hochac and his advisor Davahassi might know that the alien owners of the stolen spirit boat had gone to visit with the Tsla, but that wasn't reason enough to connect the off-worlders to these furry fishermen. As far as Langai and the rest of Hochac knew, Etienne and Lyra Redowl were far away.

So no soldiers rowed out to inspect the fishermen and the two boats were able to move safely inshore on the heels of nightfall. As soon as it was dark, Etienne and Lyra crept out on the upper deck and produced daynight scopes from their kits.

"Must be used to attacks." Etienne squinted through his monocular. "The stockade's made of wood instead of stone, but its good and high. Too high to scale easily. You can see places where the individual logs have been scarred by fire. The top is flat and lined with broken glass. Cute."

"What sign of thy spirit boat?" Tyl asked softly.

"I can't see a thing besides the stockade, but there's a helluva lot of light from the center of town." He touched a switch on the side of the scope and the tiny long-range microphone amplified sound along with the light. Homat jumped at the unexpected rush of noise while the Tsla drew back and made signs. Lyra reassured them.

As soon as Homat had overcome his initial suspicion of the scope, Etienne asked him, "What do you make of this?"

The Mai moved hesitantly nearer the source of the sounds. "Drums, pipes, flutes, high chanting: they sound as if they are celebrating." His face lit with recognition of a particular chant. "That is what it is. A gathering to celebrate their great triumph over the Aibites and their successful theft. I did not recognize it at first. Many of the words here are different from in Po Rabi."

"Then we have a chance to surprise them while they're partying."

"I don't think so, de-Etienne. They will have the spirit boat carefully watched, lest some of their own fellows try to steal it and sell it Downriver. Anyone clever enough to steal the spirit boat would not be so stupid as to trust his own people."

Etienne touched the asynaptic pistol riding his hip. "Then we'll just have to walk in and make a polite request for the return of our property." He glanced at his wife but this time Lyra had nothing to say about the prospect of wreaking havoc on the natives.

Another source did, however. "The taking of lives would be most regrettable." Tyl wore his most soulful expression.

"I'm sorry too, Tyl, but we have to get our boat back and I'm in no mood to be nice about it. Not only would its loss mean the end of our expedition, but there are devices on board that could be a real danger to the Mai themselves if they ever managed to figure them out." He wiped sweat from his forehead. The temperature was still over a hundred and ten and the humidity hovered around ninety percent.

"There's another factor to consider. Lyra and I could probably obtain transportation back down to the Skatandah Delta, but we couldn't take months of this heat."

"I do not dispute the need to recover thy property, Etienne. I only abhor the necessity of taking lives through violence."

"We'll do as little shooting as possible."

"A very exuberant celebration." Homat was still listening intently to the amplified sounds coming from beyond the stockade as the two boats slipped into the harbor. "Siask!" he suddenly snapped, dropping to the gunwale. Etienne and Lyra immediately flattened themselves below the seats.

"What is it? What's the matter?"

"A patrol, I think. What do we do now?"

"If I may be permitted?"

Etienne glanced down toward Tyl. "You have something in mind?"

"You and thy Lyra must remain concealed, for on sight of thee the alarm will surely be raised, but thy friend Homat will only be questioned, especially if we show ourselves. It is unusual, as you know, for we of the Tsla to come down to the river. These warriors should be intrigued by our presence but not alarmed, for it is well known that we love peace and harm no one."

"Good idea, Tyl. You put them off their guard long enough for Lyra and me to get close enough to bring them down."

Tyl's proboscis twitched with amusement. "That would be too risky, would it not?" He gestured toward his companions. "We will undertake the necessary action."

"Wait a minute." Lyra looked confused. "What about what you just said, Tyl, about loving peace and not harming anyone?"

Etienne shushed her. "Don't confuse our guests. Let's see what these pacifists can do when they want to, shall we? Think of it as an interesting footnote to your research."

She gave him an angry stare, but said nothing. They hid themselves beneath a section of sail as the Tsla rowed the boats into shore. He had a sudden crazy urge to pinch her but managed to suppress it.

At first the patrol ordered both boats to stand off, but on sight of the Tsla they allowed them to dock. Etienne listened hard. At any moment he expected the sail to be thrown aside and to find himself eye to eye with a long spear.

Then there was the sound of muffled struggling and he and Lyra emerged from their temporary cocoon with pistols at the ready. They might as well have relaxed beneath the cloth.

Tyl and the porters had no trouble with the patrol. Yulour in particular distinguished himself, exercising his great strength with a caution that was frightening to see. Etienne made a mental note to leave the teasing to Yulour's companions.

The entire patrol had been neatly silenced. Etienne was full of newfound respect for their philosopher-guide as he helped him and the other Tsla slip the guards into the river, but he couldn't help but wonder at this facile contravention of established Tsla tenets. Time enough later for social analysis, he told himself curtly. First order of business was to get their boat back, not discuss Tsla motivation.

Having gone ahead to scout out the approach, Homat now beckoned them forward. Soon they were standing next to the impressive palisade of logs that girdled the town. There were plenty of slots cut in the wood through which archers could aim and fire on attackers. The openings near the harbor showed only the backsides of buildings, but as they made their way around the stockade, gaps appeared which permitted a view deeper into the community.

Eventually they located a small pedestrian gate. It was unguarded and swung wide at Homat's touch and they stepped inside, concealing themselves behind a square storage building.

From the slurred shouts they could now hear clearly, it was evident that plenty of drinking and drug-taking was going on. As they moved toward the center of the town they had a glimpse of unsteady revelers falling down in unexpected places, and nearly tripped over several who had celebrated themselves into unconsciousness.

Ahead lay the town square, a place of ceremony and

money-making among the Mai. Smack in the center of the paved square, surrounded by celebratory bonfires, was the Redowls' hydrofoil. The fires were maintained at a reasonable distance from the boat, not out of any fear of harming it but to ensure the safety of the wooden cage in which it rested. The chanting was loud now and terribly off-key. Etienne looked to his wife, saw with disgust but not surprise that she was furiously whispering a description of the celebration into her note-taker. That was his Lyra: if the locals ended up boiling her in fish fat she'd spend her last moments jotting down the recipe for posterity.

"What now, Learned One?" Apparently Tyl had exhausted his limited store of strategic knowledge. Etienne felt a perverse satisfaction over the Tsla's use of the honorific.

"How can we free thy boat, Learned One?" asked one of the porters. "It seems secured most strongly."

"Doesn't matter," Etienne told him. "All we have to do is get within shouting distance. We're close enough now, but I'm worried that all this loud chanting might drown us out."

"*I* understand," said Homat confidently. "You plan to call upon the spirits that watch over your boat."

Tyl eyed him distastefully. The Tsla were not heir to the plethora of superstitions that infected Mai culture.

"How will thee regain control of thy craft, Etienne? And more important, perhaps, how are we to transport it from the center of this unfriendly village to the water's edge?"

"You'll see," Etienne told him. "Homat's not far from the truth." Their Mai guide chose not to look down his nose at the skeptical Tsla, probably because in any such exchange he was bound to come off second best.

Etienne idly noted the architecture as they worked their way closer to the central square. No grand stone towers here. This wasn't Po Rabi. Most of the buildings were of wood, thatch, mud, and adobe, though several did soar to the impressive height of three stories. He did not admire them, however. Hochac's prosperity was tainted and it throve by taking from its neighbors. Perhaps tonight they could redress a few of those wrongs, make the inhabitants reconsider their methods. He hoped he'd be given that opportunity. Lyra would disapprove of his attitude, he knew, but right now he didn't much care. He watched her coolly making notes and couldn't help but admire her. If they died here tonight, no one could say they'd neglected their research right up to the final moment.

They were halfway to the central square when they stumbled into a pair of sober locals. They looked very young and Etienne regretted having to pull his pistol. He was too slow and could have saved his regrets. Once again Tyl and his companions did their work with quiet efficiency. There were no screams and no deaths, though a single brief warning shout was lost in the shouting and chanting.

They were surprised when the arrow thudded into Swd's side. The short thick fur absorbed some of the arrow's force, but not enough to keep the porter from staggering up against Tyl. He struggled with the shaft as they sought cover beneath the overhang of a large house.

The archer stood on the porch of a building across the street. He was waving his bow toward the square now, jumping up and down and screaming high and steady. To Etienne's chagrin, Homat stepped out into clear sight to return the local's steady stream of expletives. While personally gratifying, this was a lousy tactical move. The celebrants in the square heard the row, turned to see the odd assortment of intruders, and had enough presence of mind left to scatter and sound the warning throughout the village.

A few located their own weapons and began to advance. Bows and arrows and spears might be primitive, but as the unfortunate Swd could attest, they were often as effective as any modern weapon. The differences between asynapt and arrow were neatness and convenience, not lethality. Add to that the fact that in seconds they were likely to be heavily outnumbered and there was little humor to be found in Homat's foolhardy posturing.

Wishing he was closer, Etienne cupped hands to mouth and yelled at the top of his lungs, "Execute Command Red-Ten!" Then he lowered the muzzle of his asynapt and fired at the feet of the nearest onrushing Hochacite. The Mai let out a yelp and fell on his face, paralyzed from the knees down.

That halted the charge for a few seconds, long enough for an answering rumble to rise from the central square. The rest of the attacking villagers turned and stared over their shoulders.

Lit from beneath by the dancing bonfires, the hydrofoil made a most impressive sight as it rose four meters into the air on activated repellers, lifting the wooden cage with it. It executed a slow pirouette until it was facing the direction from which the command had been given, locked in on Etienne's eyes, and started to move toward them. As it did so the downward facing air jets on which it hovered blasted flaming fagots of wood in all directions, scattering fire and natives alike. The movement caused the wooden cage to begin to break up, showering logs and planks down on the scurrying Mai.

〖 x 〗

Those Hochacites who were sober started screaming about spirits and devils as they flung their weapons aside and bolted for the nearest cover. Homat retreated to rejoin his companions, his eyes wide and locked on the hovering bulk of the spirit boat as it drifted toward them.

Lyra had to give him a shove to start him back toward the stockade gate. "Back to the harbor, everybody, before they get over the shock!"

Moving as fast as possible without conveying the impression of a hasty retreat, the intruders fled with studied dignity. Now and then a face would peek out at them as they passed along the street, but a burst from an asynaptic pistol would cause doors and windows to slam shut quickly.

They reached the narrow gate and filed quickly through it. Unable to quite clear the crest of the palisade, the hydrofoil made a satisfyingly loud smashing and crackling as it splintered several of the massive logs.

Etienne and the Tsla remained behind to guard the landward end of a pier while Lyra directed the boat over the water before retracting her husband's order. The hydrofoil settled gently into the Skar. Bending low to avoid an intact section of wooden cage, she stepped aboard.

From his position facing the town wall, Etienne was gratified to hear the start-up growl of the engine as power was transferred from repellers to jet. A few armed Mai had pushed through the gap in the stockade, but hadn't gained the courage to charge. As soon as word came that the boat was acting like a boat once more, some of the initial terror of its unboatlike behavior would fade and the Hochacites would try to recover it. Etienne had no intention of giving them that kind of time. "Now, Tyl! Get your people on board before the Mai have time to regroup!" Even as Etienne backpedaled to cover the Tsla's retreat, the bolder villagers slowly advanced.

Lyra made a quick head count and spun the wheel as she nudged the accelerator. The hydrofoil *varoom*ed out into the safety of the Skar, but not as fast as Etienne wanted. The unwieldy remnants of the cage prevented the boat from rising up on its hydrofoils. Distant shouts sounded from Hochac's harbor; pursuit was being organized.

Among the ship's tools was a heat stitch that could cut and weld. It made short work of the leather thongs that bound the sections of the wooden cage together. As Etienne sliced the thongs the Tsla heaved the heavy timbers over the side, and a few arrows *thunk*ed against the rear of the boat. Finally, with a loud splash the undersection of the cage gave way and drifted astern. The pursuing Mai were still within insult range but by now even Homat was too tired to respond.

Etienne stumbled to the intercom. "We're clear, Lyra. Raise her up."

The rumble of the electric jet became a whine as the boat rose above the surface on its twin foils and rocketed Upriver at a leisurely sixty kph, leaving the Tsla whispering their wonderment to one another and the frustrated Hochacites far behind.

"Wonderful, delicious," Tyl muttered as he peeked hesitantly over the side. "The boat flies over the water. You must explain to me how it works."

Etienne stiffened, relaxed almost as quickly. Tyl's words had sparked bad memories of Irquit and the ease with which she'd mastered the hydrofoil's security system. But there was no deception in this philosopher-teacher. Etienne felt guilty at his instinctive suspicion.

"Be happy to, Tyl. You're entitled to learn about what you've just rescued. I'll try and explain the principles to you and you must tell me more about what we're likely to encounter Upriver, especially this Topapasirut that has you so concerned."

"I will gladly do so, Etienne. But as for the Topapasirut there is little to say. It must be seen to be understood."

"Still certain we can't surmount it?"

"I still think so, yes, but after seeing what you have achieved tonight I am less certain than I was before."

That is faintly encouraging, Etienne mused. Further discussion would have to wait until morning. He longed desperately for the softness of his air-conditioned bunk. Lyra could drive for another half hour. Then they'd be far enough Upriver from any lingering pursuit to put the boat on autopilot.

At last they were on their way again, though he felt no pride in the thoroughly unprofessional but necessary diversion for which the inhabitants of Hochac were responsible. With any luck that would be the first and last interruption of its kind.

As for allowing the Tsla into the cabin, that was a necessity. They would be much more comfortable inside, where the temperature approximated that of their home. There was no fear in him. For one thing he was too tired. For another, he'd slept peacefully among the Tsla for weeks. They'd earned his trust. Besides, he and Lyra could always lock themselves in their cabin, and no curious Tsla could disengage a locked autopilot.

The morning dawned bright, hot, and stinking humid but Etienne sat comfortably alongside Lyra in the little dining nook. Tyl squatted on the floor nearby. The porters ate farther astern, in the storage area that had been turned into their living quarters. They could have joined the humans but chose not to. Etienne asked why, confident it would have some bearing on his question.

"They're ashamed," Tyl explained.

"Ah." Lyra looked satisfied. Apparently she'd been thinking along similar lines. "Because they had to fight?"

"Oh no." Tyl nibbled at his bowl, his stubby six-fingered hands probing for solid morsels. The Redowls had already overcome their distaste at seeing a Tsla rummage for food with its long snout. "They are ashamed because they were not permitted to fulfill their intentions."

"But they did," Etienne argued. "We're safe and we recovered our boat."

"Yes, but no thanks to us."

"You dispatched that patrol at the harbor."

"It was our intention to assist thee during the entire process, Etienne. Yet we could only stand helplessly by and watch while this wondrous craft," and he tapped the metal floor, "did more to save itself than did we."

"But you couldn't have done more than you did," Lyra told him. "We barely had enough time to activate the voice pickup."

"That is not the point. We know we could not have carried this boat to the river on our shoulders, but we did not have the chance to *try*. Therefore merit was lost because we did not have the opportunity to vanquish our enemy."

Lyra looked uncomfortable. "It's my understanding that your society is a pacifistic one."

"Of course, that is true."

"Then how can you talk of gaining merit by fighting?"

"Like a storm or rockfall, a declared enemy is an agent of nature. As an enemy it removes itself from the considerations of civilization."

Etienne was enjoying his wife's discomfiture enormously. "But your enemy is only acting in what he considers a civilized manner."

"He must be judged by civilized standards."

"You mean, by Tsla standards."

"Naturally. You do not think that we would adopt the standards of the Mai?" He sounded politely outraged. "A truly civilized people instinctively know what constitutes civilized behavior."

"Sounds like expediency to me."

"Not at all. Our moral standards are not nearly so flexible."

"Then you feel remorse when you kill an enemy?"

"Naturally. An enemy is one who has freely abjured his soul. How else could we feel but sorry for him?"

"That wouldn't, however, have prevented you from killing every Mai in Hochac who opposed you?"

"No, it would not. By opposing us in the recovery of your property they would have demonstrated disregard for civilized behavior, thus removing themselves from consideration by those who adhere to such behavior. I see no contradiction in this."

"No contradiction at all." He glanced at his wife. Lyra's note-taker was running and she didn't look up at Tyl. "Just wanted the point clarified."

"I thought," Lyra said quietly, "that the Tsla considered it sinful to kill."

"To kill any civilized person, yes, a terrible sin. But there is no moral restraint against defending oneself from the hostility of an uncivilized person any more than it is sinful to raise a roof to keep out the rain."

"All perfectly clear," Etienne agreed. He was content. It was clear that his initial worries about the safety of the Tsla were unfounded. For all their vaunted pacifism they were quite capable of taking care of themselves should the need arise. Killing a civilized person is a sin. Anyone who assaults me is uncivilized. Very neat.

Neat enough to quash Lyra's romanticized notions of Tsla society. Her beloved mystics were no more or less bloodthirsty than any other primitive folk. Well, that wasn't quite fair. But it was evident they could slaughter with a clear conscience so long as their victims fell below civilized standards. When you set those standards yourself it gave you considerable flexibility in establishing a defense.

Lyra continued to press Tyl for information, hoping to bolster her fading thesis of Tsla nobility. Etienne left to check the autopilot and then to see what the other Tsla and Homat were up to. He also wanted to tell the porters that, in his eyes at least, they'd acquired a great deal of merit for what they'd done in Hochac.

They were more than three thousand kilometers north northwest of Steamer Station and the distant Skatandah Delta. Cloud cover was increasing daily though it brought little relief from the heat and humidity. The Barshajagad was beginning to narrow sharply, towering walls shortening the daylight on the river. Both sides of the canyon could be seen now though the edge of the Guntali Plateau was still faint with distance. But for the first time it felt like they were sailing up a canyon.

Ahead lay another major tributary of the Skar, the river Gaja. Beyond this confluence, according to Tyl, the Barshajagad's walls drew toward one another with breathtaking suddenness, closing in to seal off the place where river devils were born, the Topapasirut. Beyond the Topapasirut lay lands unknown even to the wise men of Turput.

One thing Etienne no longer had to concern himself about was Lyra's tendency to adopt Tsla habits. After Tyl's breakfast explanation of adaptable battlefield philosophy he never again saw her in Tsla cape and toga.

They reached the place where the Gaja flowed thick and muddy into the clear Skar. The Tsla records were accurate. It was immensely wide and tinged a pale rust in color. The Gaja was another Amazon, just another tributary. He felt no amazement. Tslamaina had already exhausted his store of geological superlatives.

Beyond the Gaja the Skar narrowed rapidly. As it did so the current intensified. Submerged mountains and hills began to produce some white water, the first they'd encountered in their long journey Upriver. The cloud cover was thick overhead and Etienne saw why that section of the river had not been accurately mapped by the single orbiting satellite.

Seven thousand meters overhead, the edge of the Guntali glistened with ice and snow. The rim was now a mere two hundred and fifty kilometers distant to east or west, descending toward the bottom of the canyon in a series of steps and escarpments. Through the telescope Etienne examined one sheer wall some four thousand meters high.

One day they were cruising slowly so that Etienne could check the standard subsurface water samples. Lyra sat at the controls while Etienne was working in the lab astern. Several Tsla were watching the logging procedure with interest while Homat lay half asleep on his mat on the rear deck. Suddenly the boat tipped wildly, almost knocking

Etienne from his feet. Something had bumped the right side of the hull.

"What the hell was that?" Etienne yelled forward.

"I don't know. Something hit us from below."

"What's with the scanner?"

"Nothing. It didn't come from Upriver."

He did some fast thinking. Whatever had nudged them un-gently hadn't shown up on the scanner. Therefore it hadn't slipped down toward them. Therefore it must have come up *behind* them.

Therefore it sure as hell wasn't a rock.

Homat was shouting hysterically from astern and Etienne and the Tsla piled out through the rear door into the hot, damp air. Even as he emerged Etienne caught himself wishing for his pistol.

Not that it would have done him any good. He was staring at a slowly rising cliff black as polished obsidian. Within the cliff was a cavern, filled with acres of dripping blueblack streamers like baleen, only thicker and more widely spaced.

"Lacoti!" Homat was blubbering in fear. Etienne immediately understood how they'd missed the creature on the scanner, since it was programed only to acknowledge submerged objects which might be dangerous to the boat. The device would blithely ignore anything organic flattened out along the river bottom. The current provided food for the Lacoti, which doubtless rested contentedly in the mud of the Skar, mouth agape to receive whatever nourishment the river chose to provide.

Unless something disturbed it, of course.

If the Lacoti had eyes, they were hidden somewhere back of that vast cavernous maw. It was moving toward them, a fact that he perceived right away. He shouted toward the intercom, unafraid but having no wish for a closer view of Lacoti gut. It might be a slow swimmer but it might also be capable of a last second burst of speed. "Lyra, there's something back here that's about half the size of a starship. Move us out of here."

"What do you think I'm trying to do? I can see it on the rear screen!" Her voice was frantic. "We've got a short or something. I can't get any speed up."

"Oh hell," he muttered. "Tyl?"

The Tsla wore a fatalistic expression. "We are not river dwellers and have no experience of such creatures. We can pray."

Etienne let out a curse and dove into the cabin. Behind him the towering gullet was drawing slowly nearer. Part of the problem stemmed from the fact that it was sucking in water at an enormous rate, creating a suction the hydrofoil was hard put to counter. If they didn't lift up on foils and make some speed they were going to go down the Lacoti's throat like a cork in a sewer. He had no idea what had prodded it out of its bottom lair. Maybe the hydrofoil's engine produced a discomfiting vibration. No time now for study.

He reached the cockpit and shoved Lyra aside. She didn't protest.

"Emergency override?"

"I tried it already!"

He fumbled at the instrumentation. The stern screens were dark now and he could hear the echo of water rushing down a monstrous throat.

The familiar high whine of the jet filled the air. Lyra was thrown against a wall and the backrest of the pilot's seat pressed hard into Etienne's back. For an instant Etienne was sure he could see a thick black lip overhead as the boat slid down that endless throat. Then they were out in the light again and the stern screen showed the immense mouth receding behind them. It closed and the Lacoti sank like an island. A quick check of the scanner showed it was not pursuing, just as it revealed rocky outcrops, mudpoles, and vegetation growing atop the massive back. The thought that something the size of the Lacoti required camouflage was sobering. The sooner they reached shallower water the better he'd like it.

He rechecked the readouts before allowing himself a long, relieved sigh. "Go check our passengers."

"Don't give me orders," she snapped as she pushed back her hair and adjusted one fallen halter strap. "I know what to do. I'm just not as mechanically inclined as you, that's all."

He spoke very carefully, conscious that she was treading a fine line between anger and hysteria. "When you tried the accelerator you forgot to disengage the secondary lock on the autopilot. That's why the emergency override didn't work either."

"I know that," she murmured. She was mad at herself, he saw, not at him. "I saw that thing in the screen and I got scared. I guess . . . I panicked a little."

"It could have happened to anyone," he said softly. He didn't want to say that. What he wanted to do was let off tension by calling her a stupid, senseless little fool. But he didn't. He was gentle and understanding. It was possibly the most intelligent thing he'd done since they'd stepped off the shuttle at Steamer Station many months ago.

What really confused him was that he didn't know why he did it.

"I'm going to run a complete checkout," he told her. "That thing coming up underneath our keel gave us a pretty good jolt. I want to make sure it didn't bust something loose."

She nodded. "I'll have a look in the hold."

She was gone for several minutes, returned sooner than expected. Her expression was grim.

"Etienne, we've suffered a fatality."

"What?" He spun the seat around and stared at her in disbelief. "How? We made it clear in time."

"One of the porters. Her name was Uon. When you hit the accelerator I was thrown against the wall. Everyone out back was knocked to the deck. But Uon was standing up top, near the mast. When we shot forward she lost her footing and fell. Cracked her skull, looks like. She's dead."

Fingers tightened on the back of the seat. "I didn't have any choice," he growled. "Another second's delay and we'd have become a meal."

"I already explained that to Tyl and the others. They understand completely. They've . . . made a request."

He didn't look up. "What do they want?"

"They'd appreciate it if we could stop hereabouts for the night so they can give Uon a proper sendoff. I didn't get the details but apparently there's a lot of ritual involved. They want to anchor somewhere inshore."

"I suppose we can find a quiet place. Least we can do. I'm really sorry, Lyra."

"It was my fault as much as anyone's." She smiled slightly.

"They've accepted it with somber grace. They adjust to death very well."

Now he looked up. "Maybe better than we? If that's a sign of social maturity I'm willing to concede the point."

But his concession didn't make her feel any better.

They found a small cove, no more than an oversized pot-hole that the Skar's swirls and eddies had etched into the riverbank. The night sky was a dull starless gray thanks to the solid cover of clouds that stretched like a fluffy awning from one rim of the Guntali to the other.

Lyra overcame her sorrow by burying herself in her studies, trying to record every slightest nuance of the Tsla funeral ceremony which was performed on the open rear deck of the hydrofoil. This involved the use of torches, some special powder carried by Tyl, and much chanting and singing. Having no desire to participate or watch, Homat had relinquished his bedmat for the privacy of the bow. He lay there murmuring spirit rhymes as he leaned over the side to watch the phosphorescent motocrullers, tiny, superfast clamlike bivalves that made whirlpools of light beneath the shade afforded by the ship.

Having considerably less interest in native rituals than his wife, Etienne had retired to the comfort of their cabin. The expression on her face when she burst in on him startled him out of his reading. She stumbled against him and he put both hands on her shoulders to steady her. She looked ill.

"What's wrong, Lyra, what's the matter?" She'd left the door open behind her and the steady chant of the Tsla filtered in to the bedchamber.

"Sendoff ritual," she whispered, choking on the words. She pushed past him, toward the head. The recorder dangling from her neck bounced against her chest.

Curiosity overcame his apprehension as he left the cabin and headed astern. The rear deck was lit by the flicker of torch-light, illuminating the source of Lyra's distress. His reaction was less violent than hers. Not that he was delighted by the sight, but since he held no high hopes for the Tsla he was far less disgusted and disappointed than his wife.

The Tsla were deeply engaged in the funeral ritual and only Tyl broke away long enough to greet him. He looked concerned. This was mitigated somewhat by the blood dripping from his mouth and snout.

"Lyra left us in a hurry. I hope we did not offend her."

Etienne summoned unsuspected reserves of diplomacy. "My wife sees you and your people as being nobler than any of us have a right to be. It's a failing many humans are heir to."

Tyl's nose twitched and those big soulful eyes turned toward the doorway. "I see. But you feel differently?"

"After a fashion. I don't approve, but neither do I condemn. Neither would Lyra, if she hadn't lost sight of her scientific training."

"I am sorrowed," Tyl continued. "It is part of the ritual. It must be done the same day, as soon after death as possible, because otherwise . . ."

Etienne cut him off. "The reasons are self-explanatory, Tyl." He was unable to keep his eyes from the scene on the deck. "It's only that the customs are very different among my own folk."

"I can sympathize." He gestured backward with a hand. "Uon was much loved by her friends. We could not think of sending her soul on to eternity without properly displaying that affection."

"We feel likewise, only among our kind we choose to express such love for the departed in more metaphysical and less immediate terms."

"Customs are different among all peoples. Now if you will excuse me, I must participate or Uon's soul will not count me among its friends."

Etienne pointed. "You have blood on your face."

Tyl wiped at it. "The result of ritual contact. She struck the deck very hard."

Etienne left the ceremony to return to the cabin, closing the door behind him. Lyra sat on the bed, staring blankly at a xenological chip unscrolling on the viewer. He doubted she saw the words. He sat down behind her and put both hands on her shoulders.

"I know how you feel," he said helplessly. "It's never pleasant to have one's illusions shattered."

"Such hopes," she muttered disconsolately. "I had such

hopes for them. They seemed to have progressed so far without the corresponding technological traumas."

"They *have* progressed far," he found himself saying, to his own considerable surprise. "But it's still an alien culture, Lyra. You can't let yourself lose sight of that, let your scientific observations be compromised by your feelings for them personally. You can't anthropomorphize their culture any more than you can their physiognomy."

"If I did that," she replied, "it was out of hope."

"I realize that, which is why you're going to make your report on Tsla funeral custom as detailed and informative as any other part of your records. The balance it will provide is important. It will help confirm your objectivity. Otherwise all the rest of your work among these people will be disregarded."

"You're right, of course." She put the chip reader aside, fiddled with her recorder as she leaned back against him. "I don't have any choice, do I?"

"As Lyra Redowl you do. As visiting xenologist representing the interests of every xenologist who couldn't make this trip, you do not."

She nodded, then stood. "It was unprofessional of me to run away like that. I know better. Among the new one must always expect a shock or two."

"It's easier for me. Rocks are rarely shocking."

She smiled, not because his sally was funny but because he bothered to try and make it so.

"We're only human, Lyra."

"Yes, and the Tsla are not. For a moment I'd forgotten that. I won't forget again."

"Don't let this push you too far in the other direction. Whatever you think personally about their customs, they're still good people, and our friends. Tyl is what he's always been: a learned and compassionate friend."

"Among his own kind, yes. Etienne, you've been right and I've been wrong."

He turned away, embarrassed by her admission as he often was when he won some small portion of their private war. There was a contradiction there he didn't understand.

She started toward the hall and the stern deck, muttering as she went. "After all, one can make the argument that ceremonial necrophilia is no more barbaric than any of a half dozen other funeral rituals observed among pristine primitive cultures. Among the Canuli, for example . . ." Her voice faded as she slipped further into scholarly preoccupation.

He felt sorry for her at the same time that he was glad he hadn't chosen to share her discipline. He made a mental note to inform Tyl sometime soon that in the event he and Lyra should meet with a fatal accident, they were to be buried in accordance with human custom only.

Still, several days passed before Lyra could bring herself to talk with Tyl or any of the surviving porters. They sensed her distress and kept their distance, no easy thing to accomplish within the confines of the hydrofoil. They busied themselves with learning the art of trolling, something they could not do on the unnavigable waters of the upper Aurang.

They were now five thousand kilometers north of Steamer Station, with an unknown distance yet to cover. Unknown because the satellite responsible for the photogrammetric mapping of Tslamaina had rather neglected this portion of the northern hemisphere in favor of detailing the much more heavily populated areas around the equator and the Groalamasan Sea.

The temperature had fallen to the point where Homat was obliged to don long clothing in order to be comfortable in the ninety degree heat of midday. Of greater concern was the sharp narrowing of the Barshajagad. Towering walls had closed in on the river, compressing its volume into a much smaller channel, and the increasingly swift current was becoming powerful enough to slow their progress even though the water could gain a grip only on the two submerged hydrofoils. They encountered no white water, however, and the scanner indicated the river bottom still lay far below their keel.

But Etienne found it difficult to concentrate on such things; he was hypnotized by the canyon walls, seven thousand meters that dropped in places sheer to the river, a gorge unmatched even on gas giants with surfaces solid enough to withstand continual erosion by high winds. All that remained of the sky was a narrow strip directly overhead, masked by perpetual cloud cover, a faint gray band delineating the limits of the real world.

Each time the river bent, the rock cliffs seemed to swallow any hope of retreat. The hydrofoil seemed very small indeed as it fought that steadily intensifying current. The Redowls worked in relays now, unable to trust navigation to the autopilot. If they lost speed while they both slept and the river caught hold of them, it would crush the duralloy hull against one of the granite walls as easily as eggshell.

〖 XI 〗

Two days of this saw their speed dangerously reduced. Lyra entered the cockpit rubbing her eyes, took one clear look at her husband's and said, "Etienne, we can't keep this up. We're both exhausted and we've no way of knowing how much longer this stretch is."

He coughed into his fist. "I thought the damn track would start widening out again by now. It doesn't make sense. This much water moving downstream at this speed ought to have worn a broader canyon. But it hasn't."

"What's the current reading currently?" She half smiled, half yawned as she squinted toward the instrumentation, wishing it could produce a cup of post-Ethiopian *katfe*. Unfortunately the nearest cup of *real* hot stimulant was light-years distant.

"Have a look for yourself." He touched a button without taking his eyes off the river.

She blinked at the readout. "That's incredible," she said quietly.

"Yes, incredible. No boat was ever designed to travel against such a current."

"What about continuing on repellers?"

"Don't tempt me. Sweet of you to suggest it, but it's too risky. We could try it for a few hours, but that's all they're designed for. Hopping rapids and avoiding waterfalls, not steady travel. We'd run down the batteries and probably find ourselves stuck in an identical position farther Upriver. Can't chance it." He muttered an obscenity.

"We can't quit here! We've come too far."

She leaned against the console. "I know how much this meant to you, Etienne. But it's not worth risking our lives for."

He looked at her then. "You think we have a life?"

A new voice interrupted them. "I overhear. There may yet be a way. I have had long to think on it and would not have thought it possible, had I not seen what thy spirit boat can accomplish."

Etienne didn't turn to confront their visitor. "What way, Tyl?"

"Do thee remember the crevice splitting the east wall, that we passed the previous day?"

"No. I was too busy looking over the bow to do any sightseeing."

"I was working on my notes," Lyra added.

"I have been watching the Barshajagad, marveling long, but always watching. There was a trail along the east wall. It terminates at this crevice. I have been this way once before. I saw no reason to mention the trail, to distract thee from thy work. We were to travel by boat, not by foot. But now I see that I must mention this other possibility or all will end."

"A trail? I didn't . . . no, wait a minute," Lyra murmured. "I did see something. I thought it was an old high-water line."

"It is a trail, Learned Lyra. A trading trail."

"Where does it go?" she asked him.

"Up. Up to a high plateau. Not the Guntali. Higher than Turput but lower than that. High enough so that Tsla can live upon it. Up above the Topapasirut. The trail is steeper and more dangerous than the one that climbs to Turput."

"How much more dangerous?"

"Enough to restrict travel. But it rises beyond the To-papasirut."

Etienne gestured ahead, at the narrow, impossibly deep canyon. "I thought that this place was the Topapasirut."

Tyl executed a gesture full of amused negativity. "No. If you would take the measure of the adversary that still lies ahead, thee must climb beyond its reach. That is, if thee think thy spirit boat can go no farther."

"Point of diminishing returns, Etienne," Lyra reminded him. "Every hour we're using more power to cover less distance. Can't you calculate how long it will be before we reach the break-even point and find ourselves making no progress even at full power?"

"Soon enough. You say there's a way to get around this Topapasirut, Tyl?"

"Above, yes. Beyond, I do not know. I have not been to that place. But I have gazed on the Topapasirut. If thee would do likewise, thee must leave thy boat behind, at least until thee see for thyselves."

"Leave it where?"

"Turn back to the trail end. I would not have thought there was a place, but thy boat can rise like a bird from the water."

Etienne looked at Lyra.

"It's your decision, Etienne. You're the geologist."

"Hydrology's not my specialty, though. But it's starting to look more and more like we've come to a dead end, at least as far as this section of the river is concerned." He looked back at Tyl. "The east wall, you said?"

The Tsla nodded. Etienne turned back to the instruments. Unwilling to risk turning the boat broadside to the current, he lifted it on repellers and turned it neatly in midair before setting it gently back into the water.

There was a sharp lurch as the river caught the hull. He used only enough power to maneuver, letting the cells recharge as they raced back downstream.

"This is our best chance, Etienne. We have to see what we're up against."

"I know that, dammit. The canyon *has* to widen out somewhere above this. It can't be like this all the way to the arctic line. Too much erosion. There's a geological anomaly some-where ahead of us."

"And it has a name, apparently. Could it be another big waterfall, like the Cuparaggai above Turput?"

"No. I'm sure of that much, anyway. The water here isn't acting like that and there's no indication of a sharp rise in elevation at this point. The photogrammetrics are solid enough on that score. That's why I don't understand this intensified flow. But if this Topapasirut's only the narrowest part of the canyon, we'll see how much farther Upriver it lies. Maybe we *can* pass above it on repellers."

By midday they had returned to the section of cliff Tyl had spotted. Etienne again lifted the hydrofoil on its repell-ers, set it down on an exposed beach out of reach of the river's grasp.

The crevice to which Tyl had alluded turned out to be much more than that—it was a break in the Barshajagad wall, a sizable side canyon rising toward the sky. And the winding line against the rocks that Lyra had thought was a high-water mark did indeed show signs of use. It snaked along the granitic wall and started up the side passage.

"Now we climb," said Tyl confidently.

"For how long?"

"Several days, at least." He turned his gaze upward.

"Homat won't be glad to hear that," Etienne murmured.

"Why not leave him to watch over the boat?" Lyra sug-gested.

"Sensible. We'll leave one of the porters with him and carry our own supplies. I don't imagine he'll regret missing the chance to view the 'birthplace of all river devils.'"

"I will come with thee and leave the others behind, for I do not share thy trust of the Mai," Tyl said.

"Homat's been invaluable," Etienne replied. "Without his aid we wouldn't be here now."

"His kind are not to be trusted."

"In this instance I think you're wrong, Tyl," Lyra said. It was the first time Etienne had seen her openly dispute the Tsla's opinion.

Tyl responded with a gesture of indifference. "Then I will direct Swd to remain behind by himself. While recuperating, he will keep watch over thy property—and its other guard."

A small stream trickled down the branch canyon, which was indeed steeper than anything they'd climbed thus far. As the meters dropped behind and below them, so did the temperature. The Redowls were obliged to wear their long-sleeved and long-legged attire while Tyl and the porters re-donned their capes and togas. Since they didn't expect to find any villagers to trade with, they carried a full stock of rations.

They ascended to the cloud. At five thousand meters Lyra was having some trouble breathing, though this was due more to the unaccustomed exertion than the altitude. Due to the denser atmosphere, five thousand meters on Tsla-maina was equivalent to thirty-five hundred meters or so on Terra.

As they crested the trail head, the clouds momentarily parted. Ahead rose the peak of a steep-sided mountain that towered above them and the nearby edge of the Guntali. As they rested, Etienne took a sighting on the peak.

"Eleven thousand meters, most of it frozen."

"Aracunga," Tyl said. Etienne noticed that all the Tsla now wore their sturdiest clothing. They stood some two thousand meters higher than Turput, at the upper limit of the Tsla ecological zone. They could climb higher still, but not comfortably.

After several days of climbing to the east, they set off northward. Etienne expected Tyl to continue in that direction, but he was wrong. On the second day they turned slightly to the west, and by that evening the Redowls could feel thunder again.

They expected another waterfall, perhaps one that plunged the full five thousand meters to the river below. But it was no waterfall Tyl led them toward. It was the Topapasirut.

Must be the father of all waterfalls, Etienne mused, still unconvinced by Tyl's denials. By the fourth day the thunder had become so loud they could communicate only by signs.

The Redowls could tap out messages on their wrist computers, but the Tsla possessed no such wondrous devices and had to make their intentions known through gestures.

It grew damp around them, the rocks treacherous and slick. Yet as they hiked now through the perpetual mist, the sky overhead remained clear.

Etienne searched in vain for signs of the expected cascade. When they finally reached the lip of the abyss, all was explained.

It was raining upward. Forced into a narrow throat of the Barshajagad, the entire volume of the Skar suddenly made a sharp and unexpected bend from south to west. As a result, the swiftly flowing river cannonaded into the north cliff face that formed the base of the mountain Aracunga, five thousand meters below their feet.

This produced a spray that rose on disturbed air to drench the puny observers clinging to a granite overhang. The solid bedrock trembled under the river's impact. Tyl communicated with gestures, but any description was superfluous before the stupendous sight below.

Etienne knew that this was the Topapasirut, the birthplace of all river devils. He knew that Tyl had been more than right when he'd insisted no boat could pass through this place. The hydrofoil could not rise high enough on its repellers to clear the maelstrom.

Across the canyon, rising from the opposite side of the abyss, was a metamorphic mass that dwarfed even Aracunga.

"The Prompaj!" Tyl screamed into Etienne's ear. He took another sighting.

"Fourteen thousand two hundred meters," he informed Lyra via wrist computer. "An impossible mountain. I think the two peaks were once closer than now. See how the river bends sharply to the west before turning south again? Tslamaina's seismically stable now, but a few eons back there must have been one hell of an earthquake in this part of the world. See the signs of slippage?" He pointed to particular strata down in the roaring canyon.

"This section of the surface slipped eastward. South of here the land went west. The result was the displacement of the northern third of the Skar several kilometers to the east. I'm glad I wasn't around then."

Lyra tapped out a reply. "I'm not real happy to be here now. Let's get away. I'm cold and wet."

They lingered a few moments longer so he could chip a few more pictures, take some final measurements. Then they headed back toward the trail head, leaving the clouds and hillsides to swallow up the Topapasirut, its thunder, and the brooding massif that was called Prompaj.

They made camp that night in a small cave, drying themselves and their clothes before a large fire. Etienne watched with interest as the porters groomed each other's fur.

The Redowls said little. There was no point in belaboring the obvious. Their expedition had reached its end. They'd run up against not a brick wall but a watery one.

When the porters had finished and dressed themselves once more they gathered close around the warmth of the fire. Tyl spoke while his companions ate.

"What will thee do now, Learned Etienne? Does the spirit boat possess some magical power we have not seen that would enable it to pass through the Topapasirut?"

"It does not," Etienne replied glumly. "We do have other machines which can fly through the air and put any bird to shame, but we don't have one here. We chose to travel by boat. It's all we have. You were right, Tyl. I apologize for doubting you."

"You had not seen the Topapasirut, Etienne. No one believes until they have seen."

"That's it, then." Lyra was not as disappointed as her husband, though she strove to sound as sympathetic as possible. If they could no longer go onward, they would have to go back, and she still had work to do among the Tsla.

"You've been stopped by a geological phenomenon, Etienne. What better way to conclude your report? Think of the reaction among your colleagues when you describe this place. Maybe some day we can come back up here with an aircar."

He'd been staring at the floor of the cave. Now he looked up, determined. "They'll be fascinated, but it won't be the end of my report."

"Etienne," she said gently, "we can't get through that chute. You've already acknowledged that."

"I won't be stopped by the very river I've come to survey."

She sighed, leaned back against the inflated sleeping pad. "Maybe you'll accept it by morning."

"Maybe."

He did not, nor did he admit defeat during the long descent to the Skar. He kept to himself and brooded, causing Tyl to move next to Lyra.

"What ails Etienne?"

"He's unhappy because he knows we can't go on. That means he'll have to leave his work here unfinished."

"But it is not his fault. Nothing passes Upriver beyond the Topapasirut. He has no control over that. It is not as if he were beaten by something in himself."

"He knows all that, Tyl, but he is persistent, Etienne is. Always has been."

"I see. A Tsla teacher would accept the inevitable; such constant worry is harmful to the mind."

"True, but sometimes it can lead to solutions where none seem possible. I've seen him do it before. Within our fields, Etienne and I are well respected. We've achieved success where others have failed. It's one of the reasons we were allowed to make this expedition while other applicants were rejected. Sometimes, Tyl, blind persistence can succeed where everything else has failed."

"I still do not understand why you would sacrifice peace of mind. I can admire such tenacity, but I cannot empathize with it."

Down on the river there was a brief but joyful reunion with those left behind. Homat didn't try to conceal his relief over the safe return of his human protectors.

"All these days," he whispered to Lyra later, "trapped with that Tsla, and him mumbling and chanting to himself all the time. It was enough to drive a sane person crazy. Did you find a way to pass this Topapasirut?"

"No, we did not." To her surprise Homat looked downcast. "I thought you'd be pleased. That means we have to go back Downriver now, back to the warm lands of the Skatandah. Don't you miss them?"

"Very much so, but I have joined myself to your purposes and therefore am disappointed for you."

"That's a very nice thing to say, Homat." She hadn't expected such depth of feeling from the Mai. Nor was it a ruse. He was genuinely distressed that their journey had come to an end.

She looked past him, frowned. Etienne was deep in discussion with Tyl and looking more animated than he had in many days. She strolled over to join them.

"What's all the excitement about?"

"You tell her," Etienne suggested to Tyl, his features alive with enthusiasm.

"On the eastern flank of Aracunga Mountain," Tyl explained, "lies the Tsla trading town of Jakaie. I have not visited it myself but it is known to Turput. It is said that beyond Jakaie and the mass of the mountain, the Barshajagad once more becomes a navigable river. If thee could but convey thy craft to that place, thee might safely resume thy journey—if the story is accurate."

"An impossible if."

"Maybe not," Etienne murmured. He was tense with possibilities. "Maybe we could portage around."

For a long moment she just stared at him. Then she let her gaze trace the lower section of the steep trail that wound its torturous course up the side canyon.

"Sure we could. We'll just hoist the boat onto our shoulders and haul it five thousand meters straight up. Lost your mind?"

Her skepticism didn't even slow him down. "No, I've just found it. Look, the hydrofoil's made of ultralight material. The hull's a carbon filament honeycomb. And we can surmount the rough spots on the repellers."

"With what power?" she argued. "We'd burn out the cells."

"We would not. You're not listening. We'd only use the repellers to get over real steep places. The rest of the time we'd rely on muscle power. Porters, Lyra! Mount the boat on some kind of platform and pull it up and over."

She did some quick figuring. "I admit the hydrofoil's light, but it's a relative lightness. You'd still need a thousand Mai or Tsla to drag it up a thousand meters."

He looked back at Tyl. "Tell her."

"There is a draft animal," the Tsla explained, "that the Mai use all along the river. It is called a vroqupii. The Mai use them in teams to pull trading boats Upriver against the current. They are strong." He eyed Homat. "Well, Mai?"

The guide looked thoughtful. "We passed many trading villages below this place. Each should be home to a few vroqupii. The animals used hereabouts must be unusually powerful because the current is so fast."

"Do you think we could find enough to do it?" Etienne asked.

"I do not know." Homat gazed at the intimidating trail.

Lyra's dreams of returning to tranquil Turput were slipping away. "Assuming we could find enough animals to do the job, could we hire enough? Would their owners consent to such an undertaking?"

"If they were promised enough money, certainly," Homat replied, looking at her as if she'd just disputed a fundamental law of nature.

"What would we pay them with?"

"Our trade goods," Etienne said. "We have some left."

"If we use up our remaining supplies we won't have anything to give any natives we meet beyond this point."

"If we don't get beyond this point the question becomes moot." She had no comeback for that. Etienne turned to Homat. "Would these vroqupii be able to climb as high as Jakaie?" He translated the relevant measurements into Mai terms.

Homat looked uneasy. "We go that much higher than the home of these Tsla who accompany us?" Etienne nodded. "I am not sure. But these Upriver tribes are proud. They might see such a proposal as a challenge."

"They wouldn't freeze. It's not *that* high," Etienne said.

Tyl agreed. "Many Mai hunters hike beyond Turput in search of prey, and their blood continues to flow."

"How many vroqupii might we need?" Homat wondered. An intense discussion of weight versus capabilities ensued, before the Mai felt comfortable in announcing a figure.

"Thirty at least. Forty would be better, fifty best, and sixty delightful, but I do not think we can find that many willing to try, not even for a share of off-world treasure."

"We must try," Etienne told him.

"Then I will do my best to convince the Brul, as they who handle the vroqupii are called." His bald skull glistened in the reflected cloud-glare of afternoon and he smiled ingenuously. "That is my job, is it not?"

Etienne nodded once. "Let's get started. Lyra, are you sure you're willing to go along with this?"

She shrugged. "If you're determined I couldn't stop you anyway, Etienne. I think it's a mistake to sacrifice the rest of our trade goods on a scheme that has a good chance of failing, but I can't argue that it's your last chance to go on. Our last chance," she added with a faint smile.

"I promise," he told her, "if it looks like we're not going to make it, we'll turn back and return to Turput. I know that's what you want."

She almost said, "I want what you want, Etienne," but did not. Their relationship was based on more powerful bonds than artificial acquiescence. They did not give in to each other; they agreed on things. She agreed now and having agreed, considered how best to help.

"Tyl, do you think it can be done with thirty vroqupii?"

"I have watched them pull heavily laden ships Upriver," the Tsla replied thoughtfully. "They are very strong. But it will require more than mere strength to achieve this thing. It will take cooperation among the Mai who are involved. The vroqupii can, I think, pull thy spirit boat up to Jakaie, but not if the Brul fall to quarreling among themselves."

"They'll cooperate!" Homat declared angrily. "I'll see to it that they do."

"And why should they listen to thee?" Tyl replied without malice. "Thee are a runaway from one of the far city-states that border the Groalamasan. The river folk do not trust those who come from the lands that lie against the Sea."

"I am not of the city-states," Homat said proudly. "Not anymore. I am of," he hesitated to glance sideways at Etienne and Lyra, "I am of these folk." Etienne suddenly felt very good.

"Don't include me in that mental family," Lyra said sardonically. "I'm going along with this insanity but I don't believe in it. If Homat wants to consider himself as one with Etienne, that's fine. Idiocy knows no species boundaries." Everyone smiled.

"We'll do it, Lyra," Etienne told her, putting an arm around her shoulders. "You'll see. We'll do it! We'll get the hydrofoil up to Jakaie, around the Topapasirut, and down to the river on the far side. Then we'll be on our way again."

"Sure we will," she said softly. She inhaled deeply. "Well, I guess we'd better get on with it. The sooner this is begun, the sooner it will end."

"That's right," he replied with a grin, "but not the way you think it will."

Word was passed down the river, the call going out for the bravest of Brul mahouting only the strongest of mounts. Meanwhile the carpenters of the village of Taranau, which was the last sizable town near the narrowing of the Barshajagad, set about under Etienne's and Lyra's instructions building a platform to hold the hydrofoil. It was to be light and strong, with double-wheeled axles fore and aft. These could be bound to the platform which in turn could be attached to the two hydrofoils. Not only would the skeleton frame provide a maximum of support with a minimum of weight, the open woodwork also would not block the downward exhausts of the repellers.

Though they talked as rapidly as their brethren, the Brul turned out to be less loquacious and argumentative than their urbanized relatives. They formed a tightly knit society with rules all their own and wore their pride on their faces. It was not quite group arrogance.

Lyra learned from Homat that most of the Brul lived outside the villages in isolated clusters or in single dwellings with only the immediate family for company. Their lives were devoted to the care and handling of their vroqupii.

As it turned out the Redowls did not have to exhaust their store of trade goods. Once the nature of the enterprise became widely known, Brul arrived from distant locations not to serve for pay but simply to pit the strength and endurance of their animals against those of their competitors.

Still, the expedition was fortunate in engaging forty of the massive animals and their owners. After some discussion among the Brul the vroqupii were yoked to the boat in ten ranks of four abreast. They walked on pile-driver legs and their bellies scraped the earth. The vroqupii was all traction and muscle, its short square head set on a bull neck. A line of horny plates ran along the upper jaw and swept back to form a low ridge above each eye, downcurving to shield the throat.

It was a startling assembly, not the least because with a

few faintly yellow exceptions, the vroqupii were clad in short, bristly, rose-hued fur. They grunted and heaved against their harnesses, anxious to get moving. The Brul sat on the soft saddle behind the neck frill, alternately joking with and taunting his fellow drovers.

With the rushing roar of the Skar for counterpoint, the expedition finally got under way. At first there was nothing but good-natured jostling for position as each Brul strove to prove that his animal was the strongest. Eventually the drovers settled down to work, conversation fading as each concentrated on the task at hand.

The vroqupii plodded onward in comparative silence, even when they reached the branch canyon and the way turned steep and difficult. They were used to pulling against the constant pressure of the river, and the incline did not seem to cause them any unusual problems. Etienne knew the real test would come during the final thousand meters, when the air turned cold and thin.

Days passed and their speed slowed only slightly. What did drop off considerably was the amount of joking among the Brul, as the difficulty of what they were attempting began to sink in. Etienne had Homat weaving in and out among the Mai every night, listening for talk of discouragement or dissent.

The tension was hard on everyone, and when they finally passed the four-thousand-meter mark, four-fifths of the way to the top, humans, Tsla, and Mai were as tired as the patient vroqupii. It had been days since any joking had passed among the Brul, and the increasingly cold air was beginning to bother them if not their animals.

A few quit under the strain. One was killed when, shivering from the chill, he fell from his mount and was crushed under the heavy feet of the team behind him before it could be halted. But even those Brul who gave up left their animals in the care of friends, admonished them to return the precious creatures in good condition when the final goal was achieved—if it ever was. Forlorn and disappointed, they straggled back down the trail by ones and twos.

It was the cold that discouraged them more than anything else. By the time the temperature had fallen to sixty degrees the Brul were so wrapped up in heavy clothing it was all they could do to cling to their saddles. A steady breeze tumbled from the flanks of nearby Aracunga, and soon even Etienne and Lyra had to bundle up.

"Do you think we'll make it?" Lyra asked her husband one day as she finished the latest count of the remaining Brul. "It looks like we just might, if we don't lose too many more drovers."

"Don't you go getting confident on me just when I'm starting to have doubts," he told her. He blew into his hands. If the temperature fell much further they would have to dig jackets out of the hydrofoil's storage lockers. The Tsla also looked uncomfortable. It was chillier than it had been during their climb to the Topapasirut.

As Tyl had explained, Jakaie lay at the uppermost limit of Tsla habitation. Above that level even the hardiest Tsla crops withered and died, though one could survive by foraging and hunting. Or so it was said.

Forty-five hundred meters, forty-six, and as Etienne's nervousness increased, Lyra's spirits rose.

"We're going to make it, Etienne. You were right all the time. We're going to make it."

"I'll believe it when the boat's sitting in Jakaie's central square," he told her. "I wish I knew why you get more enthusiastic the closer we come to a crisis point, while I get more and more worried."

"We complement each other, remember? When I'm down, you're up, and vice versa."

"I thought all you wanted was to get back to Turput."

"I never thought we'd get this far. Now that we have, I'm dying to see how the Tsla of Jakaie have adapted to their harsh environment. There should be different architecture, methods of farming, cooking, everything. Society as a function of altitude. There's a whole paper in that."

"Must be a very close-knit population."

"I agree, but what makes you think so? You usually don't speculate in my field."

"They have to be close. It may be the only way to keep warm."

"Anytime you think it's getting a little chilly, Etienne, just consider the poor Mai." She gestured toward the long team of vroqupii and Brul as she and Etienne marched alongside

[153]

the hydrofoil. "I wonder how low the temperature has to fall before they become susceptible to frostbite?"

"To freezing, I'd expect, but you'd never know it to look at them now. Half of them are so cold they can't shiver anymore. Too numb."

Not one Brul had quit for several days now, however. For those who remained the climb had turned into a grim contest. None would give up so close to the goal for fear of being derided by those who stayed on.

As for the vroqupii, they could not voice any complaints, but they seemed to adjust to the colder weather much better than their masters. Their pace was slower now, more measured, but none had fallen by the wayside. Undoubtedly their short brightly colored fur afforded some protection against the changing climate. It also helped that when a particularly steep spot was reached, they were unhitched while one of the humans lifted the boat and its wheels to the next level on repellers. The Brul looked forward to such respites with relief.

Forty-eight hundred meters. Forty-nine.

"Tomorrow morning." Etienne spoke as he crouched across from the portable heater they recharged every couple of days from the boat's batteries. He longed for the comfort of their heated cabin. They slept outside at Homat's insistence. If they did not, he warned them, they risked losing the respect of the Brul. "We'll reach the top of the canyon tomorrow morning."

He put down his self-heating cup of tea and slid beneath the thermosensitive blanket. The covering was warm but the ground beneath the sleeping pad very hard. A glance showed the temperature to be fifty-three.

Tomorrow, vindication, he mused. After that, two days of steady travel overland to Jakaie. There they would find friends, shelter, and fires large enough to warm even the Brul.

Lyra still sat in front of the heater, staring at her husband. "You never would know when to say no, would you, Etienne? A bad habit, one that'll be the death of both of us one of these days." She smiled. "You dragged me all this way when I'd just as soon have quit and turned back toward home."

"Home?" His eyebrows lifted.

"Well, back toward Turput. I've come to think of that as kind of a home away from home."

"In spite of the inhabitants' unpleasant burial rituals?"

"I didn't spend much time consorting with the dead. I get to do that on the boat every night."

"Very funny." But she was still smiling. Tyl sat nearby, leading his fellow Tsla in their nighttime chant. Etienne watched her as she listened to them without reaching for her recorder. Light from the porters' fire lit her profile, burning away the years.

Ten years together. She'd been very beautiful a decade ago. Now she was hardened, toughened by fieldwork, by adversity, by too many hours spent away from the comforts of civilization—and still beautiful. All the poison in her spirit, all the acid in her voice could not change that.

She grew conscious of his stare and turned back to him. "I owe you an apology for wanting to turn back."

"How about a kiss instead? I haven't had a kiss in a long time. Apologies I can live without."

She eyed him uncertainly for a moment, then walked around the heater to bend next to him, touching her lips to his. They were warm against the night.

Then she pulled away, sooner than he wished. Too brief, too considered, not spontaneous enough, he thought. But something, it was something. It had been a long time since they'd had even that.

He turned over beneath the blanket, feeling much warmed inside—and not by the heater—anxious for morning to come.

〖 XII 〗

Screams, shouts of panic, and the hoarse trilling cries of the vroqupii woke him, the latter a sound he hadn't heard since the start of the long climb up from the Skar. Gesticulating silhouettes rushed past his sleep-filled eyes like the shadows of ghosts. Only the heater was alive, a steady glow in the darkness.

Trying to force himself awake he sat up, hunting for the source of all the disturbance. Suddenly he found himself rising from the ground. Something had placed tight steel bands around his shoulders and the back of his neck. He screwed his head around so he could look overhead, thinking how strange it was to meet a denizen of hell five thousand meters away from the center of the planet.

Four long wings beat at the air, protruding from a thick, flattened body. Wind and a fetid, corrupt odor assailed his face. Not far from his eyes, altogether too near, was a mouth full of sharp hooks. A pair of saucer-sized bright blue eyes glared down at him. The pupils were huge and yellow.

The odor of carrion was overpowered by a sudden sharp smell of ozone. The monstrosity shivered. Lyra fired again

[156]

and Etienne found himself falling. He landed heavily on his blanket and sleeping pad instead of the naked rock. With two holes burned through one wing, the creature had had enough. It lifted skyward, emitting a cry very like the sound the devil must make when gargling.

Etienne rolled over and clutched his right elbow, which had absorbed the brunt of his fall. It throbbed painfully. He was fully awake now.

Lyra jostled him as she slid on her knees next to him. Her eyes were still on the night sky. "Here," she said, handing him his pistol. "Others are still around." She gave him a hand up.

Guarding each other's backs they stumbled through the confusion and screaming, Etienne handling the asynapt with his left hand. The most immediate danger came not from the nocturnal carnivores but from the bellowing, stampeding vroqupii.

Etienne fired and fired. Though there was no recoil, his fingers grew numb simply from gripping the pistol. Eventually the night was scoured clean, however, and he let the weapon fall to his side. The stars returned, except off to the north where the air was filled with vast dark shapes, rapidly receding.

The Redowls returned to their campsite, set the heater back on its base, and sat down. All around them panic was giving way to muttered curses and exclamations in excited Mai.

Homat joined them, almost invisible in his cold-weather gear.

"What were they?" Lyra asked him. Etienne massaged his elbow, still looking to the north where a last straggler fled after its companions on ten-meter-wide wings.

"Monsters." Homat was shivering despite his bulky attire. "Very rarely do they come down to the river. They must be more common up here, where the land is better suited to monsters and Tsla!"

Other eyes joined the conference. If Tyl had overheard Homat's last words, he chose not to comment. "Strepanong," he declared, gesturing heavenward with his flexible proboscis. "Scavengers and killers." He paused. "They took two of the Brul. They rarely bother us in the fields, and never in the towns. Never have I seen so many in one place at the same time. The presence of so much meat must have drawn them."

"A bad omen, bad omen," Homat was muttering. "Perhaps we should turn back, de-Etienne."

A small invisible needle pricked his elbow and he winced. "Not after making it this far, Homat. I'm not turning back now."

"The Brul may grumble once they restore calm among their animals," Homat warned him. "They do not come this far to fight with monsters."

"Tyl, repeat what you said about never having seen so many in one place before. The chances of this happening again before we reach Jakaie are insignificant, aren't they? Tyl?"

The Tsla spoke mournfully. "I can guarantee nothing, Learned Etienne, though it would be most unlikely."

"One strepanong is too many," Homat argued.

"We drove them off," Lyra reminded him, gesturing with her pistol. "We injured several of them, maybe fatally, threw a real scare into the entire flock. I don't imagine they'll come after us again. You tell the Brul that. And from now on Etienne and I will alternate standing guard at night so we're not surprised anymore. If there is a next time they'll feast on strepanong, not the other way around."

"That is no consolation to the families of the two who were taken." Homat shuddered at the thought.

"Their families will be compensated," she promised. "Tell the Brul that if they turn back now because of a bunch of carrion eaters they're no better than children, crying for their mothers. We're only a couple of days, maybe less, from our goal, where there'll be warm shelter and safety for all."

Tyl assumed an uncharacteristically haughty air. "That much can be assured. Tsla hospitality refuses no one."

"You can also tell them," Lyra continued with a sudden burst of inspiration, "that if they insist on turning back now, we'll have to find Tsla help to take us the rest of the way."

Homat smiled at this slyness. Truly de-Lyra was becoming knowledgeable of Mai ways. "All your assurances would not convince them, but an insult to their reputations!—yes, I will tell them that. I do not think we will have any trouble."

He turned and disappeared in the direction of the vroqupii corral.

The Redowls were left alone. Lyra indicated her husband's right arm. "What's with your elbow?"

He forced a wry grin. "It thought it was a foot. I landed on it, but I don't imagine it's broken. Just feels like it. Couldn't you have managed to shoot the damned thing before it got me off the ground?"

"Sorry," she said dryly. "Be thankful we're camped on a relatively wide section of trail. You might've been dumped over a precipice."

"Wouldn't that have made for an interesting dive? Time enough for forty-eight twists with a couple dozen triple gainers thrown in. Unfortunately, I don't think I would have survived long enough to enjoy the judging."

"I'll try and come to the rescue a little sooner next time."

He was suddenly solemn as he eyed the sky. "I hope there won't be a next time. Insult to their professionalism or not, I don't imagine the Brul will stay if we're attacked again. Did you get a good enough look at our visitors to classify them? I wasn't much interested in their taxonomy myself, and I didn't have the best view."

"It wasn't a bird. I'm not even sure it was mammalian. Looked like a cross between a condor and a centipede."

"Sweet critter. I think we'll forgo any opportunities for up-close study." He grimaced as he tried to straighten his arm. "I saw enough to know it spends most if not all of its time in the air."

"I've never seen a quadruple wing arrangment like that before," she added, "except on insects, and the strepanong's no insect despite its appearance. It had feathers, and plenty of 'em."

"I know. I had to smell them." He looked toward the circle of Tsla. Tyl was watching them, the fire bright in his wide, sad eyes. "You're positive we're not more than a day or two march from this town?"

Tyl performed an elaborate gesture with his nose. "I am positive, Etienne. A passing of the sun once or twice across the sky will see us in Jakaie. I look forward to it myself, for I am curious to see how my brethren have adapted to so isolated a home. Life must be harder than in Turput."

"But not so hard they won't be able to aid us?"

"Learned Etienne, the more difficult a Tsla's circumstances, the more generous he is with his hospitality."

Lyra confirmed this declaration, as Etienne knew she would.

There was much grumbling and many more complaints than usual among the Brul the next morning as they mounted their vroqupii. That was only to be expected. Etienne thought he saw several expressions of hatred directed at himself or his wife, but Homat assured him it didn't matter whether the drovers disliked them or not. Only that they respected them.

Several of the vroqupii displayed new scars, evidence of attempts by the marauding strepanong to carry them off. At least the weather had decided to cooperate, and the grumbling rapidly died down. It was almost warm as they set out up the trail.

They reached the top of the canyon and paused for a brief celebration, which helped to raise the drovers' spirits considerably. That night they slept easy, reassured by the sight of one of the Redowls patrolling alertly with asynaptic pistol in hand.

By the following day nearly all dissension had faded away. The trail now crossed level ground and the Brul paused in their shivering long enough to study a land they'd never visited before. They realized they were pioneers of a sort and a few found they were enjoying the journey.

They were two days in from the trail head. The vroqupii surmounted the occasional ridge with ease. The beauty of the lower plateau captivated the travelers, from the rushing streams beginning their long race down to the Skar to the stunted but wide-spreading evergreens.

Lyra was particularly interested in a convoluted pile of brush that Tyl called an *aroyt*. Covering as much as half an acre, the *aroyt* was a single growth that defended its highly edible trunk with an impenetrable armor of centimeter-long thorns. There were also clumps of high mossy fungi that rose to their knees and held melt water like a sponge. Not that water underfoot was a problem. Most of the trail had been cut from solid rock. Soil was a precious rarity at this height.

They were approaching a saddle between a finger of Aracunga and a low hill when the two lead Brul who had disengaged themselves from the team to serve as advance scouts returned at a gallop. That in itself was extraordinary, since it was the first time the Redowls had seen a vroqupii move at anything faster than a walk.

Homat hurried to meet the outriders as the procession slowed. The scouts were chattering loudly to their companions as they traveled down the line.

"Maybe they've spotted Jakaie over the ridge line," Lyra suggested hopefully. Too hopefully.

Homat rejoined them quickly, his fright apparent in his expression. "The Brul are taking their animals out of harness."

"What?" Etienne looked toward the front of the team, could see the drovers working with the harness. "What the devil's wrong?"

"Exactly," Homat replied. "Many devils. Demons." His eyes were wide.

"More strepanong? Or some other animal?"

"Not animal, not animal," Homat insisted. "Demons!" Etienne could see he was far more terrified than he'd been the night of the scavenger attack.

Etienne started up the line. "They can't unhitch and quit now! We're almost there." As he spoke, several vroqupii were already moving out of file. "You've got to make them stop, Homat."

"They won't stop, de-Etienne. The strepanong they can understand, but no one can fight demons."

Desperately, Etienne turned to Tyl. "What's going on? What are they so frightened of?"

"I am not sure," Tyl murmured, "but I fear what I may know."

"Demons are in Jakaie," Homat went on. He turned to point toward the saddle just ahead. "Jakaie lies just over that ridge, but the demons are there. The Brul will go no further, de-Etienne. They say they are going back to their homes as fast as their mounts will carry them. They complain that nothing was said in the contracts about dealing with demons."

"What kind of demons?" Lyra asked, trying to make some sense of the Mai's panic.

"Ice demons!"

"Ah, it is as I fear." Tyl turned and began talking rapid-fire to his companions, the words flying almost as fast as if he were speaking Mai.

"Not the Tsla too," Etienne snapped angrily. The first retreating vroqupii were passing the boat now, heading back toward the Barshajagad. He stepped toward the nearest.

"You must stay!" he shouted in Mai. The Brul ignored him. He walked to the next in line. "You can't leave us here like this. We have a contract, an agreement." He struggled to recall the words Lyra had used to hold the drovers the night of the strepanong. "What of your commercial honor?"

"To flee from devils is no disgrace," the Brul announced with dignity, even as he looked back over his shoulder to make certain no demons pursued. And that was all any of them would say.

In less than thirty minutes the last vroqupii had disappeared over the slope behind them, its Brul urging it to greater speed. Etienne and Lyra considered their boat, marooned on a rocky plain, yoked to nothing.

"Ice demons," Etienne grumbled. "Didn't they see how easily we drove off the strepanong?"

"These are not strepanong," Tyl told him. "Thee must see to understand as thee had to see the Topapasirut to understand it. I sorrow for thee, Learned One. As for ourselves, we must go on to aid our brethren in Jakaie."

"Hey, what about us? Are we supposed to just sit here and wait for the next flood?"

"Etienne," Lyra said gently, "you're not thinking clearly. You never do when you lose your temper."

"So enlighten me."

"This town lies just over the ridge ahead." She stared meaningfully at the hydrofoil.

Realization brought embarrassment with it, though the Tsla did not perceive it. "Just ahead. We have plenty of battery power and we don't have to lift too high." Lyra nodded, turned to the Tsla. "These ice demons. They wouldn't happen to be the Na, would they?"

"What other demons of the ice are there? I thought thee knew." Tyl gestured toward the boat with his snout. "Thee will use thy spirit boat to help us?"

"To help you, yes, and ourselves, since we have to get it into Jakaie somehow. You know what to do?" Tyl nodded and moved with the porters to climb aboard. The Redowls followed.

"You wanted to see this legendary third race, the one that inhabits the Guntali," Etienne reminded her as they mounted the ladder. "Looks like you're going to have your chance."

"I'm not sure I like the circumstances, but it doesn't appear we have much say in the matter."

They checked out the boat's systems carefully. It had been several days since the repellers had been used. But the hydrofoil lifted easily off the ground and started forward on its cushion of air. The wooden platform hung beneath the hull, the huge heavy wheels spinning aimlessly. Bindings groaned but held.

Jakaie had better be as close as the Brul had indicated, Lyra thought as she guided them toward the notch in the rocks. Otherwise they'd have to squat down somewhere until the cells recharged the batteries.

Jakaie was built into a flank of Aracunga. The architecture was similar to Turput's but much heavier construction seemed to be the rule. The buildings boasted fewer windows. At that altitude the Tsla needed to conserve heat.

Off to the north lay irrigated fields filled with soil laboriously collected from notches and arroyos where it had gathered. The wall was the most obvious difference between Jakaie and Turput. It was an impressive wall; a good six or seven meters high but not especially thick.

Apparently Jakaie was high enough for creatures of the Guntali to mix with those of the Tsla ecological zone. Including, it seemed, the Na. He tried to visualize the Na in his mind's eye, using variations of the Mai-Tsla pattern—a bipedal, mammalian type. And that much was true. But the ways in which the new form diverged from those previously encountered caused the small hairs on the back of his neck to tense.

Several gates broke the town wall and no more than two dozen Na battered away at the largest. That two dozen Na would take on an entire town said more for their ferocity and disposition than all the fears expressed by the Brul.

Jakaie was large enough to harbor anywhere from five hundred to a thousand inhabitants, all of whom not only were on the defensive but appeared to be losing the battle. Tsla bodies were visible outside the wall. There was no sign of dead Na though one individual did sit some distance away from the fight. A big male, it was festooned with spears and arrows and was busily engaged in plucking them from his body as if they were so many bee stings.

As they watched from the straining hydrofoil, the gate gave way under the steady pounding from rocks and small trees. The Tsla inside scattered as the Na rushed in among them, and screams of terror pierced the clear mountain air. "Thee must hurry, Learned Ones, or many will die!" Swd called from the foredeck.

"We're moving as fast as we can," Etienne told him through the speaker membrane. "This boat wasn't designed for rapid travel out of the water."

Many primitives would have paused at the sight of so alien an object as the flying boat coming toward them. Not the Na. Either they did not possess sufficient imagination to be fearful of strange new shapes or else they were too confident in their own irresistible strength. A few bellowed in the hydrofoil's direction as it crossed over the wall, but the assault continued.

The hydrofoil bucked and rolled uneasily as they began to pass over homes and streets. It wasn't designed to compensate for such uneven terrain. Everyone aboard was glad when Etienne finally set the boat down in a parklike area near the center of Jakaie. A few anxious faces, flexible snouts aquiver, peeked out at them from shuttered windows and portholes. The noise of fighting could be heard clearly. Etienne checked his pistol as Lyra urged him to hurry. "What, in a rush to shoot some more natives?" he chided her. "How are you going to justify that in your report?"

"If this town's devastated we won't be able to find the help we'll need to get us down to the river again."

"What makes you think the Tsla here have any interest in helping us? This isn't Turput." He scrambled down the boarding ladder.

"Because we're going to endear ourselves to them by helping to repel this attack. Not that I wouldn't help them anyway." She started toward the broken gate and he had to hurry to keep up with her.

Anxious to protect her precious Tsla, he mused. But she was right about one thing: they'd do it if they had to or not. Tyl and the porters had become more than natives during the journey Upriver from Turput. They'd become friends.

Tyl and the three porters were offered arms by oldsters and adolescents. Only Homat did not accompany the reinforcements. He remained with the hydrofoil because between his bulky clothing and the temperature he'd have been useless in a fight.

It was not as if they hadn't encountered violence on Tslamaina before Jakaie, but it was still a shock to stumble onto the decapitated body of a female Tsla lying in the street. The head was nowhere around and the sounds of combat were very close.

After the Na broke through, the Tsla retreated to their strong buildings to harry the invaders with spears and arrows. Etienne and his party rounded the side of one such structure and halted only a few meters from a cluster of ten or twelve farmers who were trapped against the wall by a pair of Na. The farmers were holding the attackers off with long pikes and sharp tools, yet it was apparent that if something wasn't done quickly the Na would pick them apart one by one.

Etienne had no time to admire Tyl's bravery as their guide darted forward, weaving with the waddling gait of his kind, to cut at the leg of one Na with a curved blade. It did not penetrate the leathery skin very deeply and he had to retreat in a hurry, leaving his weapon behind.

But the Na had felt it, grunted, muttered something unintelligible, then reached down to pluck the weapon from its ankle. The creature was four meters tall and covered with a thick, shaggy pelt. Its clothing was crude—heavy sandals of some unknown leather, a leathery vest and breastplate, and a kilt of some similar material. A bone knife hung from a cord tied around the waist, the blade almost as tall as Lyra. As its main weapon, the Na clutched a club which had once been a tree of respectable size. It was panting heavily and a dark tongue lolled from a corner of its mouth.

That made sense. An inhabitant of the Guntali would have little use for sweat glands.

Without a word Etienne moved to his left, Lyra to the right. As he ran he fired. Thick hair was burned black on the back of a pillarlike thigh. The Na howled and turned its attention away from the desperate farmers.

The creature's forehead was very low and its blunt snout seemed incapable of advanced expression, but there was no mistaking that snarl of hatred. It displayed four canines, two upper, two lower. The remaining front teeth appeared to have been filed to sharp points. One did not have to be an experienced biologist to realize the Na did not exist on a diet of vegetables.

It uttered something in words of single syllables as it brought the massive club down faster than Etienne would have guessed possible. He dove wildly behind a small wagon piled high with some kind of vegetation. The club made kindling of the wagon and splinters bit at Etienne's exposed face. As he rolled to his feet he thought suddenly, *What am I doing here?* I should be behind a desk at a university, grumbling over sophomoric student reports and wondering who's going to show at the next faculty get-together.

There was no time for regretful contemplation. The club swung parallel to the pavement and he heard it *whoosh* as he ducked and it missed the top of his skull by centimeters. Then a big hand was reaching for him, six treelike fingers with hooked nails at the tips.

He stumbled backward, away from that menacing grasp, firing as he fell. The bolt passed between the forefinger and first thumb to strike the Na in the left eye. It let out a thunderous howl, dropped the club and fell to its knees, shaking violently. The Na was dead by the time it hit the ground.

Etienne tried to rejoin his companions, only to find his path blocked by the other Na. It charged forward and brought its own club down with both hands. Etienne barely missed being pulped by diving behind a nearby wall.

Freed of the need to ward off two attackers, the farmers fanned out behind the survivor. Pikes and spears and scythes stabbed and cut at muscles and tendons. The Na roared and bellowed, frustrated in its attempt to locate the snoutless Tsla who had slain his companion. As a great tendon was

[166]

finally cut, the beast fell to one knee swinging the club in a wide arc to kill a pair of Tsla who'd closed too quickly.

But now that the Na was down it no longer seemed so massive or invulnerable. Etienne took careful aim and fired at the base of the skull. The bone was so thick that it prevented the charge from penetrating to the spine, but the shock was sufficient to temporarily paralyze the creature and send it tumbling the rest of the way to the street.

It did his heart good, though Lyra would surely not have approved, to watch the peaceful, philosophic Tsla jump all over the body and start hacking it to pieces. Knowing that his help was needed elsewhere, he left the surviving farmers to their butchery.

He needn't have worried. The Na were in full retreat, harried by the persistent townsfolk. He spotted Yulour atop a crop-loading ramp and climbed up beside him.

"You don't fight here, Yulour?"

"No, Learned One," said the slow-witted porter. "I want to help, but Teacher Tyl tell me no. He say, I would only end up hurting myself."

Etienne nodded, commending Tyl's good sense. He picked his way back down the ramp.

The fleeing Na carried huge bales of some kind of dried meat from a storehouse they'd broken into, while others hauled off unknown booty in huge leathery sacks. The Tsla pursued them only as far as the ruined gate.

Etienne saw only one other Na corpse. Perhaps word of the two deaths he'd had a hand in had been enough to frighten the rest of the Na into giving up the assault. Or perhaps they'd gained what they'd come for. He could speculate on motivation later. Right now he was exhausted and more than glad to see them go.

Another folk might have pursued in an attempt to recover their stolen stores, but not the Tsla. There was no room in their philosophy for active military pursuit. And out on the open plain they would be at a disadvantage against their opponents, whose size and maneuverability would not be restricted by stone walls and narrow streets.

He slowed as he approached the shattered gate, to stare after the retreating Na. A group of curious locals began to gather around him. Smiling and making Tsla gestures of friendship, he forced his way through them to find Tyl deep in conversation with a silver-furred elder.

The guide introduced him. "This is Ruu-an, First Scholar of Jakaie. Ruu-an, make greeting to the Learned Etienne, a scholar from a world other than ours. He comes here to learn about us . . . and as thee have observed, sometimes to help."

"I am gladdened by thy presence," the elder said. His accent differed from that of Tyl and the other Tsla of Turput, but the words remained comprehensible. "Also that thee saw fit to put aside thy studies long enough to aid us in a most desperate time. I have been informed that thee helped to bring down two of the Na and thereby to hasten their flight."

Etienne holstered his pistol. "Does this happen often? From what I saw of the fight I don't see how you could survive repeated attacks."

"The Na assail us infrequently, and usually with less loss of life. Many times we will simply fall back against the mountain and let them take what they will. They are not indiscriminate thieves and never take more than they can carry. But it has not been a good time for us and it was decided this time to resist. I do not think the choice wise."

"They come to steal your food?"

"When the time is hard on us, it may also be hard on them. Nor do they know how to grow food of their own. Despite their appearance, they have a hunger for the fruit of the soil. When it is scarce on the Guntali they will sometimes come down among us. I suppose they cannot be blamed. The life offered by the Guntali must be very hard."

"You sound like you're ready to forgive them," Etienne said, eyeing the bodies scattered both in front of and behind the ruined gate.

"We always do," the First Scholar told him. "Have they not souls just as we? They are more to be pitied than hated for their ignorance and weaknesses."

"I didn't see many weaknesses, but I've already learned that you Tsla are more forgiving than we humans." Already the townsfolk were busy removing the dead. That sparked an unpleasant memory.

"After the . . . funeral ceremonies . . . are concluded, what do you do with the bodies of your deceased?" He could not look at Tyl as he said this. Sensing his discomfort, the guide discreetly allowed the First Scholar to answer.

"Here we cremate the bodies and then scatter the ashes upon our fields, so that as tillers of the soil those who pass on may help the next generation to grow better crops."

"So they can be stolen again by the Na. You ought to put a stop to it."

"That would be a fine thing," the elder said, "but alas, a thing not possible. We cannot chase the Na up to the Guntali. It is too cold for us and the air too thin for us to fight in. Up there, they are the masters.

"Similarly, they cannot fight long down here. The thick hair which protects them from the Guntali's cold soon causes them to grow too hot to exert their great bodies, and they must retreat."

"I'm glad I don't have to depend on the weather for my defense," Etienne replied. Not that it was within his province to criticize the way these Tsla managed their lives.

"Actually," the elder continued, surprising his human audience, "there are times when we trade peacefully with the Na."

"I'd been told the Tsla served as a conduit between Mai and Na, but for some reason it just slipped my memory."

"You must not judge them only by this unusual attack," Ruu-an advised him. "There are many times when the Mai also prefer to fight instead of to trade."

Etienne was glad Homat was still back at the boat. "Listen, I'm standing here taking in all this information and it isn't even my department. Lyra's the one who should be making a record of your ways." He looked past them, making a perfunctory survey of the battlefield. "Where is she, anyway? I haven't seen her since we split up to try and flank the two Na we first encountered."

"Ah, Learned Teacher Lyra," Tyl murmured.

"Yes. Didn't she stick with you, Tyl?" Suddenly he was very cold, the kind of coldness that comes from inside the body and makes the muscles of one's arms and legs start to cramp.

"No. We became separated during the fight. I have not seen her since. Perhaps we ought to return to the place where we began the combat." He sounded concerned.

There was no sign of Lyra. Not where Etienne and the farmers had slain the two Na, not in the streets nearby, not before the gate. The word was passed among the townsfolk. Surely they'd know her whereabouts. An alien fighting among them would stand out immediately.

When the word came it was devastating in its finality.

〖 XIII 〗

The expedition's aims, his hopes for a personal rapprochement, the papers they planned to present to various scientific societies, the acclaim and acknowledgment and honors, all suddenly meant nothing beside the hollowness in his heart. Ten years of hard work had been shattered like that gate which had so ineffectively protected Jakaie.

Several of the townsfolk had seen the alien female disappear into a Na sack. They were positive she was alive at the time. Two or three Tsla had been stuffed in the sack with her.

Etienne and Tyl, accompanied by the First Scholar, rushed to the narrow street near the gate, following the lead of two young Tsla. A quick search turned up several raggedy fragments of Lyra's shirt—and something more significant. Battered but still functional, her pistol lay dark against the paving stones where she'd dropped it.

Asking without wanting to ask, he looked despairingly at Ruu-an. "Why would they take her alive?"

The elder glanced at Tyl, who knew the strange creature

better than he, but no enlightenment was forthcoming. So he answered.

"I told thee, Learned Etienne, that when times on the Guntali are difficult the Na come here to find food. They are not selective in their diet. Meat is meat to them, whether recently killed on the Guntali or traded to them by some merchant . . . or the merchant himself. They take live captives to prolong their supply of fresh food, as we do with our domestic animals."

The sudden irony of it made Etienne want to laugh, but he couldn't, any more than he could cry. All he could do was stare silently through the broken gate toward the rampart marking the rim of the Guntali, more than a thousand meters higher than Jakaie.

Lyra was up there somewhere, no doubt occupying her thoughts with the unprecedented opportunity granted her to study the culture of the Na at close range. Probably she was bouncing around in her sack with her fellow captives and cursing the lack of a recorder. She'd be doing exactly the same thing when they slipped her on the spit. Her last notes would detail the eating habits of the Na. He was sure it would be a paragon of scientific explication and his wife's final thought would be regret over the fact no one else would be able to read them.

"Damn them," he muttered. "Damn her!" He let all his anger and hate and frustration flow out over the stones and an occasional curious onlooker and when he finally concluded the tirade he was ashamed of himself, because there still were no tears.

As he turned back to the patient Tyl he discovered he could speak with extraordinary calmness. It was the peace of the resigned.

"Do you think they will eat her soon, or save her for a while?" How easily the words came now, the absurd words.

Tyl looked to Ruu-an instead of replying. "It is hard to say. Certainly they have sense enough to wonder at the differences between her and us. If any among this tribe has ever seen a Mai, they may think she is kin to them, albeit from a larger tribe. They may want to sample this new food right away, but I think they may choose to make a special feast around her. Thus they would save her for a last meal."

"I have to proceed on that assumption."

Tyl eyed him curiously. "What can thee do, Learned Etienne? I am wounded for thee. I was very fond of Learned Lyra. I learned much from her and enjoyed our sharing of customs and knowledge. Both pupil and teacher she was, but there is nothing to be done for her now."

"You and your damn fatalism! She's my wife, damn it, and as long as there's the slimmest chance she's still alive I have to go after her. It's her own damn fault for being so careless and putting me in this position, and she knows it. She's probably laughing over my predicament right now knowing that I have to come after her or risk everything going down the drain. Months of work, years of preparation all at risk because she didn't have a care for her fat rear and let some big dumb cretin of a native stuff her in his shopping bag. Lost her pistol, too." He shoved the other asynapt into his belt.

"I'm going to go back to the boat for our cold weather gear. Lyra'll be lucky if she doesn't freeze to death before she finds herself on the menu. Or maybe she won't be lucky. It depends on how right your assumptions are and how fast I can move up there." He scanned the rock wall.

"One thing I can tell from here; I'll have to hike it. No way the repellers will last long enough to get me up that. What about trails? Are there foot trails leading to the plateau, or do they just follow the easiest route down?"

"Always they follow the easiest," Ruu-an said. "That is their way. They make no attempt to hide themselves, for they have nothing to fear from us. But I do not understand what thee intend, Learned Visitor. The captured are already lost. Whether alive or dead this moment matters not. Thee saw how the Na fought here in our homeland, constrained by our walls and overheated as their bodies were. Think what they will be like to confront on the Guntali, where they are at home and in comfort. I will meditate on thy mate's behalf."

"Thee meditate thy butt off. I'm still going after her." He turned to their guide. "Tyl, you'll come with me, won't you?"

"As the First Scholar tells, the captured are already lost to us. In any case we can do nothing against the Na in their own land. To do so would only be to add to the rolls of the departed."

"How do you know you can't do anything if you've never tried?"

"Logic, Learned Etienne, and common sense, dictate our actions. We are calm because we are sensible, content because we understand our role in the scheme of existence." He reached out to try and comfort his distraught hairless friend.

"Please, Etienne, friend, thee must continue with thy work. Thy Lyra would have wished it. Thee must not grieve for her."

"I'm not grieving for her, you gutless wonder. I'm going after her because she may still be alive." Then, more quietly, "I mean no insult, Tyl. I won't grieve for her unless I know for a *fact* that she's dead."

"If thee wish to perish alongside her, why, that could be understood," said Ruu-an, attempting to make some sense of an alien reasoning that flew in the face of all logic.

"I've no intention of committing suicide."

"That is what thee will do if thee persist in following the Na onto the Guntali," Tyl insisted. "I am sorrowed, Etienne, but I cannot follow thee. My teachings, my beliefs, will not allow it. You may ask of any others thee wish." He did not add that such a request would be a waste of time.

Etienne forced himself to reply as courteously as possible. "I respect your beliefs, Tyl. I don't understand them and I don't sympathize with them, I don't even like them, but I can respect them. But I'm wasting time standing here trying to convince you." He wondered what Lyra would say if she could hear Tyl's refusal.

"I'll go after her myself."

"Thee will not return," Tyl warned him.

"Oh, I'll come back. Look at it like this: I'm going to acquire additional knowledge. It will be a learning experience."

"Death is learned soon enough," Tyl said. "They who—"

"I will go with thee."

So intent was he on his mental preparations and his frustration with the Tsla that Etienne didn't hear the voice.

Again it said, "I will help thee."

"Who said that?" He turned, to find himself confronting one of the porters. The last porter anyone expected to say anything: Yulour.

"If thee will have me, Learned One."

"Have you, yes, and glad of it." He didn't think Yulour could think fast enough to be of much help in a fight, but if supplies could be piled on that willing, powerful back they would make much better time. And it would be good to have company. In that respect the porter's slowness did not concern him. He doubted he'd be much in the mood for extended conversation atop the Guntali.

"Why? Isn't it against your spiritual principles?"

"I have no spiritual principles, Learned One." Yulour fought with the large Tsla words. "I do not have sense enough to have them." He looked hesitantly past the human. "Teacher Tyl must allow. I am bound to him."

Tyl was staring curiously at the porter. "I cannot allow myself to go, nor would thy companions, but if thy conscience is clear and committed."

"What is conscience?" Yulour asked innocently.

Tyl sighed. "No matter." He turned to Etienne. "He may accompany thee as he wishes. I cannot stop him, though I would if it were in my power. All beings have free will. Remember this, though: thee will bear a heavy responsibility if he dies. It will be on *thy* conscience."

"I'll remember that." Etienne faced his one volunteer. He'd had little personal contact with Yulour, indeed, with any of the porters, preferring to give them their instructions through Tyl.

"Thank you, Yulour. I accept your offer of help. It would be better understood among my own people."

The porter shook his head sadly. "I do not understand, Learned One."

Etienne clapped the Tsla on one muscular shoulder. "It doesn't matter. All that matters is that you're willing to help."

"I *like* Teacher Lyra," Yulour said with simple sincerity. "I want to help her."

"If we can, we will, Yulour."

They hurried back to the hydrofoil, ignoring the crowd

of curious Tsla which had gathered around it. Homat was waiting to greet them.

Etienne caught his breath as a blast of superhot air rushed out of the main cabin. Inside the temperature reached for the hundred-degree line, forty degrees warmer than the air outside. Homat's reaction was exactly the opposite of Etienne's. As cold air poured inside he retreated to the pile of blankets he'd assembled on the floor of the cockpit, curled up beneath them, and peered out apologetically as Etienne strode in after him.

"Please do not be angry with me, de-Etienne," he pleaded. "Only I was left behind, and I remember how to work the device that makes the air inside the spirit boat hot or cold. I could not resist. It's the first time in many times I have been truly delightful warm."

Etienne had to smile. "Relax, Homat, it's all right. I'm not mad at you." The smile quickly vanished. "De-Lyra has been taken by the Na, by the ice demons."

Homat began to moan and Etienne hastened to cut him off. "Yulour and I are going after her."

Homat's nearly bald head emerged from the smothering blankets. "After the demons?"

"After the Na, yes."

"You will not come back."

"I really appreciate all the support I'm getting," he mumbled absently as he started rummaging through a storage locker in search of needed supplies. "I never thought I'd see the day when Mai and Tsla were in perfect agreement on anything."

"After the demons," Homat whispered. "I—I would come with you if I could."

Etienne threw him a surprised look. "That's delightful of you, Homat, but you know how much use you'd be. The temperature atop the Guntali's probably somewhere just above the freezing mark. I don't think you could handle that for very long. No Mai could. The climate here in Jakaie's at the upper limit of your tolerance."

"I wish it were not so, de-Etienne. It is wondrous that you can move so freely between the comfortable weather of the Skatandah and the roof of the world."

"Our special clothing helps to make that possible, Homat."

He held up a thermal coat just excavated from storage. "I'm more concerned about the atmospheric pressure above the six-thousand-meter line. The air will be thicker than at a corresponding altitude on my home world, but thinner than I'd like. We have some methods of compensating for that, too."

Into the large backpack went a half dozen supplementary breathers. Each consisted of a facepiece designed to fit comfortably over mouth and nose and flexible metal tubes that fit over the ears and behind the head to hold the contraption in place. The tubes contained pure O_2 under pressure and would serve equally well under water. For high altitude use they'd last much longer, since their full flow wouldn't be required.

Two ascents from the bottom of the Barshajagad had prepared him for the coming climb. All that he feared was the possibility of having to do some running at high altitude. He wondered how Lyra was handling the thin air and low temperatures. She was wearing long clothing when the Na had attacked, but that wouldn't suffice if the nighttime temperature dropped below freezing. It might be that all that stood between her and freezing to death at night was the warm presence of her fellow captives.

"Yulour, will you be warm enough?" he asked his sole companion when all was ready. The porter wore several layers of toga and two capes, in addition to a cloak pulled tight over his head.

"I will be fine, Teacher. Please not to worry about me. It upsets me when I see anyone worrying about me."

Tyl and Ruu-an waited at the main gate to see them off. With typical Tsla matter-of-factness, masons and carpenters were already hard at work repairing the broken barrier. Ruu-an presented one stocky villager who would guide them to the base of the incline the Na usually employed for their travels.

"Do they ever leave a rear guard behind, or anything like that?" Etienne asked the First Scholar.

Ruu-an made a negative movement with his trunk. "They have nothing to fear from us since we never pursue them."

That sense of invulnerability should be my greatest ally, Etienne mused. Once safely back in their own territory atop the Guntali the Na would relax. Counterattack would be the last thing they'd expect. The shock should be considerable. But he didn't delude himself into thinking that they'd run off in panic. The Na weren't the type to run.

No, he'd have to rely on surprise. Even with two fully charged pistols he doubted he could hold off an entire tribe of the giants for more than a couple of minutes.

"We're wasting time." He led their local guide toward the wall beckoning to the east, moving as rapidly as practicable. Yulour fell in step behind, the big pack bobbing easily on his broad shoulders.

Tyl and Ruu-an watched them go.

"What a strange folk," the First Scholar declared. "I listen in amazement to the accomplishments you tell me they have achieved, and then something like this is done, something which a child of but a few years can see is useless."

"They are full of contradictions." Tyl's gaze was still on Etienne's retreating back. "One moment they are very wise and the next, foolish as little Mai. I think their souls must be in perpetual confusion."

"Thee believe they have souls, then?"

"I am convinced of it, though other teachers of Turput argue otherwise."

"It may be that their minds are variable, that they are adults one moment and cubs the next. Very strange folk. I am glad I was able to meet and talk with one of them before they died."

"Yes, I will miss them. The female came to me day after day and asked endless questions, which allowed me to make a close study of her and her ways. Now that they have left us we will have only that to remember."

He turned and helped the elderly Ruu-an as they started back toward town, continuing the discussion as they walked.

There were plenty of switchbacks which over the years the Na had developed into a recognizable pathway, so the climb was not as difficult as Etienne first feared. He still had to stop at regular intervals to catch his breath. Common sense insisted on calling regular halts while his nerves tried to force him to greater haste. The supplementary breathers wouldn't last forever and he tried to ration the flow of the one clamped over his face.

Despite the frequent pauses they reached the plateau sooner than he'd dared to hope. Gaps in the thick clouds afforded only an occasional glimpse of Jakaie and its valley sitting far below and behind them. Above the rest of the real world brooded the mountain called Aracunga. A thick cloud of ice crystals trailed southward from its crest, looking like smoke flowing from a volcano. In the distance rose a white ghost, the impossible bulk of the sky-scraping Prompaj Massif.

A few trees stood ready to greet their arrival, thin wispy branches applauding their achievement at the behest of a steady wind. Nearby, green-brown bushes clung to the ground. Etienne bent to examine the nuts they produced, found them hard to extract from the poor soil. They hugged the earth with hooks of wood.

In the light dusting of snow they saw tracks of animals that walked on broad but delicate feet, with long strides. Etienne visualized something tall and thin running fast. As they left the rim they encountered larger spoor, indication that a large predator had recently passed.

Whenever their course was in doubt Yulour would drop his head toward the ground and employ his oversized proboscis to sniff out the scent of the Na.

"Not far," he told Etienne by the end of the day.

"No reason for them to cover ground." Etienne squinted into the growing darkness, an occasional snowflake tickling his skin. "Probably they've picked a comfortable spot to relax and reminisce about their attack on Jakaie. If they have that much sense, that is. We should come up on them soon, then?"

"Yes, soon." Yulour straightened. "Then what we do?"

"I'm not sure. Depends on how they set their camp."

They saw the glow from the earth before Yulour caught the scent of the tribe. The fire itself wasn't visible because it lay in a depression. Heeding Etienne's request for silence, Yulour followed the Teacher as they crept up the side of the low ridge and found themselves looking down into a small crater in the rocks. It was deep and offered excellent protection against the wind. On the far side, stone overhung part of the depression, and the alcove was packed with sleepy, sated Na. Only a few of the primitives were moving, mostly to tend to the roaring fire. The odor from the burning chips was strong.

For the first time Etienne saw Na females, along with two-meter-tall cubs. Unlike the children of most species, the offspring of the Na were not cute. They moved nervously in their sleep, their bare feet kicking toward the warmth of the fire.

Vegetation was unusually abundant in the depression, not only due to the presence of nutrients unintentionally supplied by Na but also because the hollow served as a watertrap. The pool lay directly below Etienne, the fire on the far side. A large pile of dried animal dung helped to reflect as well as freshen the blaze.

Yulour pointed and whispered with childlike excitement. "Look there, Teacher, look there!"

Etienne's gaze traveled to the right of the fire. Stone and bone had been heaped together to create a crude kitchen. Attached to a long bone suspended over a smoking fire was a shape that he didn't immediately recognize. It took him a moment to see that it was a dead Tsla shorn of its fur. He glanced sideways at his companion. There was no fury, no hatred in the porter's face.

"It doesn't bother you?"

"What bother me, Teacher?"

Etienne gestured toward the firepit. "They're cooking one of your own kind down there."

"Everyone must eat," Yulour said ingenuously.

Etienne turned away. Obviously a great deal more research would have to be performed before they could fully understand the Tsla.

Of more immediate interest was the cage that rested against the far right-hand base of the depression. It was made of the curving rib bones of some big creature, lashed together with cured sinew. Four—no, five—Tsla were clustered together within. Along with one figure clad in bright blue. His pulse raced, threatening to set his fingers trembling.

Lyra was alive and apparently intact, from what he could see. The collar of her shirt was buttoned all the way up over her neck and her long hair was wrapped around her face.

The Na had left their carrying sacks in with the prey, and Lyra lay beneath one for further protection from the cold.

A single young male squatted sleepily in front of the cage, idly tossing pebbles into the fire and ignoring his charges.

"Soon he may sleep, Teacher," Yulour said of the guard.

"He'd better." Etienne checked to make sure both pistols were readily accessible, along with the supplementary breathers. Then he backed carefully down the slope and circled the depression.

When they climbed up again they topped the rise directly behind the cage. Then they waited.

It was well after midnight when Etienne stirred himself for another look down into the hollow. Tslamaina's moons were masked by cloud and most of the light in the depression came from the central bonfire. He watched the motionless guard for another half hour before he could be certain the Na was asleep.

"What must I do, Teacher?" asked Yulour.

"Just stay here and keep quiet, and wait for us."

"Be careful, Teacher."

"I will, Yulour."

"I will come down if thee need me," he added anxiously as Etienne slid on his belly over the top.

"I know you will. You're a good friend, Yulour."

"I thank thee, Teacher," whispered the porter, over-whelmed by the compliment.

Etienne half-slid, half-crawled down the incline. The tribe dozed like the dead beneath the rocky overhang. He checked his wrist. It was twelve degrees below freezing. He was quite comfortable but he worried about Lyra. If the temperature fell much further she would have difficulty walking until he could get her into her own thermal suit, which was stuffed into Yulour's copious backpack.

He reached for a purchase only to see the rock tumble down the slope. It came to rest against the back of the cage. The guard did not stir. Etienne followed the stone as rapidly as practicable, assuming a kneeling position behind the cage.

"Lyra," he whispered intently, shifting his gaze from her to the guard and back again. Bodies stirred within the cave but no one rose from sleep.

"Lyra!" Her head jerked around in the darkness and she shoved her hair aside.

"Etienne?"

"Who the hell else would it be?" He pulled one of the pistols and carefully adjusted the setting after quickly inspecting the lashings holding the cage together. "I'm going to try and burn through the material holding these bones. Be ready, for God's sake!"

He started working, the pistol's faint hum absorbed by the wind overhead and the crackle of the central fire. Lyra moved quietly to wake her fellow prisoners. They had enough presence of mind to keep quiet, save for one who whispered in surprise, "It is the mate of the stranger who is with us!" Lyra shushed him.

"Here, as Etienne cuts these loose, take them up and lay them somewhere aside." The Tsla moved silently to comply.

He smiled to himself. Fatalistic in philosophy the Tsla might be, but clearly that didn't extend to sitting dumbly by if the chance of escape presented itself.

"Etienne, what the devil are you doing here?"

"Saving fair maiden from an incipient barbeque." Another lashing split and he started on the bonds above it. One of the Tsla males gripped the base of the loosened section to prevent its falling.

Lyra sat clear of the humming pistol, shook her head. "Somehow I never thought you capable of the heroic gesture, Etienne."

"Lyra, shut up. I'm busy." Another series of sinews gave way and he started on those holding a second bar as the Tsla carefully removed the first.

The second bone popped clear easily and again the Tsla moved it aside. Lyra was first out and Etienne caught her as she stumbled. Her muscles were numb from cold and confinement.

For an instant he thought she might have suffered some unseen injury. She quickly dispelled that concern.

"I'm in one piece, though I thought I'd suffocate in that damn stuffsack." The Tsla were filing out wordlessly behind her, looking around in bewilderment. "We're up on the Guntali, aren't we? The sack was opaque, so I couldn't get any bearings." He nodded. "No wonder I'm so cold."

"Fill me in on the details later," he advised her, looking anxiously past her toward the dozing guard.

"We are grateful," said the senior Tsla among the captives.

"Be grateful when we're safely back in Jakaie," Etienne admonished him. "Follow me and stay *low*." He started up the slope on his belly, glancing back once to make sure Lyra was on his heels. "You need any help?"

"No. It just feels good to be moving again."

As soon as they dropped over the dark side of the depression he extracted her thermal suit from the supplies. She was so cold it took her three times as long as normal to climb inside.

"I am gladdened to see thee, Teacher. We feared for thee."

She looked at Yulour in mild surprise, peering past him to see the others who had come with her husband. Her disappointment in the darkness was evident.

"Etienne, you wouldn't believe the habits of these Na. Their cruelty isn't studied, of course. It's simply their way. But their victims suffer needlessly. As a matter of fact I'd have to say that based on preliminary studies which admittedly were not carried out under the best of conditions, they have no redeeming social characteristics whatsoever."

"You'll think of some as soon as you get warmed up. You'll end up with a balanced report. You always do."

"Maybe, but I don't feel I'm in a very balanced mood right now."

When the last of the Tsla captives reached bottom Etienne addressed them hastily. "As you know, I am Learned One Lyra's mate. We're going back to Jakaie. Stay together and no talking unless it's absolutely necessary. We have to travel as rapidly as possible. If anyone gets lost or falls behind for any reason..."

"We know what we must do," said the senior Tsla. "But we do not know the way back to our home."

"We do, so stay close by us." Holding Lyra's hand tightly in his own he turned to follow Yulour. The rest of the Tsla trailed behind in perfect silence.

⟦ XIV ⟧

They shambled on through the cold and wind all the rest of that night, following Etienne's lead. He glanced constantly at the instrumentation on his wrists, but was glad he could rely on Yulour's sense of smell for confirmation of their course. The rising sun was welcomed not only for the warmth it provided but as a further aid to direction. Aracunga was a more reliable beacon than any readout on a tiny screen.

They were well down the trail toward home when a boulder the size of a small house fell past them in awesome silence, to pulverize a basaltic outcrop below. It missed Etienne and Lyra by a few meters.

Instinctively he pressed his back against the cliff. "Landslide," he muttered.

Yulour made a quick, sharp gesture of disagreement, looked upward. "Na slide."

A glance toward the Guntali showed a single enormous hirsute shape leaning over the edge, gesticulating angrily and stomping the ground. The mouth made sounds that were swallowed by the wind. Then the figure vanished.

"Coming after us," Etienne commented with unexpected

calm. "I'd hoped they wouldn't. I wonder how many of them there are." He pulled on Lyra's hand. "Can you run?"

She clutched her pistol firmly, nodded.

"Remember now, hon, we don't want to harm any more of the native population than is absolutely necessary," he said dryly.

"Pardon my lack of objectivity. The rotten cannibalistic bastards."

"No time for gory details, love."

Trying to make as much speed as possible, they raced down the pathway. No more small mountains crashed down around them, but by the time they reached the base of the cliff they could hear bellows and roars behind them.

Twists and turns in the descending trail made it impossible to tell exactly how near their pursuers were. Voices could carry a long way in the clear mountain air. Then they broke out of the talus at the base of the cliff and found themselves running along a well-beaten road.

The Tsla who'd joined Lyra in escaping shouted warnings to the farmers who toiled in the fields. Tools were flung aside, seedlings left in pans as everyone ran for the safety of Jakaie.

Yulour put a hand on Etienne's shoulder, bade him turn as he pointed with the other. "There, Teacher!"

Etienne saw, no raiding party this time, but the entire tribe stumbling down the cliff face in pursuit. Females and awkward adolescents brought up the rear. Evidently the rescue was an outrage sufficient to infuriate the Na beyond reason.

They ran slowly but with ground-eating strides. Out in front and much too close behind were males hefting clubs bigger than a man.

"Come on, move it!" he shouted at the farmers who had begun to lag behind.

"We'll make it with plenty of time, Etienne." As Lyra spoke her right foot located the only hole in the road and she went down in a heap, immediately rolling over on her back to clutch her ankle. Pain replaced confidence on her face as she cursed her clumsiness.

"Not broken," she was finally able to gasp out.

"I know that, stupid," he said as felt gingerly of the already swelling knot. He looked past her. He couldn't tell if the Na had seen her go down. The farmers and escapees were nearing the town wall now.

"Hurry, Teacher," Yulour implored him. "There's little time."

"Get up, Lyra," Etienne ordered her. She threw him a look of anger mixed with determination. Using his shoulder and an arm for support, she struggled to her feet. They limped toward Jakaie. The agony in her ankle started her crying silently, but she didn't stop.

Etienne did so, however. "Too slow. We'll never make it." He bent under her and her pain gave way to startled surprise.

"Etienne!" She was across his shoulders. "Put me down! You'll end up killing both of us."

"Lyra, you talk too much." She bounced awkwardly on his shoulders as he ran. There was no pain, but the considerable weight soon had him panting heavily. Without the supplementary breather's steady flow of pure oxygen he couldn't have done it.

"Teacher, can I help thee?" Yulour waddled alongside them. Something went *whomp!* against the earth off to their left, smashing a small bush to kindling. The Na club was much larger than the unlucky shrub.

Etienne wanted to look back to see how close their pursuers were but he couldn't spare the wind. The city gate was very near now, the repaired entrance gaping invitingly. This time armed Tsla waited on the walls, waving and shouting to urge him on. Encouragement was one thing he didn't need. Already his legs felt like lead determined to sink toward the center of the planet and Lyra, lovely sweet Lyra . . . if only she were a little less voluptuous.

Something struck the small of his back and he almost went down. But he staggered, regained his balance and ran on. A dull flame began to burn just above his coccyx as waiting hands reached out to relieve him of his burden.

They set Lyra down alongside him as he sucked at the last of the breather's air, breathing like a man who'd just finished a long underwater swim. Shouts and yells penetrated his exhaustion.

"I'm too tired to sit up," he wheezed. "What's happening?"

"Don't ask me. I'm the one with the sprained ankle, remember?"

"Pity you couldn't have sprained your mouth."

"Be of good cheer, Teacher," said the solicitous Yulour. "I will find out." He moved toward the gate.

Long moments passed with Lyra massaging her ankle and Etienne slowly regaining his strength.

"That was a dumb thing to do," she finally told him. "You could have gotten a hernia."

"Excuse me," he said between gasps. "Next time I'll drop you."

"Next time I shoot myself before I let them take me." She saw the expression on his face and looked away. "So it's bad xenology. I can't help it. I have feelings too. What on earth made you try something like that, anyway?" When he didn't reply she pushed at his shoulder. "Roll over. I want to see your back. I saw the tail end of that club hit you."

With an effort he turned onto his side. Her fingers moved across his waist, making him wince.

"Could have busted your spine," she murmured gently. "You've got a hell of a bruise."

"I can tell. Where's Yulour?"

She looked toward the gate. "I don't see him, but so far it looks good. There's still a lot of yelling and screaming on the walls, but the new gate looks much stronger than the old one." Her eyes returned to him. "You're an idiot, Etienne. You saved my life."

"That was the idea."

"Why?"

He slowly rolled back, stared blankly at the sky. "Damned if I know." His face contorted as the fire in his back spread to new nerves.

"It never ceases to amaze me, Etienne, how often you can do the right thing and then say just the opposite. Stay there. I'll get something from the boat." She started to rise, flopped back heavily. "I forgot. I can't walk."

"What a sensible, always alert pair we make," he murmured. "If only our sponsors could see us now." He would have laughed if he hadn't been so tired.

"Thank you for saving my life, Etienne, whatever your motives."

"Anytime. Don't mention it. Do you think you can help me sit up?"

"Be careful," she warned him.

Several faces were suddenly staring down at them. One was familiar.

"Hello, Tyl." Etienne clasped his knees toward his chest, trying to alleviate some of the pain in his back. The nerves there argued with every millimeter of effort.

Tyl executed a most profound sideways Tsla bow. "We did not expect thee to return, Learned Etienne. Thee were in the right and we in the wrong, and most grateful am I to be proven so. It was a grand thing thee did. Songs will commemorate thy deed. And this one's, whose service is unprecedented." He indicated Yulour, standing in front of the crowd.

"I don't understand, Teacher," Yulour said.

"Dear, sweet, brave Yulour," Lyra murmured. "I know thy customs and why thy kinfolk did not come, but why did thee?"

"It seemed a good thing to do, so I did it." He looked embarrassed.

"I'll make it up to you," she told him.

"Make . . . up to me? I do not understand."

"I know you don't. Do you understand what I mean when I say that Etienne and I thank thee very deep?"

"Thee are welcome," the porter replied gravely. "Now I must go and find my friends."

Tyl watched him go. "A peculiar soul, but many-times blessed, I think."

"He certainly has our blessings," said Lyra. She looked toward the wall. The shouting had ceased and the Tsla were leaving the top of the palisade, chatting easily among themselves.

"It seems the Na have given up and gone away. Do you think they might attack again?"

"They vented evil gestures and many shouts," Tyl informed them, "but I think they will not come back for some time. They are not animals and know they cannot break into

Jakaie without first surprising its people. This time there was no surprise, so they have gone."

"So we're safe?" Etienne mumbled.

"Yes, all are safe now. Jakaie owes thee a debt for the dead thee have restored to them alive."

Etienne's back improved slowly under Lyra's ministering hands. The worst of it was the body wrap she made him wear. It enveloped him from beneath the armpits to below his waist and he walked like a recently resurrected mummy.

Among the prosaic Tsla the novelty of the rescue quickly wore off and they returned to their daily chores. But there were frequent, shy visits from those he'd saved and from their relatives and friends to thank him.

The debt they owed, they insisted, could never be repaid. Until Tyl came aboard the hydrofoil one morning to see the patient.

"There was a meeting." The temperature in the main cabin was seventy-five and Homat sat shivering off in a corner.

"What kind of meeting?" Lyra asked.

"A community meditation. I am sorry thee were not invited, but there was no time. I have made the people aware of thy problem. Thy wooden undercarriage is still serviceable, is it not?"

"The wheels haven't fallen off, if that's what you mean," Etienne replied.

"There are not here the large draft animals like the Mai have. No vroqupii. There are *lekkas*, but they are for riding, not for pulling. Unlike Turput, here the land is cultivated mostly by hand. But we are Tsla. The Tsla are strong." He flexed both arms and they saw the muscles ripple beneath short fur.

"All Jakaie will assist. Will it not be easier to lower thy boat back to the bottom of the Barshajagad than it was to bring it up?"

Etienne considered their guide's words, trying hard to restrain any excitement. Excitement hurt his back.

"Sure it would be easier, but still a difficult descent."

"I have talked long with Ruu-an and the other elders. There is a way north of here that descends to the Skar and bypasses the Topapasirut. They say also that the way is longer and gentler than that which climbs the side canyon we used. They say, Etienne and Lyra, that it can be done."

"Who am I to dispute Ruu-an?" said Etienne. He felt like shouting but restrained himself lest he strain something.

"When can we start down?"

"Soon. The families of those thee saved demand the honor of taking up the ropes nearest the spirit boat, where the work will be the hardest."

"Our thanks go out to them," Etienne said.

"Thee can thank them thyself." Tyl readied himself to leave. "It will take some time to organize provisions and find the rope sufficient to secure thy craft. Thee will have ample time to thank thy new friends and repair thy back."

"Wait a minute," said Lyra, frowning. "What about the Na? What if they come back when the town is nearly deserted, or catch everyone out in the open?"

"This too was discussed during meditation. They will not come near Jakaie for a long time, so embarrassing to them was their defeat. And after a few days of descent the temperature will grow much too hot for them to follow us."

"We won't argue with that, will we, dear?" He stared meaningfully at Lyra.

As usual, she wasn't intimidated. "If the townsfolk feel confident of their security, I don't see why we shouldn't permit them to bounce you all the way down to the river."

In contrast to the agonizingly difficult haul up from the bottom of the Barshajagad, the descent to a rocky beach northwest of Jakaie and the bulk of Aracunga mountain was almost relaxing. There were a few rough places, easily surmounted by the hydrofoil's repellers, but as the Tsla promised the slope was far gentler than the steep side canyon route on the southern side.

Chanting in unison as they leaned into the heavy ropes, the Tsla were able to lower the boat on its wheeled cradle faster than the Redowls expected. It was hard to imagine the vroqupii and their Brul doing the job any more efficiently than the citizens of Jakaie. It helped that there was none of the sense of competition among the townsfolk that there had been among the Mai. Homat grudgingly conceded that sometimes cooperation was worth more than skill and strength.

When at last the wooden cradle was removed from the hull and the boat bobbed once more in the waters of the Skar, Etienne passed among the villagers trying to thank personally each and every Tsla for their help.

Ruu-an chided him. "Too many thanks. If thee would truly thank us, thee may share thy knowledge with us when thee return this way. We will be waiting to take you up and past the Topapasirut a second time."

No obstacles ahead to hold us back now, Etienne thought excitedly. No more blank spaces on the topographics, no second Topapasirut. According to the Mai, the Barshajagad began to widen once more north of that place. For the moment they still floated between immense sheer walls, but now that the birthplace of river devils lay behind them the stark cliffs no longer seemed quite so forbidding.

The seven of them reboarded and the Redowls settled into their boat with a sense of relief. It had become their home and refuge, and it was good to be surrounded once more by familiar objects and the comforts of an advanced technology.

As Etienne let the boat float free in the current, the townsfolk assembled on the shoreline set up a plaintive, haunting chant of farewell, as different a music from the whirling frenzy of the Mai as Ligeti is from Gregorian chant. The swift current pushed the hydrofoil out into the center of the river.

Lyra stood on the foredeck alongside Tyl, executing with him the Tsla posture of good-bye. The song of farewell was beginning to fade with distance when Lyra turned and called to her husband. "Don't you think that's enough? Let's move." He made a face up at her. Suddenly she was concerned.

"What do you think I'm trying to do?"

She pressed her face to the plexalloy. "What do you mean you're trying?" They were accelerating steadily, but in the wrong direction. Only the boat's internal stabilizers kept them from spinning in helpless circles like a leaf caught in a flash flood.

"Everything's functioning except the intake feed."

"Dammit!" She rushed for the nearest gangway.

As she looked aft she saw the canyon narrowing further behind them, forming the immense granitic funnel which

Etienne had theorized constituted the upper limits of the To-papasirut. In the distance and coming rapidly closer she could make out thickening mist and the first faint, threatening rumble of water attacking rock. She dropped through the gangway and in seconds stood alongside her husband.

"Everything checks out, everything. Except the intake feed. Every time I try to open her wide she locks shut on me."

"Emergency override?"

"Forget it. I'm still trying, though."

"Repellers?"

"No way. We used our stored power during the descent from Jakaie. We need time to recharge or else we can recharge by moving Upriver. Of course, if we could move Upriver we wouldn't need to recharge." He worked rapidly at the diagnostic computer, canceling unhelpful replies to his queries. Unfortunately, those were the only type of reply he could extract.

The rumbling astern was becoming thunder. Dense mist enveloped the narrow cleft of the canyon. He switched the stern scanner to sonic and tridee black-and-white graphics appeared on the screen as ultrasound penetrated the obscuring mist. In a very few minutes the current would slam the helpless boat into the unyielding sheer cliff that was the upside-down waterfall, the Topapasirut. Fragments of the hydrofoil would boil out of the water Downriver, to be wondered at by any Mai who encountered them on nameless beaches. Of the crew there would be only a memory. Nothing so fragile as flesh and blood would survive the coming concussion.

The boat was enveloped in a storm as the river rained toward the sky.

"Do something!" Lyra shouted above the crash of the water.

"Do something yourself!"

She eyed him a moment before turning to disappear below. Her voice reached him via the engine room intercom.

"Everything looks okay. The fuel cells are produc—"

"I can see that on the readout!"

"Just letting you know what I see down here. The engine's quiet, and—wait a minute."

"That's about what we've got left." The boat vibrated anxiously beneath his feet. Would they know when they hit the cliff? He couldn't begin to calculate their velocity.

"Try it now!" Lyra ordered him.

He ran numbly through the restart procedure, was startled when the *Function* light turned green. He stabbed the accelerator, bringing thrust up to maximum.

For an eternity they hung motionless in the vortex, suspended in fog between open water and oblivion. Then very slowly the hydrofoil began to creep Upriver. To Etienne their progress seemed infinitesimal. His anxiety was heightened by the knowledge that whatever had shut down the flow of water to the jet once could do so again at any moment. Gradually their velocity increased to the point where the boat could rise up on its hydrofoils. As the river fell away beneath the hull, relinquishing its grasp, they started to make some real speed. Thunder faded behind them.

As they left the mist Lyra emerged from belowdecks. Her hair was strung like paint across her face, alternating with rivulets of sweat. She stank of Skar.

"What did you do down there?" He spoke without looking at her, refusing to take his eyes off the controls lest something else fail before they were out of danger.

"Emergency surgery." She slumped into a seat. "Very complicated." She held up something in her right hand. As he turned to look he saw that she was wearing heavy-duty insulated work gloves.

A half dozen glistening worms twisted in her grip. They had dark heads.

"These were glued to the conduit just above the main feed to the jet. Watch this." She held up a small diagnostic probe with her left hand, touched it to the tail of one worm. A loud buzzing filled the cockpit and the readout on the front of the tool went berserk.

"Local relative of the terran gymnotids. Generates quite a current for its size. They must have thought they'd found themselves a nice new home when they slipped in through the mesh intake strainers on the foils. Every time you ordered the boat to open the intake feed they responded with a corresponding jolt. No wonder the computer couldn't locate the source of the short-out in the system. It was external. You'd

[193]

order the feed opened and these little cuties would short it shut, countermanding the directive."

She rose and turned to open one of the ports in the cockpit. With great deliberation she flung her slimy acquisitions as far out into the river as possible. Then she closed the port and spoke toward the stern.

"You can come out now, Homat."

Hesitantly their Mai guide emerged from the heated storage locker in which he had secreted himself. "We're not going to die, de-Lyra?"

"No, we're not going to die. Not today, anyway. The spirit boat is functioning normally again."

He crept out to join them, still encased in his cold-weather gear to combat the cabin's air conditioning. Soon that air conditioning would no longer be required. That would be no comfort to Homat, who would continue to pile on clothing the nearer they drew to Tslamaina's arctic circle.

The population of Jakaie was still assembled along the riverbank. As the spirit boat reemerged from the mouth of destruction, alien voices expressed relief. The villagers lined up quickly and once more the occupants of the hydrofoil were treated to the chant of farewell as Tyl and his companions performed the gestures of good-bye.

"Calm acceptance," Lyra murmured, "no matter what our fate." She was standing on the foredeck alongside their Tsla friends. "Tell me, Tyl, what would the reaction have been if we hadn't come back out?"

"There would have been no reaction that thee could have seen, save that after a suitable time they would have begun a funeral chant instead of one of farewell."

"There didn't seem to be any panic as we slipped downstream."

"Why should there be? There was nothing they could do to help us," he explained patiently. "Thee should know, Lyra, that we are not given to violent displays of emotion in public."

"I recall. Would any of them have grieved for us in private?"

"I imagine so. But they could do nothing to help us."

"Just as nothing could be done to help those who'd been taken by the Na." Etienne spoke from inside the cockpit, addressing his wife in terranglo. "I don't care what the level of mental serenity is among these people, they're not going to make much progress until they dump this fatalism. If they don't watch out, the Mai are going to push forward to develop a complete, advanced technological civilization. The Tsla will end up becoming wards of the Mai, just as it will be the Mai who will push out to tame the Na and the Guntali."

"Specious argument for radical change," Lyra shot back. "The Tsla are content as they are, much happier than the Mai."

"Sure, and the ancient Polynesians were happier and more content than the caucasoids who ministered among them, and we remember what happened to *their* culture."

"Etienne, the analogy doesn't apply here. The Tsla are a different race, occupying a radically different ecological niche. It's not the same thing at all." And she launched wholeheartedly into a lengthy dissertation on history and anthropology that both Homat and Tyl desperately wished they could understand.

Upriver, according to the best information available to Ruu-an and the elders of Jakaie, two last immense tributaries fed into the Skar: the Madauk and the Rahaeng. Beyond that lay the far narrower but still impressive Upper Skar, and unknown lands.

Several hundred kilometers above the Topapasirut the geology of the land altered radically. The gorge of the Barshagajad widened and the river rose in frequent steps, reducing the depth of the canyon. The Redowls were constantly being wakened from sleep by the insistent beeping of the computer. Since the boat could not negotiate rapids on autopilot, Etienne or Lyra would stagger sleepily forward to run the whitewater or lift the hydrofoil past it on repellers.

The steady rumble of the rapids was in stark contrast to the silent river south of Aib. At night Tslamaina's four moons transformed the streaks of white water into thousands of pale crystalline tentacles. Not all was difficult, however. There were quiet stretches of relatively calm water of great beauty.

They began to relax for the first time since leaving the Skatandah. As the temperature grew chillier and the river climbed its ancient bed they encountered fewer signs of settlement, as the land was fit only for Mai hunters and gatherers. Occasionally they saw a few ramshackle houses clustered around poorly irrigated plots. No elaborate terraces had been built there.

Shaped by a harsh land, the local Mai were a hardier breed than their southern cousins. They were also open and much more honest. Or perhaps they were just so startled by the appearance of the hydrofoil and its strange inhabitants that the urge to thieve never crossed their minds.

"I'm not sure that's it at all," Lyra theorized one day. "The truism seems to hold among nonhuman primitives as well as among our own kind that the poorer the people and the more isolated their homes, the more trustworthy and helpful they are. Hardship seems to breed a need for companionship which extends to lending assistance to any who come your way."

Etienne did not argue with her because he was more interested in the locals' openness and lack of fear. They were startled but there was none of the fearful paranoia or jealous awe the Redowls had encountered farther south. He surmised it was because everything was new to these pioneers. For all they knew the Redowls came not from another world but from some unknown distant city-state bordering the Groalamasan. When one shares a world with two other intelligent races it's not difficult to accept the existence of a third.

They expected to encounter a few Tsla villages, but Ruuan told them to expect none, and the information supplied by the elders of Jakaie turned out to be accurate. Whether the abandonment of the northern latitudes by the Tsla was a decision of choice or due to some unknown circumstances, Lyra could not determine. Homat and Tyl argued about it long into the nights, with the Mai staking a claim for greater adaptability among his kind and Tyl retreating into calm conviction that a perfectly good reason existed for shunning such a barren land.

A considerable surprise awaited everyone aboard the boat, however, when they reached the confluence of the three great rivers. Where the Madauk and Rahaeng joined their volume to that of the Skar, several small villages had grown, trading posts, no more.

It was not their existence or location that shocked the travelers, but rather the population—Mai and Tsla traders and hunters mingled freely, working side by side with a lack of self-consciousness that was stunning when compared to the uneasy peace maintained by their southern relatives. The need to work together to survive in a harsh land had overwhelmed ancient suspicions and inhibitions. Homat and Tyl were startled as much by the implications as by the reality.

"It bodes well for the future," Lyra commented. "Maybe when the Mai gain the technology that will enable them to live and work in colder climates and the Tsla the ability to move more freely through the humid river valleys, they'll discover this living example of racial cooperation waiting up here to show them the way."

"They cooperate here in order to survive," Etienne argued. "Without that external pressure, technological advancement may only heighten ancient conflicts, not solve them."

"You're such a damn pessimist!" she said angrily.

He shrugged. "I look at things the way they are, not the way I want them to be."

"And so do I, or are you making one of your frequent criticisms of my objectivity?"

"It's just that it's so much easier to be objective about this." He hefted a sample of dark schist chipped from the riverbank where they had anchored inshore the day before. "On Earth this would be called precambrian or Vishnu schist. It's much older than its terran equivalent, however. There's nothing subjective about it."

"Lucky you."

"Nobody forced you into xenology. You chose it."

"I sure did, because it's a damn sight more exciting and interesting when the subjects of your studies can talk back to you and help you with your research. Better that than a life of drudgery and dirt. My work provides me with new revelations every day."

"All well and good, so long as you don't get personally involved with your revelations." Too late to retract, he thought furiously. Once more his mouth had moved faster than his brain.

She eyed him strangely. "Now what's that supposed to mean?"

He tried to escape into silence, stared at the rock walls about them. The cliffs on either side of the river were barely a thousand meters above the water now.

"When we first arrived in Turput," he mumbled, concentrating on his instruments instead of looking at her, "you spent an awful lot of time," he hesitated over the right word, "meditating with Tyl."

"It was very instructive," she replied. "I'm still not following you, Etienne."

"I thought maybe you were diving a little too deeply into your work."

"I don't—" she broke off, gaping at him. Then her expression twisted into a smile. "Well I'll be damned. You're jealous of Tyl, aren't you? Jealous of a primitive mammalian alien."

"I didn't say that," he snapped quickly. "There you are, jumping to conclusions again, seeing things the way you want to see them."

"Well you can relax, Etienne." The smile grew wider. "Among the Tsla the length and shape of oversized probosces are important sexual characteristics, but a flexible shnoz holds no attraction for me whatsoever."

His head jerked round and he stared at her. "I just said you were spending a lot of time with him, I didn't mean to imply that—you've got a dirty mind, Lyra."

"You mean a dirty husband. Etienne, I can't believe you. I don't know whether to be flattered or insulted."

"Oh hell," he muttered, embarrassed to the soles of his feet, "be busy." Footfalls sounded behind them. "Anyway, our passengers are coming in."

"So what? They can't understand terranglo."

"Don't be so sure. I'll give the Tsla this; they're quick on the uptake. Don't be too surprised if we learn that they can draw a few inferences from our private conversations, especially when their names are mentioned."

"Not just a dirty mind, a dirty paranoid mind," she murmured, but she broke off when Tyl and his companions trundled in.

Homat was sandwiched between two of the porters, a ball of thick cloth and fur among which only eyes and mouth were visible. "I can't go outside anymore, de-Etienne," he whimpered. "No more."

〖 XV 〗

Days passed and the temperature fell slowly, but outside the hydrofoil the climate was working dramatic changes on the landscape. Though sheets of frozen water hung from the much reduced cliffs, hundreds of fast streams flowed into the Skar.

Homat was squatting in the main cabin behind the cockpit, heavily bundled and warm but far from comfortable.

Etienne had been mulling the problem for several days. Now he spoke to their Mai guide. "Maybe we can fix something up for you, Homat."

"No matter, de-Etienne. I will not go outside any more."

"Lyra, what about trying to fit him with one of your spare thermal suits? You've got two backups. You two are about the same height, though you're much more—"

"Watch it," she said warningly from her seat.

"—Rubensesque. Homat would swim in a suit, but couldn't you concoct some kind of strap so that the sensors would stay close enough to his skin to function, and adjust the thermostat for Mai comfort?"

"I'll see what I can do." She escorted the nervous Homat down to the lower deck.

Several hours later they reemerged. The thermal suit ballooned around Homat's arms and legs but she'd managed to secure the fabric around his torso.

"It's still a little loose. I had a hard time convincing him he couldn't wear his furs inside because the thermal sensors had to have some skin contact. He finally gave in, but I thought he was going to turn blue before he finally got out of his old attire and into the suit. It wasn't hard to adjust the circuitry." She put a hand inside one sleeve, pushing back the elastic material. She drew her fingers back hastily.

"Are you sure you're okay like this, Homat? It's hot enough in there to burn."

Their guide was jubilant. "For the first time in many many days I am truly comfortable," he replied. "So delighted I am! Thank you, de-Lyra, thank you all much!"

"What about you, Tyl?" Etienne asked the Tsla who rested on the floor behind him. "Will you and the others be able to handle the weather here if it's necessary to go outside?"

"We have our double capes and hoods, Etienne, and we can tolerate colder climes than thee. We will be all right, as long as it does not prove necessary to remain outside for too long."

Etienne unexpectedly leaned forward and the hydrofoil lurched sharply to port. "Sorry. Instinctive reaction." He pointed. "What's that?"

A small mountain stood in the shallow water by the riverbank. The mountain had a half dozen legs, two of which were busy in the water. As they watched in fascination the multi-ton beast brought up a twisting hundred-kilo fish in hooked claws, transferred the catch to a long snout lined with sharp triangular teeth. For so massive a creature it moved with blinding speed. Long black hair covered the entire body and dragged in the water.

Eyes with narrow pupils peered out at them from beneath bony ridges. Etienne edged the hydrofoil toward shore for a closer look. As he did the beast turned with a deep grunt then galloped away on all six legs, its catch clutched firmly between extended jaws.

"I have never seen anything like that before, de-Etienne."

As he spoke Homat made rapid protective signs across his chest and stomach.

"I have," Tyl said softly. "A Hyral. I have seen only two such before and both were dead, having fallen over the edge of the Guntali."

As they stared the hirsute fisher crested a slight slope, where it dropped its catch between its mate and two massive roly-poly cubs before turning to throw a penetrating, high-pitched roar toward the boat.

Lyra was staring through her recorder as she committed the new discovery to their records. "Family group. I wondered what else the Na ate."

"Speaking of the Na," Etienne said as he steered the hydrofoil back into the middle of the river again, "it's cold enough here for them to come right down to the water, but we haven't seen any."

"Perhaps they stay away from the river out of superstition, some kind of taboo."

"I wouldn't think that. Not with all the fish to be had in these waters."

"Maybe the air's too thick here. We're not nearly as high as the Guntali near Turput. It wouldn't matter. The river's still wide and deep enough to protect us." She looked thoughtful.

"Something will have to be done about the Na, Etienne. We've seen proof that Mai and Tsla can work together, but the Na appear too primitive and combative to be brought into any worldwide interracial process without extensive education and a great deal of care. Just because I'm not fond of them doesn't mean I want to see the other two dominant races exterminate them.

"They're not animals. They're intelligent and have developed a rudimentary society. If you consider the amount of territory they control then a case could be made that they and not the Mai or Tsla are Tslamaina's dominant life form."

"I'm glad we don't have to make the ultimate decisions," he replied. "Someone else will have to decide whether it's right to intervene in local affairs to protect the future of the Na, and that's a long way down the road."

* * *

Though the Skar's course twisted in a steady curve farther eastward, they continued to travel north toward the planet's sole ice cap. The occasional appearance of the sun through the uneasy clouds did little to warm them. Despite this Homat spent an inordinate amount of time out on deck, luxuriating in his thermal suit and the freedom it provided, a freedom to laugh at temperatures that would have frozen an unprotected Mai in minutes.

They saw evidence of the ice cap before they set eyes upon it. It announced itself as a brightening ahead, where the ice reflected the sun back against the undersides of scudding clouds. The next morning they lifted on repellers to clear still another rapid, turned a bend in the river, and saw the southernmost edge of the frozen rampart.

The once awesome canyon of the Barshajagad had been reduced to a meandering river valley. Numerous waterfalls tumbled down the melting edge of the cap. They would freeze solid again during the night.

They did not have to trace dozens of the streams to locate the source of the river Skar. The much shrunken but still navigable stream emerged from a huge hole in the wall of ice, having eroded a tunnel a hundred meters high at the entrance. Etienne guided the hydrofoil in until it floated beneath the lip of the vast cavern. Then he carefully nudged the boat ashore, scraping bottom several times before beaching on the gravel.

Overhead the ice had thinned and sunlight poured through the translucent, frozen ceiling, tinting the ice a pale blue and illuminating the river for a distance of several dozen meters from the entrance. Then it was swallowed by cold night. Cold water dripped from smooth icy stalactites, stinging the upturned faces of the crew as it stood on the deck to examine the surroundings.

"What a beautiful place," Lyra murmured. Somewhere a faint echo concurred with her opinion.

The four Tsla kneeled in a circle, chanting and making signs. The Redowls waited respectfully until the ceremony had concluded before Lyra inquired as to its purpose.

"We give thanks," Tyl explained. "We feel in our souls a great warmth, as must thee, for thy journey has been far longer than ours."

"We couldn't have made it without your help," Etienne told him, "and without the aid of your people."

"All given freely in the pursuit of knowledge. We were glad we could help." Swd and Yij likewise expressed their feelings, while Yulour stood nearby and looked on with bemused contentment.

"What do we do now?" Homat inquired, peering out through the eyeslits in the cloth that covered his face. "Do we begin our return tomorrow? A long journey."

"I know you're anxious to go home, Homat, but we've come all this way to see the source of the Skar and we're not leaving until we do so."

Homat sounded puzzled. "But have done so, de-Etienne." He gestured at the spacious cavern and the distant darkness. "What other source can there be?"

Etienne smiled as he turned to point into the blackness beneath the ice. "This isn't the river's source. Somewhere back there it emerges from the mass of the ice cap, probably in the form of a hot spring. I can't think of another mechanism which could have bored so deep a cave in the body of the ice. I need to record it."

Homat's eyes grew wide. "You can't mean to go back in there, de-Etienne! This is the top of the world. Who knows what devils and monsters lie in wait for us in the night which lives throughout the day?"

"Why should any lie in wait," Lyra asked gently, "since no one ever comes here? If any did live back in there they'd long since have given up hope of any meals coming to visit them."

"You argue very plausibly, de-Lyra. My mind wishes to believe you, but my insides are not convinced."

"If you'd feel safer you can camp on the shore here and wait for us to return. I doubt the river runs very far back, hot springs or not."

"No, no, I will come with you," the Mai insisted bravely. "I would rather do that than stay here alone. You are certain there is not far to go?"

"I can't be sure, but I'd be willing to bet we'll have less than an hour's journey in the boat. If the water becomes too shallow, we'll travel the rest of the way in on repellers."

"Why do your words not make me feel confident, de-Etienne?"

"Relax, Homat." He turned to Lyra. "When we reach the source I want to take some core samples. This must be very old ice and the geologic history of the planet is stored here, conveniently waiting to be thawed out for study."

Lyra offered no objection. Their goal was within reach. Soon they would begin the long journey back to warmer climes. Let Etienne enjoy his fieldwork for a day or two. There was no reason to rush now that they'd arrived at their intended and eventual destination.

He looked to his right, deeper into the cavern. "There's a nice wide spot. I'm tired of rocking. The water there is gentle and shallow. I'll move us over and set the foils down on the gravel. Be nice to sleep without rocking for a change."

"Second the motion," Lyra said. "It should be safe enough. There's no sign of carnivores about, no bones or dung on the beach, and the water should keep any small vermin clear of the boat, assuming this enviroment is benign enough to permit their existence."

"I'll run a good charge through the hull. That ought to keep off any late-night visitors."

"It would be delighted to sleep so quietly," Tyl agreed.

"Then it's settled. We owe ourselves the rest," Etienne declared. "First thing tomorrow morning we'll go Upriver to the source so I can get my samples. With luck this ice may predate the collision that created the Groalamasan. That will give me plenty to do on the way back Downriver."

"You did enough griping about the heat down south to fill a book, and now you can't wait to get back to it," Lyra chided.

"I've always been cold-natured, Lyra, you know that. It doesn't mean I enjoy sweating down to skin and bones, though." For a change the argument was friendly. In its own way that was as great an accomplishment for the two of them as was reaching the head of the Skar.

Lyra was sound asleep when the muffled scream woke her. She blinked as her head lifted from the pillow and she stared across the cabin. Soft green lights from ship's instrumentation lit the darkness. A soft wheeze alongside indicated that her husband still slept.

The scream had barely faded and she was beginning to wonder if she'd dreamed it when suddenly a cluster of the green lights changed to red and a warning horn started to blare. Etienne woke instantly, slid off the bed and struggled with his pants.

"False alarm?"

"I don't know," she told him, still straining to hear. "I thought I heard something yell." The horn continued its racket as a soft knocking sounded at the door. Lyra opened it as she fought with the seals of her blouse.

"What is happening?" Tyl asked sleepily. The remaining Tsla clustered in the corridor behind him. "There are strange noises outside and Swd thinks he smells something even though we know we are protected from the air outside."

"Noises and smells and you think you heard something," Etienne muttered as he sealed his coat. "That settles it." He pushed past Tyl on his way to the cockpit.

The light of three of Tslamaina's four moons poured through the transparent plexalloy. The horn continued to shout as Etienne strained to check the instruments. "Don't see anything outside. No abnormal readings. We haven't moved from where I parked us yesterday evening and the hull's still electrified."

"I'll check astern," Lyra told him. She removed her pistol from its charging slot.

"Watch yourself," Etienne admonished her.

With the Tsla following curiously she worked her way aft. There was no sign of Homat, but that didn't worry her. Anything less than a complete upset of the boat would not be enough to pry him from the comfort of his overheated cubicle.

Cautiously she cracked the stern doorway. Freezing air brought her all the way awake. The rumble and gurgle of the shallow river was the only sound as she stepped out onto the rear deck.

A glance forward showed only darkness. There was no movement in the upper reaches of the cavern. Outside only the moons moved in patient procession against the sky. Something shorted out, she thought, wondering if some other strange local critter was somehow playing havoc with their instrumentation.

A heavy weight landed on her right shoulder. She went down hard. The asynapt went flying across the deck. A big chunk of dead log lay next to her.

The Na who had thrown it now peered over the gunwale, eyes glittering in the moonlight. Several similar hairy faces joined the first. One huge, muscular arm reached over the top of the railing and Yij disappeared over the side.

Tyl and Yulour took Lyra under the arms and hauled her toward the doorway. A second club flew toward them. It landed short, booming across the metal deck.

Through the wash of pain that radiated from her shoulder Lyra gasped, "The gun...get my gun!" The source of the scream must have been a Na who'd made contact with the electrified hull as it tried to board the hydrofoil.

Careful not to touch the metal another Na took aim with an axe. The bone blade was a meter across. At the last instant Swd lunged into its path, to fall gushing blood and life back against Lyra, the weapon's intended target. Yulour had to kick the nearly split body aside as they fell inside.

Etienne was there to help, his eyes on Lyra's shoulder where the club had struck. She moaned when he touched her.

He closed the hatch, then ordered her to move her right arm.

"Hurts like hell, but it works," she told him.

"Rotate," he said curtly. She did so, turning the arm palm up, then palm down. "Lucky you."

"Not so lucky," she told him painfully. "My pistol's outside. That's twice I've lost it when I needed it most. Going to have to work on my grip." She glanced at Tyl. "Did you see where it landed?"

"The lightning thrower flew through the air. I saw not where it landed."

"The little metal tool," Yulour mumbled frantically, trying to keep abreast of what was happening, "I saw where it is."

"Why didn't you go after it?" Lyra asked him. "I told you to go after it."

Yulour looked away, hurt. "We were more concerned with saving thee, Lyra," Tyl told her. He looked at the porter and said gently. "It's all right, Yulour. Tell us where the lightning thrower landed."

"In the water," he said brightly.

"Oh hell!" Lyra looked up at her husband. "I'm sorry, Etienne, I'm sorry. I never saw them. We went out on deck, everything seemed normal, and then something landed on me like back taxes."

"Never mind that now. Just take it easy with that shoulder."

Something went *whang* atop the cabin and everyone looked upward, but the metal held. Thin as it was, the alloy was far too tough to yield to mere bone and stone.

"What will we fight them with?" Tyl wondered. "It is dark and they are very close."

"We don't have to fight them with anything, Tyl. Help Lyra forward."

Outside the cockpit was a choice scene from Dante. The hydrofoil was surrounded by at least thirty of the towering aborigines, who were jumping up and down, howling and spitting and gesturing angrily at the boat. The Na carefully avoided all contact with the hull and when one of them attempted to express his feelings by urinating on it, they no longer tried that either. They did use long spears and the ubiquitous clubs to hammer on the sides. The wood and stone were poor conductors and the Na had discovered they could flail away at the hull without risk to themselves.

As the Redowls watched, one especially massive warrior tried to vault over the railing. He didn't quite make it and grabbed a hold with his hands. His lower body slammed into the hull and he lit up in a shower of blue sparks. When the thick fingers finally let loose the huge body splashed into the river.

Etienne assumed the pilot's chair, his fingers flying over the controls. A muffled roar sounded aft as the engine came to life. The hydrofoil lifted half a meter on its repellers and shot forward, scattering Na. One didn't dodge quickly enough, and a sickening *thud* sounded from the bow as the aborigine was knocked aside.

Nightscope screens came alive, revealing the rest of the war party falling astern. Several bodies bobbed in the shallow water together with pieces of the individual run over by the boat and a smaller silhouette: Yij. Angrily Etienne spun the hydrofoil on its axis and sent it roaring down on their attackers, plowing through the now panicky Na and sending several additional bodies flying. The sound of metal meeting flesh momentarily filled him with an unholy delight and he damned himself even as he pivoted for another run.

As the Na threw their weapons aside and scrambled onto the beach he bashed through the survivors two more times. By then they were in full retreat outside the cavern, not even turning to hurl an occasional insult back at their intended prey. Etienne slowed as he beached the boat on the far side of the Skar.

"The middle of the river's still deep enough here to prevent them from crossing after us," he muttered. "Stay here." He took his pistol as Lyra assumed the pilot's seat, favoring her injured shoulder.

"One nighttime stroll on deck's enough for this little lady." He smiled thinly at her by way of reply.

Tyl and Yulour followed him aft. The doorway opened easily, readmitting the night. He had a sudden thought, closed the door immediately and directed the Tsla to wait for him as he disappeared belowdecks.

He reappeared carrying a pair of long metal rods, showed one to Tyl. "These are for making seismic soundings in spots inaccessible from the boat. Never mind what I mean, just take them." The Tsla did so.

"Those are explosive charges on the tips. Small lightnings. There are five charges on each pole. You press this here," and he showed the fire buttons to his companions, "after you've touched the end of the pole to your target. They're difficult to use, but they were not designed as weapons. They'll be effective if you have to use them, though."

"I understand, Etienne," Tyl told him, lightly fingering the fire button. Etienne turned to the other Tsla.

"How about you, Yulour? Do you understand? See, you press there after you touch whatever you want to stop with the other end of the pole."

The porter eyed him blankly, his expression a bovine mixture of sadness and confusion. Sighing, Etienne carefully set the second pole to one side.

"Never mind. Stay close as we go outside."

He cracked the doorway to the deck for the second time. Outside it was silent as the departed, an unfortunate simile.

Holding the asynapt out in front of his body he edged out, keeping low and nearly stumbling over the cleaved corpse of Swd. The porter had been a faithful worker, obedient and always ready to lend a hand. Now he was only a lesson in Tsla anatomy. Etienne found he was too mad to be sickened by the sight.

Tyl and Yulour stayed tight on his heels. Three Na bodies lay draped over the stern rail where they'd perished in a last-ditch attempt to board the boat. They looked even bigger up close than they did from a distance. Etienne inspected the shore. Nothing moved on the gravel. The river itself and the mouth of the ice cavern were equally devoid of life.

"Shouldn't have let them surprise us like that. Always underestimating. You'd think we'd have learned our lesson by now."

"I am sorrowed," Tyl said solemnly.

"Nothing for you to be sorry about, Tyl. The responsibility's ours. We're the 'masters of superior technology.'" He let out a rueful laugh. "Some joke. It's just that we haven't seen Na or signs of Na since that day back in Turput and I didn't expect to encounter them this far north. Shows how adaptable they are. I didn't think. I'm the one who should be sorrowed." He gestured at Swd's body.

"Now two more of your people have died."

"Death comes to all of us eventually," Tyl replied. "You ask that I not sorrow for thee. Now I ask that thee sorrow not for us. Swd and Yij achieved what they could not have in a dozen lifetimes, because of thee and thy mate. Their souls are grateful to thee, not angry."

"Well I'm angry! Damned angry. Angry at myself, angry at . . ." the wind went out of him with a rush as Yulour struck him in the midsection and drove him backwards. As a result the small spear passed beneath his arm and pierced his side instead of his spine.

Tyl whirled and leaped to jab the end of the seismic probe against the neck of the Na who had thrown the spear. He pressed the fire button. With a sharp report, the Na's head blew off its wide shoulders, arching into the darkness in a spray of blood and bone fragments. It landed in the water with a splash.

Yulour was rolling away from Etienne, who lay on his

back, staring up at the roof of the ice cave. With great care the porter extracted the spear. Blood quickly rushed from the wound. Tyl rose to alert Lyra but she'd heard the explosion and now joined them on deck.

Her eyes widened as she saw the extent and depth of the wound. She vanished belowdecks again and reemerged moments later carrying the boat's first-aid kit.

Etienne was breathing raggedly as she worked to halt the flow of blood. His pulse was racing and uneven.

"What happened?" she asked the Tsla as she worked.

Tyl explained while Yulour looked on helplessly. "That one," and he indicated the decapitated body of the Na who had thrown the spear, "was not dead but only pretending."

Lyra saw that the headless corpse was spraddled across the two other bodies. "It was shielded from the full charge. It lay still, waiting for its chance. They have that much intelligence, anyway. Too damn much intelligence by half, the hairy bastards." She glanced up at Yulour. "Throw them over the side, and be careful not to touch the metal outside. It's still holding a charge, a spirit death."

"Yes, Teacher."

Yulour showed his considerable strength by disengaging each corpse in turn and shoving the dead weight into the water. Then he returned to carry Etienne into the Redowls' cabin.

Both Tsla looked on respectfully as Lyra ministered to her husband. A third figure joined them later.

"I didn't know what to do, or how to help." Homat looked very small alongside the two Tsla.

"Be quiet, Homat." To his credit the Mai said nothing more, remaining silent alongside his taller companions.

They watched as Lyra slowly passed a small plastic device over Etienne's side and chest. When she finished and put it aside her expression was grim. Etienne tried to reassure her by smiling, but the pain made it difficult.

"Well . . . doctor?"

"You're bleeding internally. I can stop it temporarily. I'm afraid it may be an arterial lesion. I have to stop it, Etienne, or you'll bleed to death. I wish I knew more surgery."

"Thank God you don't," he whispered. "You've spent

twenty years messing up my mind. I don't need you fouling up my insides as well."

"We've got to get you back to Steamer Station where they can fix you properly. You know how good the thranx physicians are."

"I know. It's funny when you think that they're better than human surgeons, them not having any bones and all. How long can you 'temporarily' stop the bleeding?"

She didn't look at him. "I don't know. The spear went a long way in, Etienne. I can seal the break and stop the bleeding and close you up, but there's no guarantee it won't break open again anytime. If it does, I don't know if your circulatory system will accept another heat patch.

"The computer says you should rest as much as possible. Some medication will help. But you can forget about jumping around boulders and cliff sides or you'll tear your guts open again."

"I'll be a good little boy." Despite the mild sarcasm his ready acquiescence confirmed the seriousness of the damage. Normally she had to strap him down to get him to take a vitamin pill.

She tried to take his mind off the injury by explaining how the surviving Na had lived long enough to fling the spear.

"We won't be that careless again," she finished. "Not that I think we've anything more to fear from this particular band. First thing in the morning we'll start back Downriver. As soon as we get within reception range of the Station we..."

"No," he said sharply.

"No? No what?"

"No we can't start home first thing in the morning. We're not finished."

"Maybe we aren't, but you are. We've come all the way."

"Not quite, Lyra. We go on to the end of the river first, then we can turn back. Not before then. I'm not leaving until we reach our last goal. If you try to stop me I'll throw a tantrum and kill myself."

"Listen to me closely, Etienne, because I may only be able to say this once," she said softly. "You are an utterly impossible man. You have no more sense in you than a

[212]

sponge. You would try the patience of Job, let alone a tired little woman like myself."

He squeezed her hand tightly. "I love you, too."

"That's what I said. Who would I shout at if you weren't around?"

"I know. A good target is hard to find."

"I agree." Angrily she rubbed at the moisture welling up in her eyes. "Which is why I'd like to keep you around for another couple of days or so. My shoulder still hurts. That we can keep joking about. There's nothing funny about the hole in your ribs."

"You're telling me?" He let loose of her hand. "Lyra, you have to do this for me. I'll be very careful. No climbing, no quarrying. If I can help it I won't even bend over. Yulour can help me get around, can't you, Yulour?"

"Yes. Yulour is strong, Teacher. I can carry thee wherever thee wishes to go."

"Too risky, Etienne. You *must* let that side heal as best it can."

"On the way back I promise I'll stay in the cabin for months. It can heal then. But it would be insane to turn around and head back when we're only a few hours from the end of our journey. I want those ice samples! We don't have anything else to compare to them and taking them from the edge of the ice cap won't mean nearly as much. If you insist, you and Tyl can take the corings and I'll just watch." He paused, added quietly, "Besides, if this turns out to be my last expedition I'm damned if I want anything left undone."

"Don't talk like that," she said quietly. "I'll kill you if you talk like that."

Somehow he manufactured another smile. "Then we'll go on?"

"All right. No more than half a day. I don't want to spend a night in glacial darkness. Whether we come to the hot springs or whatever, we go on for half a day and then we turn around."

"Fair enough. I wouldn't want the repellers to fail in here, anyway. And I promise to let you do all the heavy work."

"You're so good to me." Twenty years, she mused. Twenty

[213]

years of performing in the same play together and they each had their lines down pat.

She prayed she would be allowed to keep acting opposite the same male lead.

〖 XVI 〗

He slept soundly the remainder of the night. Lyra knew because she stayed awake at his bedside monitoring his condition. The computer's diagnostic program indicated that the internal bleeding had been halted. Getting the arterial wall and surrounding flesh to heal would be a much slower and more difficult process.

The machine assured her of an eighty-five percent probability of survival for her husband, provided that he adhered to all instructions, took his medication and ultrasound treatments regularly, and received proper surgery within six months. There would be no permanent damage except possibly to some torn lemnisci in the area. That would keep him out of any gymnastic competitions. She greeted the evaluation with relief.

They would have to be exceedingly cautious during the return journey. No chances could be taken, no more violent encounters with belligerent life forms, intelligent or otherwise. Her studies among the elders of Turput would have to wait.

One half of a component whole was useless, and it took at least two to make a team.

Exhaustion and darkness finally conspired during the early hours of the morning to send her into a deep sleep. When she awoke it was to discover that most of the morning was gone. He was upset when she woke him for his breakfast but didn't argue very strenuously. Instead he sought refuge from his discomfort and fear by making delicious wisecracks about her cooking and waiting on him. She enjoyed every criticism.

At Etienne's insistence Yulour carried him forward and they installed him on a raised pallet so he could see out through the cockpit bubble. Lyra settled herself behind the controls.

The hydrofoil hummed as it lifted above the water. She turned inward and sent the boat toward the black maw that was the rear of the cavern. There was no sign of the night's attack. The current had mercifully carried off the three bodies Yulour had shoved over the side.

Lyra would have been gratified to learn that her husband's opinion of the Tsla had risen several notches. Not because of their calm acceptance of their fates or their precocious knowledge of the intricate workings of the mind, but because of the way in which they handled themselves through one crisis after another.

Ice swallowed distance and daylight until the mouth of the cavern had been reduced to a distant dab of white ink. Lyra switched on the hydrofoil's running lights and fore and aft search beams, bringing gasps of surprise and admiration from Tyl and Homat. From the pilot's chair she used the two beams to scan the opposite shore. The river continued to narrow beneath them. Fish fled from the intruding illumination.

Surprisingly, the ceiling of the cavern remained far overhead, testament to the length of time the Skar had been flowing. They flew slowly along the winding tunnel beneath millions of tons of permanent, ancient ice.

"Spirits live here," Homat murmured nervously. "This is the top of the world. Spirits live here." Beneath the roof of the planet even the thermal suit was hard pressed to keep him warm.

"We should be taking periodic samples from the shore gravel," Etienne told Lyra.

She eyed him uncertainly. "Think you can handle the controls?"

He grinned. "They're no heavier than the breakfast you fed me. Yulour, give me a hand up, will you?"

After making sure Etienne wasn't working in pain, she donned her own thermal suit and a long-handled scoop and went out on deck. She gathered samples for another thirty minutes before she was obliged to scream at him.

"Stop the boat, stop the boat!" Her tone was urgent, not alarmed. He nudged the requisite controls and the whine of the hydrofoil's repellers died as it settled into a meter of frigid water.

"What is it?" he called toward the speaker membrane in the bubble wall. His first concern was that she had spotted signs of Na, but that didn't jibe with her attitude. She was standing by the railing, staring off to port.

At the shout, Tyl had bundled up and rushed out to join her, with Yulour close behind. Homat crowded close to Etienne.

"Come out on deck, if you think you can make it without hurting yourself." Now she sounded funny, he thought.

"What is it, what's wrong?"

"Everything's wrong. You'll see." That was all he could get out of her as he painfully worked his body into his own cold gear.

As he started for the gangway Homat reached out with a delicate hand. "Don't go, de-Etienne. Spirits live here."

Gently he disengaged himself from the Mai. "Lyra's not confronting any spirits, Homat. We don't believe in spirits."

"No one does, until the spirits come for them."

"A good point, but I'm willing to bet they're not coming for us here."

Yet when he stood on deck and stared at the cause of his wife's excitement he found himself seriously considering Homat's warning. For while the spirits did not present themselves for inspection, they had left ample evidence of their presence.

The Redowls gazed quietly at the shore until Tyl broke the silence. "What is it, Learned Etienne?"

"I'm not sure, Tyl. I think they're machines of some kind. At least, they look like machines."

Using the tiny remote control he'd brought from the cockpit he aimed both searchlights. The powerful beams swept into the side cavern Lyra had discovered, illuminating unpredictable metallic blue forms and piles of twisting, curving gray shininess. Yellowish-white coils of tubing connected separate structures and smaller adjuncts of green and deeper yellow protruded from the larger shapes.

"You don't know what this place could be?" he asked the Tsla.

"I have never heard of it, Etienne. No Tsla has ever visited here, to my knowledge."

Lyra's breath congealed in the cold still air of the cave. "We've got to have a closer look." She glanced over at her husband, her companion in discovery. "If the Tsla didn't build them it's almost certain the Mai didn't."

"Then who? Surely not the Na?"

"You ask the simplest questions. Get back to the controls and move us over before you fall down."

He nodded, returned to the cockpit. As those on deck steadied themselves the hydrofoil lifted out of the water once more. Etienne pivoted the craft and moved inshore, setting down halfway between river and revelation.

Lyra broke out hand beams from the ship's stores and distributed one to each of their three companions so that even Homat, who had to be half-dragged from the cabin, had his own source of light. In addition they could control the spotlights mounted atop the boat by means of two remotes. Thus armed against the dark they climbed the polished gravel toward the alien construct.

It was clear that the facility had not escaped the ice intact. Bits and pieces of metaloceramic matrix littered the ground. But the damage seemed minor.

"Wonder how old this place is?" Lyra whispered.

"No telling 'til I can run some analyses." He bent carefully at the knees and picked up a section of some tubular material. Tiny strands of opaque metal were embedded in the core and protruded slightly from the ragged end. He ran a finger along one of the flexible filaments.

"Not glass."

"Poured quartz?"

"Silica-based, anyway. That's not all." He handed it over.

Her arm dropped a centimeter before she could recover from the initial surprise. "My god, that's heavy. Any ideas?" She turned it slowly in her hands, examining the metal.

"Alloy of iridium; something in the platinum group, anyhow. Hard to say for certain just looking at it."

Homat could not understand the strange alien words, nor was he sufficiently versed in metallurgy to comprehend even if the Redowls had spoken in his own language. It did not matter, because regardless of what the humans decided, he *knew* what this spirit home was constructed of.

Solid sunit.

More sunit than *jreal* addicts saw while lying dazed and doped on their dream-couches. More sunit than the most avaricious philosophers could conjure up in their imaginations. More sunit than even Moyts possessed.

The old merchant's story was true, his dying admonition to the Zanur of Po Rabi founded on fact. He had been to this place of spirits and had returned with the proof of his tale. Homat swelled with pride. No Tsla had visited the spot before, but an old Mai had done so. His travels had killed him, but not before he had made truth his tombstone. And of all the Mai only he, Homat, had duplicated that epic journey.

Not all the strange shapes and terrifying forms were pure sunit, but there was more than enough laying about to shock the members of the Zanur who had sent him on the journey in the guise of a scout. Here was wealth enough to buy more than businesses and trading vessels, storehouses of grain or gems or the services of others. Here were riches sufficient to buy a city-state entire, to purchase all of Suphum or Ko Phisi—or both.

Enough wealth to purchase the world.

Stunned by the visions before him, he wandered among the spirit buildings, hardly daring to touch the solid gray masses of the precious metal. Lyra warned him not to stray too far. She was concerned by the obvious effect the discovery was having on their Mai guide, though she did not realize its source.

Some of the constructions towered two hundred meters

toward the ceiling of the cavern, where the ice cap had drawn away from the metal. The reason for such spaciousness was self-evident, revealed by mere touch. Much of the metal surrounding them was comfortably warm.

"Not a great deal of heat," Etienne commented, "but a lot of energy is involved. Some kind of mechanism is still functioning here, protecting this place from encroachment by the ice."

"No sound," she replied.

"Insulation. Makes sense in a cold place."

"It's more than that," she said, running her fingers over the smooth frostfree flank of a contorted metal ellipse. "There's nothing moving anywhere, no vibration from within. I think the heat may be a characteristic of the alloy." Removing one of her gloves, she searched the ground until she found a short thick chunk of the yellowish material.

"This has broken away. See the ragged edge?" She leaned back. "Probably fell from somewhere higher up. There's no telling how long it's lain here, but it's just as warm as the intact stuff. Generation of heat's a property of the metal. The damn stuff's exothermic."

"All right, I'm convinced. And not only is it exothermic, I think the property's variable. The temperature of the metal is just high enough to hold back the ice without melting a big hole in the ice cap."

"Maybe," she said quietly, "this installation was built before the ice cap moved so far south. Maybe the glaciers moved over and around it, burying it here."

"That would make this place a minimum of ten thousand years old, given what little we know of Tslamaina's geological history." She said nothing.

They continued their examination, but they found nothing to suggest the nature of the builders. Everything was a solid mass, seemingly formed whole from molds. They found no doorways and no windows, nothing to hint at the builders' size or shape. Only smooth-sided featureless geometric forms. Equally striking was the absence of visible controls.

"If this is a fully automated installation," Lyra pointed out, "designed to function for a long period of time without supervision, there would be no reason to expose sensitive controls to the cold."

"Possible. We'd have a better idea if we could tell whether it's operating now, or dormant, or kaput."

"Instruments," she murmured. "Sit down and rest, Etienne. I'll be back in a minute." She turned and jogged toward the hydrofoil, gathering up the two Tsla as she ran.

With their help she set up several sensitive probes next to the hull, aimed them at their discovery, and began to take readings. Some of the instruments operated efficiently from a distance while others required her to pass among the structures with remote sensors.

Except for the heat emanating directly from the metal, from the standpoint of radiant energy the enigmatic erections were dormant. The residual readings that appeared on the instrumentation matched the output of their flashlights and the hydrofoil's batteries. Though the examination could hardly be considered exhaustive, considering the limitations of their equipment, the Redowls agreed that regardless of what the constructs had been designed to do, they weren't doing anything now.

A library search informed them that self-exciting exothermic metal alloys had existed only in theory—until then. As for the machines themselves, their design did not match the technological architecture of any known civilization.

However old it was, most of the alien technology seemed to be in excellent condition. Though fragments littered the ground, there was no evidence of extensive degeneration within the metal or ceramics themselves.

While they couldn't give a date to the installation or a name to its builders, they could determine the composition of the materials used. In addition to iridium, Etienne noted the presence of two dozen alloys that defied chemical and spectroscopic analysis, including one thin metallic whip that the computer insisted was an alloy of metallic sodium, despite the fact that in the damp air of the cavern there wasn't the slightest evidence of oxidation on its shiny surface. When they dipped it in the river and nothing happened, the Redowls thought they could hear Homat's beloved spirits move a little closer.

Much of the spirit boat was still strange to Tyl, and he was having trouble finding the fresh lightning pack that Lyra called a battery cell. He rummaged carefully through the storage bay, trying to disturb as little as possible. A noise overhead caused him to pause.

Curious, the Tsla climbed the walkway. His snout was extended, the tip probing the air. The sounds drew him up from the hull, through the second deck and onto the upper. He walked past the humans' sleeping quarters, past the place of food they called the galley, until he was standing in the passage that opened into the open bubble of the cockpit. He stared for a long moment before speaking.

"What do thee here, Mai?"

Startled, Homat spun around. When he saw who confronted him he relaxed. "I am simply curious. We Mai are always curious about new things."

Tyl gestured with his snout, a mildly insulting display. "Thee should be outside helping our friends."

"I know, I know. I'll be there again soon. But it's so cold out there, so cold." He shivered.

"I am cold outside also, but the coldness is settling now inside me."

"I don't understand you, meditator."

"Thee linger too long and too frequently over the important places of this craft. For several days now I have noticed this. Thee have always stared as our friends worked here, but never more so since the attack by the Na. I think that this interest has escaped the attention of our friends, who though sophisticated in many ways are childishly naive in others. They are preoccupied with their study of our world and ways. But I am not so occupied, nor so naive. This unnatural interest of thee must be remarked upon." He turned to leave.

"Stop there, meditator!" The chill had suddenly slipped from Homat's body into his voice.

Slowly Tyl turned. His gaze fell to the device the Mai clutched firmly in his left hand. It was heavy for the six-fingered grip and Homat had to support part of it with his other hand. But the correct end was pointed at Tyl. He had seen the device in operation often enough to know that much.

"Mai," he whispered, managing to combine a whole paragraph of insults into the inflection he wrapped around that single noun.

Homat was neither impressed nor intimidated. The Tsla

usually overawed the Mai, but not him, not Homat. The hairy ones were bigger and stronger, but not necessarily smarter. No, size was no indication of intelligence, as he fully planned to prove.

"Do you know what this is?" he said, enjoying himself thoroughly as he gestured with the device he held. "This is the humans' lightning thrower. I have seen it operate many times. It may be difficult to build, but it is very simple to use." He pointed toward the clip holsters attached to the lower part of the control console.

"They sit there in their little homes, drawing strength from the spirit world until they are ready to serve the humans. These spirits are stupid. They do not respond to sacrifices or prayers or offerings, but will serve any who learn the rituals of operation. I have made an extensive study of such rituals these past many months."

"To what end?" Tyl inquired softly even as he estimated the distance between them.

"You have seen the sunit that sleeps here, and the other metals. Enough wealth to buy half the world."

"I am sure," Tyl said carefully, "that the humans would not object to thee returning with enough of the gray metal to make thee wealthy until thy passing."

"I'm sure they would allow me to bring a small amount, but not any more than would interfere with the plain rocks de-Etienne has already collected, for example. Why should I bow and scrape for a beggar's pouchful when I can have all that the spirit boat can carry?" He produced a thin Mai smile. "I can have the spirit boat itself. The sunit will make me master of Mai. This vessel can make me master of the Groalamasan."

Tyl's initial anger dissolved into sadness and pity. "Poor Mai. Thy dreams are so much larger than thy body."

"Are they?" said Homat hoarsely. "I planned to wait, but you push me toward delightenment. The Tsla have always pushed the Mai. In the end we will overwhelm you. See, how simple the humans' spirit devices are to work? You just touch this little round thing here . . ."

Etienne looked up from the base of the metallic mass he was studying, using the crutch Lyra had fashioned for him from a scoop net, and glanced back toward the boat. The glare from the two powerful spotlights made him squint.

"Did you hear something, hon?"

Lyra lifted her eyes from her work. She was trying to decide if some scratches they'd discovered on one wall might be writing. "Hear what?"

"The boat. I thought I heard something arc."

She shrugged. "Missed my ears."

He thought a moment, glanced to his right. "Yulour. Did thee hear anything from the spirit boat?"

The patient Tsla was sitting on the ground, playing with some colored stones. "I heard nothing, Teacher."

Just then Etienne saw a shape approaching them. "Here's Homat. Maybe he heard something."

Lyra returned to her studies and Etienne waited until their guide emerged from the glare. "Homat, you were near the boat. Did you hear something?"

"Yes, Etienne." He sounded odd, Etienne thought, though he couldn't define the difference. "I heard. It was your lightning thrower dealing spirits."

Lyra heard that, slowly rose from where she'd been sitting.

Etienne spoke precisely. "The lightning thrower? You mean it went off? How did that happen?"

"The way it always happens." The Mai was careful to keep his distance from Etienne, despite the severity of the man's injury. He removed the pistol from the pocket of his thermal suit. Etienne stiffened and Lyra backed toward the metal wall behind her.

"It happened," Homat continued, his confidence starting to build, "when I touched this place you call the trigger. I touched it and called upon the lightning spirits. I, Homat, did this."

Etienne struggled to choose the right words. "That's a very dangerous thing to do, Homat. You don't know what you're doing. The lightning spirits can be very unpredictable. You could hurt yourself."

Homat laughed softly. "You clever humans. You come here from another world, with your wonderful magical devices, and you try to make us think none but you can make

[224]

them work." He shook the asynapt at them. "Well, *I* can make them work!"

"Where is Teacher Tyl?" Yulour asked uncertainly, looking past the Mai toward the hydrofoil.

"Be quiet, simpleton. The meditator is dead. I killed him, with this." He shook the pistol again.

"But *why*?" Lyra cried as she looked toward the boat.

Homat's voice was as icy as the air around them. "To make certain that I did know how to call upon the lightning spirits. Truly it is very easy. You just touch this trigger place here." One finger eased toward the firing button.

Etienne negotiated a couple of awkward steps backward, leaning on the crutch.

"Don't be frightened," Homat told him. "I don't think I have to kill you. Besides, I need your arms and your backs."

"What for?"

Homat looked past him, his eyes afire. "To load the spirit boat with the gray metal, the sunit."

"The iridium alloy? Your people value it too?"

"More than any other thing of this world. It will make me master over much of it."

"We don't care if you take some sunit back with you," Lyra said. "Enough to make you rich, if you wish. We promised you a reward for helping us."

"The meditator said much the same thing. I take my own reward, Lyra. I want to take back as much sunit as the spirit boat will hold. We will make room by throwing out the useless things you have gathered during this journey, bits of plants and rocks and clothing and cheap trinkets."

"Homat, you can't! We need to take samples of your world back for study."

"You don't listen, Lyra. What is important to you does not matter now. It doesn't matter that your civilization is smarter than that of the Mai. It doesn't matter that you are smarter than me, though I am not so sure of that anymore. It does not matter that you are larger and stronger. This is all that matters now." He gestured with the asynaptic pistol. "I have not touched it since we fought the Na. It slew the meditator. I am certain it can slay you. This is something even we simple Mai can understand."

"Irquit wasn't the Zanur's representative," Etienne said accusingly. "It was you all the time."

"Oh, no, Etienne, she was a representative of the Zanur. We both were. But she was in charge over me, and I couldn't have that. I did not need her around, watching as I made careful study of your magic. I knew we would fail at Changrit."

"So you're a traitor then. To your city-state of Po Rabi, to your Zanur, to your Najoke de-me-Halmur."

Homat dug his toes into the ground, a sign of disrespectful disgust. "From this moment on Najoke de-me-Halmur is nothing. He is become less than the grains of gravel that roll from the mouth of this cave, less than the droppings of the *prewq* upon the fields. The Zanur is become nothing. Po Rabi itself is as nothing beside the wealth that lies here. If I choose I will buy Po Rabi for a winter home. I will be Moyt over all."

Lyra fought to restrain her temper. "Now listen, Homat. Maybe you can operate that pistol without burning your foot off, but running the spirit boat is another matter entirely."

"Is it so? I have watched for a long time now while you thought me shivering and cowering behind you for protection. Already I have steered the spirit boat once. I think truly it is not so complicated to use. A very few controls run it mostly, and one allows the spirits within to run by themselves."

"Even an autopilot needs occasional instructions."

"Does it? I think you try to deceive me. We will see."

"And what happens," Etienne pressed him, "if we don't return and our friends come looking for us? They'll find the boat and they'll find you."

"Perhaps. If they do I will shiver and cower some delighted more and explain that you were slain by the Na and that I, Homat, not knowing what else to do, was returning the spirit boat to its rightful owners. I think they will let me keep the sunit and award me honors for my bravery and dedication."

"Even assuming you could run the boat," Lyra said, "how can you get it past the Topapasirut without the help of the Tsla of Jakaie?"

"I think they will believe my story also. If they are reluctant to believe, there are other ways." He gestured past them toward the mountain of metal. "The Tsla are also traders. They are not immune to the promise of great wealth. Not all the hairy ones sit and meditate their lives away. They work hard in their shops and fields and when they come down to the Skar, wealth changes hands. And there is another reason why I know this can be done."

"Another reason?"

"An elderly merchant of Po Rabi preceded us to this place. Without lightning throwers, without this wondrous delighted clothing you have given me, without a spirit boat, he came to this place, stood perhaps on this same spot, and returned to Po Rabi with proof that he had done so. With all your wonders at my command, I cannot fail to do as well.

"But why this talk of your not returning? I bear you no malice, and I need your strength to load the sunit into the spirit boat. Then we will see. It would be easier if you agreed to help me return to the Skatandah. Perhaps I will even let you keep your boat. You will not have the useless rocks and weeds that you have gathered, but you will still have the magic images you make of them.

"One thing is certain: you have no other choice but to help me. If you do not, it will take longer to load the sunit with the help of only this simple one," he gestured toward Yulour, "but it will be done nonetheless. And I will surely kill you."

"Yulour and I will help load your precious sunit," Lyra said bitterly, "but Etienne cannot. If he does much lifting he stands a good chance of reopening the wound inside him."

"If he does that you can fix it again."

"I don't think it can be fixed again, at least not in the same way with the tools we have on the boat."

"He works like you and the Tsla or he dies now. I cannot spare the attention to let him sit and watch for a chance to surprise me."

Etienne limped forward. "I'll watch myself, Lyra, don't worry. I can rig a sling and work with my left arm."

"Our specimens," she muttered disconsolately. "Everything we've worked so hard to assemble, the first pieces of the puzzle that would enable us to start bulding a picture of this world's ecology, all thrown away."

[227]

"They won't do us any good if we don't live to deliver them."

"Not so stupid," Homat said approvingly. "I didn't think you were that stupid." He gestured again with the muzzle of the asynapt. "I do not like this place. Let us hurry."

Though he worked very carefully, the pain in Etienne's side never let him alone. The internal bleeding didn't start again, but Lyra ached in her own heart as she watched him struggle to load the heavy alloy.

Homat supervised the loading silently and displayed not a twinge of remorse. The lower hold was filled and they began stacking piles of broken metal on the second deck. Yulour carried twice his share of the load as he toiled quietly next to his human friends.

Several days later an exhausted Lyra, sweating inside her absorptive thermal suit, slumped to the ground and spoke sullenly to Homat.

"That's all she'll carry."

"No, there is yet room," Homat insisted. "Much more room. You must continue."

"Listen to me, Homat. The sunit, the metal, is very heavy. If you stack any more on the upper decks you'll ruin the boat's stability. All the sunit in the world won't do you any good if you turn over in the middle of the Skar." She held her breath as she dropped her gaze to the ground. Actually the hydrofoil could carry another ton or so in comparative safety, but she doubted Etienne would last another day.

Homat looked uncertain. "Very well. That is enough. Enough to buy two cities, and I can always come back for more."

"Fine," Etienne commented. "Now let us help you deliver your damned fortune so we can go our separate ways, which won't happen soon enough for me."

"Or if you insist on trying to take the hydrofoil back by yourself," Lyra added, "at least let us go with you as far as Turput. We can find transportation back to Steamer Station from there, and by the time we reached our outpost you could be halfway around the Groalamasan."

"And then what?" Homat inquired suspiciously, his inherent Mai paranoia surging to the fore. "Then you'll organize your friends and come looking for poor Homat with more of your strange weapons, to punish him and steal his glory." His grip on the asynapt tightened.

Slowly Lyra got to her feet. "Homat, don't be a fool."

"Truly that is not my intention."

Etienne was backing toward the silent mass of alien metal. He stumbled and Lyra rushed to help him, her eyes never leaving the pistol.

"There's no need for you to do this, Homat. We won't come after you. It's not worth it to us. It's not worth the spirit boat. We can always get another."

"Can you?" She knew enough of Mai psychology to see that he was working himself up good and proper, trying to excite himself to the point of pushing the trigger. Killing Tyl was one thing. Mai and Tsla disliked one another and sometimes fought. But the thought of slaying them was something new. There were powerful spirits involved, strange alien spirits, and he was still unsure of himself.

He was going to do it, though. She could see it in his eyes, read it in the way he stood, hear it in his voice. The scrawny bald little humanoid primitive was going to kill the two of them in cold blood there at the top of his world, beneath a ceiling of ancient ice, their backs to an enigma that would now never be properly studied.

"I will keep the slave," Homat said solemnly. He gestured toward Yulour, who stood nearby looking worried and confused. "I will make use of his strength on the homeward journey. Him I do not fear, but I do not trust you. I cannot stay awake all the time to watch you. As soon as I slept you would forget all your promises, set aside your assurances, and toss poor Homat into the Skar to take his chances with the fish.

"It is not I who is destined to be food for fishes. Not Homat the brave, Homat the great." He took aim with the heavy pistol.

"When he settles on me," Etienne whispered as he took a step forward, "run for it. I'll take the shot and if you can get beyond the ship's lights you'll have a chance."

"No, I won't..."

"Don't be an idiot!" he said huskily, taking another step forward. "Now of all times." The muzzle was shifting to cover him, Homat's finger moving toward the trigger. "Use your legs, Lyra. For both of us."

The tears were coming again, blinding her worse than the glare from the spotlights. She didn't know what to do and there was no time to make careful decisions. If only Etienne wouldn't be so damn logical! But he was right. If she could hide in the darkness of the cavern there was an outside chance she could slip aboard the hydrofoil without Homat seeing her. She was bigger and stronger than the Mai.

Homat saw her start to back away and moved the muzzle back to cover her instead of Etienne. It was impossible to outrun the charge, but the heavy weapon was awkward in Homat's grasp. Etienne saw that he was anticipating Lyra's flight and steadied himself to leap between them to take the shot.

He didn't have to. The same thought had occurred to someone else. Certainly no one, least of all Homat, expected Yulour to interpose himself between the pistol and its intended targets.

Etienne didn't have time to wonder at the Tsla's unaccustomed assertion. He was shoving at Lyra with his left hand.

"Now, run now."

Lyra was gaping at the Tsla. "I don't understand. Yulour doesn't act on his own."

"Don't worry about it now, shut up and run!"

She left him leaning on his crutch as she whirled and bolted for the blackness to their left. Homat turned to aim at her, but once more Yulour made certain his body was between hers and the gun.

"Get out of the way, moron!" Homat shouted. Yulour stood quietly, holding his ground. "I said get out of the way! I need you for the journey Downriver."

He could hear the gravel flying from beneath the human female's boots. Of course, he could abandon both of them, leave them to die slowly, but he was furious that his carefully rehearsed triumph might be spoiled by a simpleminded Tsla. He stared over the barrel of the lightning thrower.

"You brought this on yourself, idiot. I'll just have to get along without you. Downriver I'll find plenty of willing backs with sensible heads atop them." He touched the trigger.

There was a bright, crisp flash of light as the asynapt fired, accompanied by a familiar faint crackling sound. Etienne shouted, "No!" and tried to throw himself at Homat. Given the distance that still separated him from the Mai, it was a futile gesture. A sharp pain ran from his side down his left leg and he crumpled despite the support provided by his crutch.

Dust stung his eyes as he lay staring dumbly across the gravel. Yulour had not fallen under the impact of the charge. He hadn't fallen because he was no longer there.

But something else was.

⟦ XVII ⟧

For an instant Etienne was positive that the charge had struck him instead. That would explain the illusion. Or perhaps the silent Yulour possessed the power of old. He blinked, and the illusion remained. His side still flamed. His nose was running. It was real.

Where Yulour had been, what Yulour had been rose four meters toward the roof of the cavern. It was slim and silvery. The coldly viscous sides twisted and flowed like the ripples that spread out from a pebble dropped in a pond. Indeed, what had been Yulour looked a lot like a tower of opaque water. Where an internal ripple reached its apex the silvery hue became suffused with other colors: gray and white, blue and purple. They spread in irregular chromatic blotches across portions of the unstable tower, fading gradually back into the silver.

Homat stood motionless, the asynapt still clutched convulsively in both hands. Probably he could not have dropped it had he wanted to. Suddenly all the terrors, all the childhood fears, all the old Mai stories of demons and devils and evil spirits that he had automatically absorbed as he had matured had solidified before his bulging eyes. He started to tremble and lost control of his bowels. He was trying to scream but only a thin whispery whine passed between his parted lips.

Through his pain Etienne thought he heard Lyra shout from her hiding place back in the artifacts. She wasn't trying to maneuver behind Homat now. All she could do was stare in wonder at the tower of pulsating quicksilver that had been Yulour. Of the three who saw, it might have been that she was the most stupefied of all, for only Lyra Redowl was familiar with the folklore and mythologies of half a hundred worlds, and thus only she knew that what stood before them in the cavern had a basis in hypothesized reality.

It had been seen before—or had it? No one was certain because no reputable evidence was ever presented to conclusively prove the existence of such a creature. Rumors gave it different names, of which the one that stuck was more hopefully descriptive than verifiable.

"I'll be damned," she murmured in awe, "a Mutable."

Etienne heard and the word sifted through his numbed brain. A Mutable. Folktales spoke of them not only on commonwealth worlds but on the worlds of the AAnn empire and the inhabited globes that turned in emptiness outside the boundaries of the principal political entities. Every space-traversing civilization had legends of encounters with true shape-changers, silhouette shifters, metamorphs.

Mutables.

But myths and fraud dissolved in the dank cavern before the glittering reality that had been Yulour the slow-witted Tsla. Legend or folktale or hallucination made real, whatever it was it had saved Lyra's life. Its intentions beyond that were shrouded in speculation.

As Etienne lay there staring at the rippling silvery shape, it occurred to him that he and Lyra were likely the first human beings ever to see a Mutable in its natural state.

It had protected Lyra. That was all that really mattered.

He wondered if the body's constant movement might be an indication of some permanent instability. As he wondered, the tower turned slightly, showing a suggestion of what might be an eye near the top. The deep gray oval swam in a sea of silver. A second might drift alongside the first, beyond his sight. It might have a half dozen hidden duplicates.

Traveling like a tree on greased treads, the Mutable moved toward the hydrofoil. The motion was silent. A single pseudopod emerged from the center of the tower, formed tentacles that reached for the asynapt in Homat's shaking fingers. As he watched, Etienne wondered how the creature had shaken off the effects of the burst from the pistol.

He wasn't given the opportunity to observe the result of a second shot, because the Mai let out a single final massive shudder, then fell sideways onto the gravel. The gun fell from limp fingers.

At this the tentacles withdrew. It mattered not to Homat, whose crumpled form lay motionless now near one of the boat's hydrofoils, knees drawn tight against the thin chest, all hint of aggression fled along with the life force. The cause of death was clear and no autopsy could have made it any clearer: Homat had died of fright, murdered where he'd stood by his own guilt and thousands of years of accumulated racial fears.

The Mutable inclined forward over the Mai's body. Then it straightened, pivoted slowly, and moved away. Rocks and gravel were depressed where it had passed, as if a large, heavy ball had rolled across the ground where the Mutable moved.

Despite its size the creature traveled with ease and a graceful fluidity. Lyra kept her eyes on it as she helped Etienne back to his feet and handed him his crutch. She could recall no legend of a Mutable's harming anything, but that was small comfort as she stood in that cold, dark place supporting her badly injured husband.

Though no pupils were visible, Lyra thought the pair of large gray spots atop the silvery mass were focused on her.

"Please do not be afraid," the Mutable said. It spoke clearly, in Yulour's familiar voice, though without that Tsla's slowness. "Yes, I am what you call a Mutable. I am the native you knew as Yulour. Please do not be alarmed." The upper portion of the tower inclined toward the hydrofoil. "I did not mean for that one to expire, but as are all his people he was a prisoner of his own private terrors. You, however, are more mature and not subject to such."

"Don't give us too much credit just yet," Etienne found himself mumbling. "I'm scared as hell."

"You must not be frightened." The Mutable's voice was almost painfully gentle.

"Mutables don't exist except as rumors," Lyra murmured.

"That is how we prefer to exist. It simplifies much."

Lyra left Etienne to stand on his own and stepped forward, extending a hesitant hand. "I don't want to offend, but—could I touch you?"

"If it is required to establish my existence in your mind."

"It's not. I know you're here. It's just something I'd like to do."

"Then please do so."

She lightly pressed against the silvery flank, discovered that it felt like warm vinyl. It took an effort of will not to jerk her fingers away, not because it was too hot but because the surface was in constant motion. She stepped back, her palm tingling.

"If you two don't mind," Etienne said, "I'm a little tired. I think I'd better sit down." It was a measure of his exhaustion that he allowed Lyra to help without his uttering a single wisecrack.

"You said, 'it simplifies much,'" Lyra repeated. "What does it simplify?"

"Our work. We are caretakers, we Mutables."

"Caretakers? For whom?"

"For the Xunca."

Lyra frowned. "Never heard of 'em."

"But you know of the Tar-Aiym and of the Hur'rikku, who dominated this grouping of stars, this galaxy, until they destroyed each other in a great war."

"Yes, I know the histories," Lyra replied. "Both races have been gone, from this portion of the galaxy, anyway, for at least a hundred millennia."

"The Xunca predate both. They are so ancient little more than their memory remains. We are their caretakers. Whether we are an independently evolved race or machines fashioned by them, we ourselves do not know. We know only our work."

"These Xunca lived and ruled before both the Tar-Aiym and the Hur'rikku?"

"They did not rule. They simply were. Their probings reached regions that can be expressed only by pure mathematics. Reached beyond this galaxy, beyond the satellite clusters of stars you call the Magellanic Clouds. They went such places."

"You imply a technology capable of traversing an intergalactic gap," Etienne observed. "Such technology is not possible."

The Mutable admonished him gently. "Did not your own kind once say the same of faster-than-light travel, before they learned of space-plus and null-space? I say to you that they the Xunca did this thing.

"This world you call Horseye and that the dominants call Tslamaina is itself a product of Xunca technology."

"This planet is a construct?"

"No." Thoughtfully the Mutable moved to its right so they could observe it free of the glare from the hydrofoil's lights. It was a gesture of courtesy and Etienne let himself relax further.

"The Xunca did not build this world, they modified it to suit their needs. The asteroidal collision which produced the oceanic basin now filled by the Groalamasan's waters was not an astronomical accident."

"Why do that?"

"The Xunca required a large body of water which would circulate only in one direction, whose currents would never change. The positioning of the four small moons assures this. Here the oceanic currents flow eternally in the direction you call clockwise.

"This perpetual motion, driven by lunar gravity, never needs refueling or maintenance. It exists and was designed to drive great engines buried in the ocean floor. Since Tslamaina is tectonically stable and has been for eons save for one regrettable massive earth tremor, there is no danger of the machinery's being destroyed by subduction. It sits and waits, ready to be driven by the mechanism of the ocean currents. The currents that scour the bottom of the Groalamasan are very powerful by the standards of most worlds. This construction was necessary because there are no other stable oceanic worlds in this area. The machinery is shielded against detection by space-going peoples. It has lain dormant for tens of thousands of your years."

"How many tens of thousands?" Lyra wondered aloud.

"Enough to total several hundred millions."

"And you've been 'caretaking' the facilities all that time?"

"We are long-lived or well-designed," the Mutable explained matter-of-factly.

"I don't care," Lyra argued. "*Nothing* lives for a hundred million years!"

"The rocks beneath your feet do. Our internal structure resembles them more than it does yours. You may be interested to know that a smaller installation, similar to that which sleeps beneath the ocean of this world, exists on yours."

Lyra started. "On Earth? Nothing like what you describe has ever been found. Is the shielding against detection that effective?"

"Yes, but that installation was destroyed by your world's continental drift. It was emplaced when your continents were one large land mass and there was a single, much larger, world ocean like that on Tslamaina. The Xunca were not omnipotent. They could not plan for every eventuality.

"But that was only a small relay and its loss not vital to the system. The main transmitter was constructed on this world. The three local intelligent life forms evolved independently long after its emplacement. They do not suspect its existence. None do." He gestured past them.

"This is a tiny portion of the transmitter's antenna system. Most of it lies beneath your feet. It is our task to see that it remains in operating condition, together with the extensive relay network to which it can be linked."

"Can it operate through the ice cap?"

"No. In the event that the transmitter system becomes active, a portion if not all of this ice will be melted."

Etienne's thoughts moved rapidly. "That would raise the level of the Groalamasan enough to flood every major city on Tslamaina."

The Mutable sounded apologetic. "As I have said, all this was designed a very long time ago, and the Xunca could not foresee everything. However, it is possible this will never occur. The system has not become active in all the hundreds of millions of years since it was fashioned. Who knows how many millions more will pass before anything happens? Nothing may ever happen."

"Nobody builds something like this," Etienne muttered, "thinking it will never be used."

"Why not, Etienne?" Lyra said with disarming calmness. "What about the security alarms people put in their homes?" She looked startled. "Is that what this is?"

"We do not know what the system is for," the Mutable replied sadly. "Not one of us knows. We are only caretakers, not operators or builders. We do what we were instructed to do eons ago. Watch over the system and insure that it remains intact.

"Do not think that we merely sit and wonder. We discuss and debate. We have our own culture. Now and then we assume one of the shapes of the space-going races and visit each other, for only one of us is assigned to each world. We assist one another in diagnosing and solving problems, but generally there is little to do. The Xunca built for the ages. But as to the purpose of the system, only the Xunca themselves know that."

"What happened to them?" Etienne asked. "If they were such masters of science, why did they let the Tar-Aiym and the Hur'rikku usurp their place?"

"The Tar-Aiym and the Hur'rikku usurped nothing. Both races rose to power in the vacuum left by the departure of the Xunca. They did not force the Xunca to leave. The Xunca were never forced to do anything. They departed because they found something their technology could not cope with."

"Then why leave this elaborate system behind? To let them know when it was safe for them to return? You must know something about it?"

"Only that it will become active if whatever it was intended to react to manifests itself." The Mutable hesitated. "We do know that it involves one particular section of space."

"Can you be any more specific?"

"It lies in the direction of the constellation you call Boötes, as seen from your Earth, but farther out. It is an area of modest size, some three hundred million light-years across, encompassing a volume of approximately one million cubic megaparsecs."

Etienne frowned for a moment until the figures quoted by the Mutable linked up with something in his memory.

"The Great Emptiness. We've known of it for hundreds of years. It's a 'modest' region, all right. It ought to be as filled with galaxies and nebulae as any other section of space, but it's not. There's nothing there, astronomically speaking. Some free hydrogen and a few isolated stellar masses of uncertain composition."

"This we know," the Mutable admitted. "What we do not know is *how* the Xunca transmitter is involved."

"I'd rather it were connected to something simpler to explain," Etienne muttered. "We humans are a gregarious bunch. We like crowds, not big emptinesses."

"You are concerned."

"It seems the Xunca were. Don't you sense some kind of threat?"

"We do not worry, nor should you. Too much time has passed without anything happening."

"Then you *do* think a threat of some sort is involved."

"We have had much time in which to evaluate possibilities. When one's entire existence is devoted to a single task, there is a fair amount of time to devote to idle speculation. I must admit that some of us believe the Xunca system to be a warning device."

"Strange, but your words don't give me much comfort," Lyra muttered.

"I wish that I could allay all concerns. We wish no less for ourselves. You should know that. We have had to content ourselves with a saying: 'the Xunca moved in mysterious ways.'"

Etienne forced himself to think of more immediate matters. All the talk of vast empty sections of space, of alien devices lying dormant for incalculable eons waiting for some unknown problem to manifest itself, of caretakers who could change their shape moving unobserved among different civilizations, was making him dizzy.

He needed to talk about something he could relate to. "Your task, then, is to ensure the inviolability of the Xunca system."

"That is so."

Etienne drew Lyra close to him. "Then that means you must have decided by now what you're going to do with us."

"It has been a very long time since this transmitter was checked," the Mutable said quietly. "In that time this river has enlarged the cavern considerably around it and opened a wide entrance. That must be sealed with ice."

"You're avoiding my question. What about us?"

"I have enjoyed the opportunity to study you for many days, Etienne Redowl man. It would have been simple to let the native dispose of you or to do so myself." Lyra's arm tightened against her husband's back. "But after hundreds of millions of years of dedication to a single task, one develops a high respect for indigenous life forms that have succeeded in developing intelligence without destroying themselves in the process. When one is governed by insights that may be more than a billion years old, one develops laws and insights of one's own. And there is one thing more."

Etienne allowed himself to hope, wondering what ancient philosophical conclusion might stay the executioner. "What's that?"

"I like you. You are simple, uncomplicated, primitive. But you are likeable. Many peoples do not place likeability high on the list of survival traits. We do. I do. I like you for yourselves and for what you are, what you represent. We are not merely components of a carefully constructed machine. We are also individuals. As such we can admire individuality in others. Your persistence and dedication, your"—was that a *smile* atop the silvery column?—"immutable devotion to your chosen professions reminds me of our own."

"I'm glad you like us," Lyra said. "I think we like you. But how do you plan to insure that we don't bring others of our kind back to this place, to tell them the story and show them the tip of the transmitter?"

"I will see to it not only that this cavern is sealed, but that the transmitter is moved—and shielded so that your most sensitive instruments cannot relocate it no matter if they spend years scanning the northern hemisphere of this world.

"As for relating what I have told you to your colleagues, we have observed enough of humankind for me to believe that you would not be taken seriously. And there is a third protection. You will give me your word."

Lyra glanced at her husband, then back at the Mutable. "I hope to live a while longer yet, but I never expect to be flattered like this again. For what it's worth you have our word."

"Thank you, woman. It is done, and I am much relieved."

"I only wish," she added, "that Tyl could be here to give his word also."

"I am sorry. Revealing my true nature is not something done lightly. I held back in the hope that the Mai would spare you and I could then help you return safely without exposing myself. I could do nothing for the Tsla."

As they stared the Mutable's exoderm began to flow and ripple violently. They stepped back as the silvery skin started to cloud over with patches of dark gray. These changed to white, pale yellow, and then became a rich hazel color. Simultaneously the sentient tower began to collapse, the internal structure shrinking and compacting. The transformation was accomplished in utter silence. Once more Yulour the Tsla stood before them.

"I thought you would find my company during the return journey less unsettling in this guise. I hope my company will not upset you. I have already set in motion the machinery necessary to conceal the transmitter from potential prying minds." Indeed, as she stood there listening Lyra was certain she could detect a rising hum from behind them, and a slight vibration beneath her feet.

"I enjoy your company," the Mutable went on, "and have not had the opportunity to spend much time among your kind since I have never been assigned to a human-occupied world. You are an interesting adolescent race."

"You're certainly welcome to our interesting adolescent company," Etienne replied dryly. As if they could prevent the creature from accompanying them if it so desired. "Whatever your motives, you did save our lives, even if you did compel us to share a mystery that we know won't be solved in our lifetime, let alone *your* lifetime."

"Myself," Lyra said dreamily, "I prefer to think the Xunca went away for personal reasons and that they left this relay system behind to help whatever intelligences might arise in their absence. That's a nice thought, anyway. I'd rather think of any people that brilliant as altruistic rather than indifferent."

They started down the slight slope toward the hydrofoil. Yulour moved to help Etienne, who flinched, but only for a moment; the fur against his arm was real, the smell pure Tsla.

They gave Tyl a formal farewell, and Lyra restored some lightness to a situation weighty with solemnity by suggesting Etienne carry out the standard Tsla funeral ritual. That sparked an affectionate exchange of insults to which Yulour listened with interest.

Etienne finished it by doing something he hadn't done in quite a while. He took Lyra in his arms and kissed her long and hard. They stood enfolded in each other for a long time, and Yulour watched that with equal interest. Such mayfly relationships were not for his kind, but there was a decided poignancy to them that forever escaped those condemned to near immortality. The Mutable sighed an ancient, silent sigh, no louder than the winds that move the hydrogen between the stars. Existence for these people was a brief explosive flash of consciousness, then limbo. A breath of life blown by in a rush of emotion and a few hasty thoughts.

The Mutable could only empathize. For it life was an infinite march toward an unknown end. Besides, there was work to do.

Etienne assumed the pilot's chair, nudged several touchplates, looked uneasy. Lyra moved next to him.

"Trouble?"

"Looks like it. We've had these spotlights on for a lot longer than we planned. The batteries are drawn down too low to power the engine, much less the repellers. We're going to have to drift out until the current and the sun can recharge us."

Yulour studied the control console for an instant. "I think I can help. No reason not to, now."

The un-Tsla's right arm began to change. Fur and muscle became a single thin strand of faintly radiant metallic silver. The tendril slipped through the small opening of a power socket. A tremor ran through the boat as a half dozen readouts suddenly flared brightly.

[242]

"Sorry. The resistance was less than I thought," Yulour explained as the silver tendril was withdrawn and became an arm again. "It is not only that a Mutable is powerful. A Mutable *is* power."

"Also handy to have around for a difficult trip. Nothing like a couple of hundred million years of specialized evolution to give you an effective jump-start, though it does seem a bit disrespectful somehow." Lyra seemed bemused.

Etienne tried again and the engine whined to life. The hydrofoil rose two meters above the gravel and pivoted toward the river. Spotlights illuminating their way, they commenced the long journey down the Skar toward Turput, Steamer Station, and eventually, home.

There they would take a long sabbatical to write their official report, one which would be haunted by memories. Somehow that report no longer seemed as important as it had when they'd started their expedition up the Barshajagad. Very little seemed important anymore, beyond the way Lyra clung tightly to Etienne and how he played with strands of her hair.

Behind them the visible tip of the Xunca transmitter was engulfed by arctic dark. It brooded motionless now but soon it would move. Within the seemingly solid mass pimesons and guons and bits of matter and bits of stuff that wasn't matter traveled their assigned pathways at speeds approaching that of light—as they had for uncounted centuries.

Unnoticed by uncomprehending humans or caretaking Mutables, one tiny section suddenly showed signs of activity where for ages there had been none. The unusual movement at the subatomic level within might intensify or it might shut down again.

But something was happening. Something had triggered a minute portion of the machinery beyond that which was responsible for normal maintenance. How soon the something might require attention, not even a watching Mutable might have said. "Soon" was a relevant term, an abstract, a precession through infinity. For a more specific explanation of what it meant in this instance the Xunca would have to be consulted.

Wherever they were.

ABOUT THE AUTHOR

Born in New York City in 1946, Alan Dean Foster was raised in Los Angeles, California. After receiving a bachelor's degree in political science and a Master of Fine Arts in motion pictures from UCLA in 1968–69, he worked for two years as a public relations copywriter in a small Studio City, California, firm.

His writing career began in 1968 when August Derleth bought a long letter of Foster's and published it as a short story in his biannual *Arkham Collector Magazine*. Sales of short fiction to other magazines followed. His first try at a novel, *The Tar-Aiym Krang*, was published by Ballantine Books in 1972.

Foster has toured extensively through Asia and the isles of the Pacific. Besides traveling, he enjoys classical and rock music, old films, basketball, body surfing, and karate. He has taught screenwriting, literature, and film history at UCLA and Los Angeles City College.

Currently, he resides in Arizona with his wife JoAnn (who is reputed to have the only extant recipe for Barbarian Cream Pie).

W9-ANT-788

Develop Your PR Skills

Develop Your PR Skills

Neil Richardson and Lucy Laville

KoganPage

LONDON   PHILADELPHIA   NEW DELHI

Publisher's note

Every possible effort has been made to ensure that the information contained in
this book is accurate at the time of going to press, and the publishers and authors
cannot accept responsibility for any errors or omissions, however caused. No
responsibility for loss or damage occasioned to any person acting, or refraining
from action, as a result of the material in this publication can be accepted by the
editor, the publisher or either of the authors.

First published in Great Britain and the United States in 2010 by Kogan Page Limited

120 Pentonville Road	525 South 4th Street, #241	4737/23 Ansari Road
London N1 9JN	Philadelphia PA 19147	Daryaganj
United Kingdom	USA	New Delhi 110002
www.koganpage.com		India

© Neil Richardson and Lucy Laville, 2010

The right of Neil Richardson and Lucy Laville to be identified as the authors of this
work has been asserted by them in accordance with the Copyright, Designs and
Patents Act 1988.

ISBN   978 0 7494 6045 7
E-ISBN 978 0 7494 5971 0

British Library Cataloguing-in-Publication Data

A CIP record for this book is available from the British Library.

Library of Congress Cataloging-in-Publication Data

Richardson, Neil.
  Develop your PR skills / Lucy Laville, Neil Richardson.
       p. cm.
  Includes bibliographical references.
  ISBN 978-0-7494-5970-3 -- ISBN 978-0-7494-5971-0 (ebook) 1. Public relations.
I. Laville, Lucy. II. Title.
  HD59.R47 2010
  659.2--dc22
                          2010000342

Typeset by Saxon Graphics Ltd, Derby
Printed and bound in India by Replika Press Pvt Ltd

Contents

Introduction

First, thank you for buying this book. Having bought it, you are now one of our customers, which means a lot to us. Throughout the text you'll see the theme of public relations (PR) being a major driver of stakeholder satisfaction and competitive advantage. These are arguably the most important factors for many professionals.

If you're not a PR practitioner, you may wonder whether it really matters. Suffice it to say that substantial research has proved the need for good-quality PR for most companies. As Senior Lecturers at Leeds Business School, we have considerable experience of teaching across the whole range of ages, industrial experiences, organisational types and markets. In teaching professional students (working towards Chartered status) we are often asked a diverse range of questions. We've encapsulated these questions in this text and offered honest, sometimes critical, answers. The professional students, studying in their spare time, are truly representative of the whole spectrum of organisations and businesses.

PR can benefit all organisations, whether public, private or third sector. It can help you identify, build and maintain relationships with your publics, including customers and

prospects, as well as wider groups of individuals who may influence your organisation. Understanding these groups and how to communicate with them effectively is crucial in maintaining and developing your organisation's reputation.

This book is designed to provide those with little or no understanding of PR with a practical guide on how to use it to enhance and develop your business opportunities. So whether you work for a small company, multinational, charity or sole trader, or if you simply want to explore the opportunities of a career in PR, this book will provide you with the foundations to understanding how PR can help you build your success.

This text is aimed at practitioners who do not have the time to trawl through 1,200-page tomes. That said, our approach, using examples to apply PR theories, will offer insights into the theories missing from many key texts. We're confident you will find new information that will enable you to develop your knowledge, skills and, hopefully, attitude.

Throughout the text we've suggested activities designed to encourage you to re-evaluate your surroundings. Questions are posed throughout with answers at the back (not that you'd cheat). There has to be a test! Despite having decades of private-sector experience between us, we're academics, after all!

So once again, thanks for the order and enjoy the book.

1

Public relations in business: an introduction

Many people consider PR to be all about media relations: how to get your name in newspapers and trade magazines, or on radio or TV, whether at a local, regional or national level. Many PR practitioners do indeed spend a lot of their time developing press opportunities and they now have the added challenge and huge opportunities offered by internet communications via social networking sites and blogs as well as websites.

We explore these areas of media and new media relations in more detail in later chapters. It is, however, important to understand that PR is much more than media relations; it can be highly effective in helping you to manage relationships with staff, suppliers, members, community groups, investors, influencers, and new and existing customers as well as in dealing with crises and issues in an ever-changing world.

What is PR?

In its simplest form, public relations is about developing and managing relations with stakeholders. Taking a strategic approach

to public relations will ensure that the tactics you implement, from sending press releases to the media to communicating with staff, investors and other audiences, are most effective and sustainable.

The profession

PR's roots in business can be traced back to the 19th century, when the showman, entrepreneur and 'icon of American spirit' PT Barnum famously said, 'Without promotion something terrible happens, nothing!' In the early 1900s, Edward Bernays, a nephew of Sigmund Freud, was a publicist for the arts who wrote books about the power of persuasion and techniques for success that are still influential today.

Public relations is a relatively new profession, although fundamentally it is about engaging communication tactics to influence the public, which has been done by governments, dictators and key influencers for hundreds of years. The growing profession is represented in the United Kingdom by the Chartered Institute of Public Relations (CIPR), a professional body that was established in 1948 and awarded chartered status in 2005. PR is used in a vast range of industries and professions, with different skills and competences being employed by practitioners. It is still emerging as a discipline and is therefore difficult to define in a simple way.

Despite its relatively new arrival as a recognised discipline, it has become one of the most popular professions for graduates, and a range of professional and academic qualifications have been developed over the past decade.

Industry definition

The UK's CIPR defines PR as:

> being about reputation – the result of what you do, what you say and what others say about you... Public relations is the

discipline which looks after reputation, with the aim of earning understanding and support and influencing opinion and behaviour. It is the planned and sustained effort to establish and maintain goodwill and mutual understanding between an organisation and its publics.

In essence this definition, if used in its truest form, is about PR becoming so embedded in an organisation's culture and vision that it permeates through all aspects of the organisation. Whether it needs a dedicated PR practitioner to implement this is debatable, but it does require the desire of the managing director or CEO and top management to embed this culture within the organisation, whatever its size and the complexity of its business.

The people involved

PR practitioners, at a tactical level, are often called 'PRs', press officers, media relations managers or communications officers. At a strategic level, PRs may be called PR managers, heads of PR or communications directors. A recent survey of FTSE 100 companies revealed that, while all have a PR/communications department, most have a PR/communications specialist at board level, contributing to strategic decisions about the direction of the organisation.

Investment at board level is obviously expensive but demonstrates how important big businesses view PR as being – as a discipline that adds value to their organisation. Similarly, public-sector organisations, including (in the United Kingdom) the National Health Service, councils and government departments, invest heavily in PR campaigns and activities to build and maintain relations with their publics.

What PR is not

PR is not marketing, advertising, sponsorship, sales or any of the more obvious expensive tools that send a message directly to

'customers', often saying, 'We are great, buy our products.' PR is
more subtle: 'You may have heard about us; get to know us and we
may have a long and happy relationship.' PR does not need to
involve the big costs that advertising and sponsorship incur, and
while it is often used to complement these tactics, it can be just as
effective as a stand-alone discipline.

Propaganda and spin

The PR industry has been associated with propaganda, no more so
than during times of war or when used by dictators, when the
messages communicated are based on ideals rather than reality.
Criticism is often aimed at businesses and organisations that do
not 'practise what they preach', or spin the story to include a
heavily biased opinion in favour of the message sender. Spin
doctors – PR practitioners representing political parties – are
frequently criticised for their part in manipulating the truth or
being economical with the truth.

In the United Kingdom there are certain laws to protect
individuals who are exploited by these means. Cases of libel
action being brought against PR practitioners are rare, but high-
profile practitioners such as Max Clifford, who would regard
himself as a publicist rather than a PR practitioner, have found
themselves facing High Court rulings for promoting stories that
were falsified. Similarly, newspapers are treated with the same
legal action for reporting stories, often promoted by PRs, that are
defamatory and may cause huge anxiety for those misrepresented.

Despite this reputation, the result of activities practised by a
small minority, there is much valuable work done by PR
practitioners who represent charities, businesses, political
parties and public-sector organisations as well as individuals.
The chartered status of the profession and the public debates
around morality and mutual benefit have led to a valued
profession with growing respect as a creative and strategic
industry. The relationship between PRs and journalists is
increasingly based on mutual respect, with much fluidity

between the professions. People with a background in journalism make up a large number of PRs as they look to diversify and develop as communicators. Salaries and working conditions are often more favourable in the PR industry than for most journalists working in a media industry that is in decline as more of us turn to the internet to get our news.

Credibility and trust are paramount in good PR. Communicated messages based on fact and the credibility of the message sender are crucial to effective PR. The audience, whether they are reading about you in a newspaper or on the internet, or are hearing you speak at an event or conference, must believe you have the authority, based on truths and trust, to engage in a mutually beneficial relationship. As the communicator, you must recognise that gaining this trust is important to building mutually beneficial relationships with your audiences that will sustain positive outcomes for your organisation.

Strategy or tactics?

Mutual respect is the most effective way to develop your reputation and build long and fruitful relationships with your stakeholders, whether they are customers, staff, investors, suppliers, community groups or even activist groups that may oppose the activities of your business. This is crucial to developing an understanding of the value that PR can add to your organisation. Identifying your target publics, the effect they have on your organisation and how to develop a mutually beneficial relationship with them is crucial to implementing effective PR.

Planning a sustained programme of PR activities that has clear aims and objectives, and evaluating the results, will ensure that you maximise the PR potentials for your organisation. A PR strategy might involve a six-month campaign focusing on one specific element of your business or a broader and longer campaign that involves a company-wide strategy. Whatever your PR strategy is aiming to achieve, it can be supported with a range of individual programmes of PR activity and tactics being

implemented. Chapter 3 explores in more detail how to plan a strategic campaign and provides a framework for developing your own PR strategy, which includes setting objectives, developing tactics and evaluating outputs and outcomes.

Many companies will use regular PR tactics such as media releases, corporate literature, events, in-house magazines, or attending industry conferences without fully understanding the impact of these individual strands of activity, never mind the collective impact of using a range of tactics. We all know that it is important to maintain communication with audiences via a range of activities, but understanding the aim of these individual and collective activities will ensure that the most successful ones are used to their maximum benefit and that any ineffective activities are improved upon or not deployed in the future.

Whilst many consider PR to be a relatively cheap alternative to other communication tools such as advertising, sponsorship and many marketing activities, it still requires a big investment in time and resources, and must be taken seriously and with great consideration as to its ongoing effects and outcomes.

Legal boundaries

In an increasingly litigious world there are legal frameworks that regulate business and ensure that it operates legally, ethically and fairly. A number of Acts of the UK Parliament have certainly provided a framework for PR practitioners within which to operate both legally and ethically. The Libel Act 1792, the Data Protection Act 1998, the Freedom of Information Act 2000 and the Privacy Law 1987 are crucial to protect the activities of many practitioners as well as act as a boundary for ethical practice.

The EU Directive on Information and Consultation of Employees (2004) gives employees of 'undertakings of 50 or more employees' rights to be informed and consulted about issues that affect their employment and the prospect of the business. This, in turn, has led to the need for employers to communicate more effectively with staff via internal communication strategies that

are increasingly designed and delivered by PR practitioners rather than human resources (HR) departments.

Practical considerations

The following chapters will give you the tools to be more proactive and effective in managing PR activities and will show you how to use it, from getting the most out of employees through to encouraging journalists to say good things about your business.

Many small to medium-sized enterprises (SMEs) outsource their PR activities, or alternatively it may be the sole or part of the responsibility of a single individual. Often these activities will be monitored or actioned by managers who see PR as an important part of business development and critical to the success of the organisation. Larger organisations may well have several PR practitioners employed by the business as well as using the services of PR agencies, especially for specific campaigns that require specialist knowledge that PR agencies can provide. Many PR agencies specialise in sectors or disciplines because, for example, they have strong contacts in the trade publications, understand legislation, have relevant government or financial expertise or have experience of key stakeholder relations.

If you want to explore developing a PR role within your organisation, you can gather information about practitioner responsibilities by studying the jobs pages of *PR Week* and the Media supplement of *The Guardian*. Both have websites with job adverts and a list of specifications for practitioners as well as salary guides. Chapter 10 explores in more detail the cost implications of using PR practitioners, from recruiting staff to using PR agencies and consultancies.

Hiring a PR agency

There is a wide spectrum of professional support available to you via agencies. If you're unsure about which communications tools to

use (and assuming you can afford the fees), it may be wise to use an agency. But which sort? The United Kingdom has some of the world's most innovative and successful PR agencies. They include the large, full-service agencies such as Saatchi & Saatchi, which can create, develop, plan and execute any manner of communication campaign as they employ specialists in all aspects of communication and have vast resources. Hence, such organisations can service the whole of the marketing communications (marcomms) mix (see Figure 2.1, page 14) on your behalf.

Alternatively, you could use an independent specialist PR agency. This choice would be generally cheaper as smaller companies do not have vast overheads to service. However, while they could create fantastic PR for you, you might still need additional types of communication, such as a sales promotion. The benefit of using a full-service agency is that it will house all marcomms specialists under one roof and can therefore cross-coordinate all communication activities on your behalf. However, it comes at a cost.

If you are thinking of hiring a PR agency or consultant, you may find the following useful:

- *A good degree of fit.* Different PR agencies specialise in different areas. Some are better at promoting established businesses, whereas others are more focused on newly formed companies. The PR agency should have local, regional and national press contacts; its previous work should illustrate whether that is the case.
- *Company and sector knowledge.* It is imperative that the agency understands what your company does – its culture, its marketplace and what makes it special or unique. Be cautious if the people you talk to do not appear interested in taking the time to understand your company.
- *Track record.* It's a cliché, but 'a good PR agency is a busy PR agency', so ask for copies of press releases and media coverage that the agency has generated for clients in the past. Ask for testimonials from clients. You need to benchmark them, as agencies charge differing amounts

for various tasks. Issues such as typical rates are addressed in Chapter 10. However, rates alone will not tell you the full story. The key to establishing a reasonable PR budget is to determine what agencies charge for a range of services and how many hours of creative time it takes to complete these projects.

Summary and activities

Key points

- PR provides benefits for *all* organisations – big or small, public, private or not-for-profit. SMEs particularly are often unaware of the benefits of good PR.
- There is more to PR than simply media relations.
- Before you decide which communication tools to use to deliver your message from sender to receiver, there are a number of factors to consider that will help you choose the most appropriate communication tools and, indeed, the configuration of the message you send.

Questions

1. At which levels of business does PR operate?
2. How do legal constraints impact on PR?
3. Who can undertake PR responsibilities?

Activities

The following represent UK- and European-based PR websites that host a wealth of information:

- The Chartered Institute of Public Relations' website, http://www.cipr.co.uk, has useful sections such as

'Looking for PR,' which includes definitions, a glossary and a guide to hiring a PR consultant, plus a PR directory.

- MediaUK (website: http://www.mediauk.com) is a forum for discussion and information for UK PR professionals plus an excellent UK media internet directory and a listing of the latest media news.

- The European Public Relations Confederation (website: http://www.cerp.org) is the umbrella organisation of national and professional PR associations all over Europe.

- The Science, Technology, Engineering and Medicine Public Relations Association (website: http://www. stempra.org.uk).

2

Where PR sits with advertising and marketing

Over the years, companies' marketing communications (or comms) activities have increased in importance, becoming a key factor in our lives. Whether we create and send messages to the marketplace or receive (and react) to them, it's fair to say that 'comms' activities are part and parcel of our daily routines. A criticism aimed at marketing in general is that there are so many products and services competing for our attention that we're subjected to a barrage of chatter or 'noise'. This wall of noise is regarded by some as being all-pervasive and as interfering with how you conduct basic comms with your customers and prospects.

There are a variety of different comms techniques and tools (Figure 2.1), and they can be used to achieve a large number of differing objectives. The diagram is not exhaustive and the list of objectives is changing every day – often driven by new technological developments.

Many language theorists argue that written words are more powerful than spoken words. However, most marketers (academics and practitioners alike) believe that 'word of mouth' is the most powerful means of communication. This has now morphed into 'word of mouse' in the domain of blogs, social

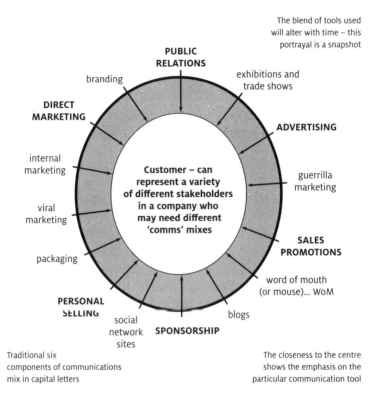

The blend of tools used will alter with time – this portrayal is a snapshot

PUBLIC RELATIONS

branding

exhibitions and trade shows

DIRECT MARKETING

ADVERTISING

internal marketing

guerrilla marketing

viral marketing

Customer – can represent a variety of different stakeholders in a company who may need different 'comms' mixes

packaging

SALES PROMOTIONS

word of mouth (or mouse)... WoM

PERSONAL SELLING

social network sites

SPONSORSHIP

blogs

Traditional six components of communications mix in capital letters

The closeness to the centre shows the emphasis on the particular communication tool

Figure 2.1 Expanded comms mix

network sites, public forums and comparison websites. In 2009, Twitter became the marketing channel of the chattering classes. Followers could read the tweets of supposed style leaders. Numerous celebrities then employed skilled communicators to tweet on their behalf – which seems to defeat the point. Hence, if you intend using such tools you'll need to develop an aptitude for understanding which tool, or combination of tools, will allow you to achieve your objectives.

Some authors use the term 'promotional mix', but this can be confusing as some customers (or prospects) may believe you're referring to 'sales promotions' rather than 'communication'. If you keep terms clean and simple, less confusion will result. Also,

promotion implies a monologue whereas 'comms' suggests a dialogue, which is healthier and in the long term more profitable.

PR and advertising

Let us consider the chapter title as a series of questions. That is, where does PR sit, say, with advertising? You'd think that this question would be simple to answer. However, as with most things in life, understanding how marketing works is more complex than most people initially believe.

When you watch advertisements on TV, it's often easier to remember the gimmick (eg the drumming gorilla) than the central message (eg the chocolate). Cunning puns and use of synonyms can avoid this (eg 'compare the meerkat' versus 'compare the market'), but often the message is lost. If you doubt this, try a quick exercise. Write down in the next 10 seconds the advert you saw yesterday that made the biggest impression on you. It doesn't have to be a favourable impression – just the one that really sticks in your memory. What was the brand? What was the central message the advertiser was trying to communicate? Now write down the adverts that preceded and followed your initial choice... Struggling? Join the club! It's an exercise that most people tend to struggle with. Why can't you remember a few ads and their central messages? This is a by-product of noise.

Hence, you need to develop (or buy in) the skills used by good communicators in order to realistically appreciate challenges presented by the aforementioned noise. You need to create comms that penetrate the all-pervading clutter so that your message is the key piece of communication your customers and prospects actually identify with, recall and respond to.

Some think PR stands apart from marketing, and certainly most business schools teach it as a stand-alone discipline with links to the CIPR. Leeds Business School has always had very close links with the CIPR and is deemed by many to be the leading PR higher education provider.

Some think PR leads a brand's comms and marketing activities, while others regard it as a key tool within the comms mix (Figure 2.1). Sadly, some see PR and marketing as oil and water – two disciplines divided by the same language, to paraphrase an old adage.

What do the marketers think of PR types?

According to the Chartered Institute of Marketing (CIM), PR can be defined as:

> [k]eeping good relations between a company or a group and the public so that people know what the company is doing and approve of it.
>
> *Dictionary of Marketing Terms*, 2003

Well, this is a nice enough start, if somewhat simplistic. How about PR is

> [t]he form of communication management that seeks to make use of publicity and other non-paid forms of promotion and information to influence the feelings, opinions, or beliefs about the company, its products or services, or about the value of the product or service or the activities of the organisation to buyers, prospects, or other stakeholders.
>
> *Dictionary of Marketing*, 2008

Again a pleasant enough definition that brings in the customers' perceptions of what you offer – which is, after all, what business is all about. The other stakeholders need a little more development, so how about: PR is a

> [c]onscious effort to improve and maintain an organisation's relationships with such publics as employees, customers,

shareholders, local communities, trade unions, with a view to strengthening reputation, ie building corporate image.

The CIM Marketing Directory, 1996

Now this is more like it. Marketers must consider the role of internal stakeholders and/or publics.

The idea of internal marketing (Figure 2.2) has long been discussed, and PR is a powerful tool for improving perceptions among your peers. It can counter misinformation and whispering campaigns, which are often based on gossip. As you know, a problem shared is a problem spread around the office! Some companies have taken draconian steps such as banning Facebook at work, purely with a view to controlling such internal 'noise'. Well, banning such tools can only be part of the solution, and stopping negativity is much easier when you have a positive message to fill the vacuum.

The reference to building relationships should chime with everyone as we all need to build relationships and not simply be transactional. We'll discuss this more in Chapter 6 when we consider PR as a tool for developing relationships with stakeholders through internal marketing.

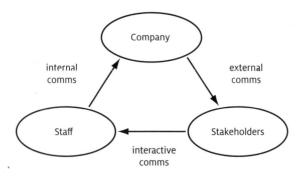

Figure 2.2 Communications links (adapted from Kotler *et al* (2005): 635)

Further to these definitions, the CIM website goes on to state that

Marketing is all about stakeholder communications, whether the stakeholders are customers, shareholders or employees of your organisation.

The phrase 'all about stakeholder communications' is the operative idea. Whether for someone who is predominantly a marketer or is predominantly a PR expert, this statement must ring true. The definition brings to the forefront the idea that PR is a key tool for communicating with your internal stakeholders.

So to answer the question, PR practitioners have the skills to provide solutions for, or with, marketers. The CIM has over 50,000 members worldwide. However, this is the tip of the (marketing) iceberg. Often these marketers are at board level and hold the budgets that PR agencies target, particularly in SMEs. Larger organisations often have directors of corporate communications, many of whom come from a PR background. Since marketing is 'all about stakeholder communications', then in truth PR practitioners and marketers are part of the same continuum and both serve the customer.

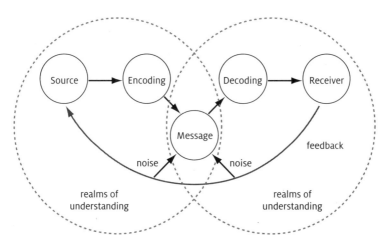

Figure 2.3 Model of communications (based on Schramm (1955) as cited in Shannon and Weaver (1962))

Always bear in mind that communication is a non-linear, continuous process (Figure 2.3). Why? Because as the world changes at what seems to be an increasing rate, the needs, wants and desires of our stakeholders and publics respond to these changes. Hence, so must our communication activities. Our messages need updating and, as stated earlier, technology has had a profound effect on this area of marketing. The nature and means of how we get our message to our receiver have never been more exciting with the options we now have available.

How do marketers use PR?

Well for a start, PR is more common than most people think. Let's consider a traditional marketing model to illustrate the usefulness of PR, namely the product life cycle (PLC) (Figure 2.4).

Every product is different, as is every PLC, and every new version of a product has a different PLC. Hence, the opportunities

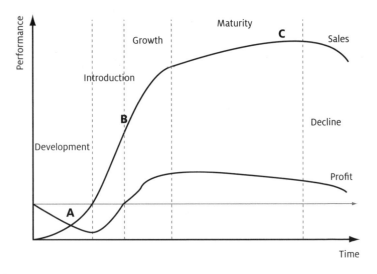

Figure 2.4 The generic product life cycle (PLC)

for PR are almost limitless, but let's consider the three scenarios depicted in Figure 2.4.

- *Zone A.* Your company is spending money developing and testing the product prior to release. Here you'd use press releases in publications relevant to your field. If it is a high-value product, you'd target top-of-the range magazines, possibly aiming to inform the early adopters. The campaign could be a teaser campaign or alternatively aimed at seeking input from opinion leaders and consumer leaders.
- *Zone B.* Your product has launched successfully and you want to extend the rapid growth so as to recoup more of your R&D costs. You may have set up social network sites and/or liaise with users' clubs. In either case, you'd seek testimonials explaining the benefits they've had from the products. You'd aim to feed positive feedback via the mass media as well as informing your customer base – that is, those clients who've so far held onto their old models. You could simply advertise. However, that's expensive and suffers from being 'marketer' dominant. That is, people expect you to say good things about your products but will gladly accept the word of real customers or other opinion formers.
- *Zone C.* You're seeking to extend the maturity section. Here you'd use PR to explain the reliability of your products. You'd recycle good feedback from magazines such as *Which?*, social network sites, user fora, comparison websites, and so on. If at all possible you'd want this to get into the mass media, so you may seek a new angle.

This principle of PR being a key tool for marketers is also evident in other models such as the diffusion-adoption curve and the new product development (NPD) process.

FAQ   Why do we need to know about opinion leaders and opinion formers?

People turn to others for support and guidance, therefore when you create your communications activities, you may reach others who are not the intended target. If they can influence the purchase, you need to draw them in so that they can support and ultimately influence the purchaser. The terms 'opinion formers' and 'opinion leaders' are what many marketers refer to when considering the communication process and the influence certain persons can have upon it.

An opinion former is somebody who, usually through their education and profession, has expertise to which you listen and respond. Think of it this way. If Toyota say, 'The new Toyota IQ is the best small car in the world', your reaction is usually muted as you expect them to say it (ie it's marketer-dominated information). If, however, Jeremy Clarkson of *Top Gear* fame says, 'The new Toyota IQ is the best small car in the world', the chances are that you'll listen to the message and (whether Jeremy denies it or not!) it will have more credibility. This is what we call non-marketer-dominated information and you trust it because Jeremy Clarkson is an opinion former or a maven. The reasons are as follows:

- **He has more knowledge in this area than you (or most people, for that matter).**
- **He has access to the latest cars and has test-driven more varieties than everyone you know put together.**
- **He is fiercely independent of the car manufacturer (as, by the way, is the magazine *Which?*).**

The combination of these attributes makes for a powerful communicator who can build trust and credibility for your brand. There's a risk, though, as you need to be confident that your product isn't going to be panned!

Opinion leaders have a social standing or closeness to us that lends their opinions credibility. Remember that a key *raison d'être* for your 'comms' is to support stakeholders, for example customers as they make purchase decisions, or colleagues who are

going through changes... and yes, you'll have internal opinion formers as well as external, as we'll discuss in more detail in Chapter 6.

Summary and activities

Key points

Before you decide which communication tools to use to deliver your message from sender to receiver, there are a number of factors to consider that will help you choose the most appropriate communication tools, and indeed the configuration of the message you send.

Questions

1. What does the term 'noise' mean?
2. Why is communication a process and not linear?
3. What is the difference between an opinion leader and an opinion former?

Activities

The CIM suggests the following, representing a small cross-section of PR websites that host a wealth of information:

- **PR and Marketing Network (website: http://www. prandmarketing.com). For the latest news and strategies in US PR and marketing. You need to subscribe to access the archives.**

- **10 Elements of an Effective Press Release (website: http://netpreneur.org/news/prmachine/pr/default.**

html). Part of the Netpreneur Exchange. It includes a link to a sample press release.

- The Public Relations Society of America (website: http://www.prsa.org).

- *O'Dwyer's PR Daily* (website: http://www.odwyerpr. com). Good for breaking US PR news, opinion and archived articles. It also has a directory of PR companies, 'counsellors' and service companies.

- PR Museum (website: http://prmuseum.com). Has excellent profiles of US PR 'gurus', plus a bibliography of books held at the Museum Library regarding the history of PR.

- The International Association of Business Communicators (website: http://www.iabc.com). A professional network of more than 13,000 business communication professionals in over 60 countries.

- The International Public Relations Association (website: http://www.ipra.org). Has a directory of PR associations worldwide, plus summaries of conference papers, but you have to be a member to gain access.

3

Understanding strategic public relations

Planning your PR activities is fundamental to success. If you only do PR because you think you should, without understanding why you're doing it, you could be wasting valuable resources, including time and money.

All consumers' opinions on the products or services they have bought and used are formed by direct experience, word of mouth, reading reviews and engaging in online discussions. Companies seeking to identify and manage consumers' perceptions may use PR to build awareness and influence our opinions. It's not a coincidence that global brands like McDonald's, Google, Virgin and BMW generate opinions, whether consumers engage with their products or not. Sustained PR campaigns, combined with other marketing initiatives, ensure that these brands remain dominant and 'manage' their reputation while controlling messages being discussed by stakeholders. This involves strategic thinking, including investment in planning, implementation and evaluation.

FAQ Why is planning important?
PR is most effective when it is considered, planned and evaluated on an ongoing basis. You may make some errors on the way but

you'll learn from these and build on your experiences, ultimately making PR work well for you. While simply reacting to industry needs may reap short-term rewards, PR is more effective if the your company takes a lead – that is, is proactive. It's worth taking time to stop the daily PR activities (responding to journalists' requests, staff, community groups, etc) and question how you benefit by only reacting.

Stop reacting. Get focused and be strategic in your PR activities.

Identify opportunities and plan ways of engaging with them to make sure you're maximising positive outcomes. A company that:

- **isn't ready to respond to the media will soon fall out of favour with them, resulting in poor relations with journalists, resulting in weak or no coverage in the press;**
- **proactively engages with the media, getting to know what kind of stories they're looking for (and their deadlines), is going to be asked to give comments and gain more positive press coverage;**
- **fails to explain (to its staff) what is happening in the company, such as new structures, products, achievements and business concerns. will demoralise and disengage its workforce with subsequent ramifications, such as absenteeism and poor customer relations;**
- **engages with employees through consultation, newsletters, e-mail updates, events and meetings will produce motivated and positive employees who understand the value of good customer relations and are proud to represent their organisation.**

Planning your PR

So whether your plan is short term, based around a specific event, or a long-term programme of activities that affects the whole business, the same principles apply. Good planning will improve

your understanding of why you're doing what you're doing. Planning allows you to:

- focus on what matters and ensure that time isn't wasted on unnecessary activities;
- say no to unplanned activities and be able to justify why you're not prepared to spend time and effort on unnecessary activities;
- create cohesion in short-, medium- and long-term activities;
- reflect on current activities that will influence and impact on longer-term activities;
- be more cost-effective, as you'll be able to demonstrate past achievements to create effective programmes of activity in the future;
- engage all stakeholder groups in a timely manner by identifying their needs, and opportunities to contribute to your plan;
- work proactively and be in control of the agenda, allowing you to identify issues and opportunities and plan actions to address them.

There are a number of key elements that must be considered before PR tactics are implemented. You must ask yourself:

- What is it we want to achieve?
- Why do we want to do it?
- How, where and when are we going to do it?
- Who is going to do it?
- What is our budget?

To address these elements it's wise to think strategically and adopt a plan (Figure 3.1), which we'll now discuss in more detail.

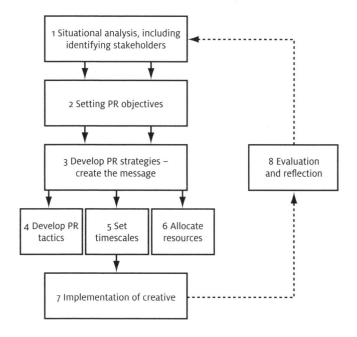

Figure 3.1 Strategic PR overview

Situation analysis, including identifying stakeholders (Stage 1)

In order to understand what needs addressing, you'll need to conduct a situational analysis by monitoring and understanding your external, uncontrollable environments (Figure 3.2). PESTEL is a widely used framework that you can use to conduct this analysis.

By monitoring your macro- and micro-environments objectively, you will better appreciate the challenges and opportunities available. This audit will enable you to develop a credible and effective PR plan based on clear objectives. It's best completed by an independent team who can provide input

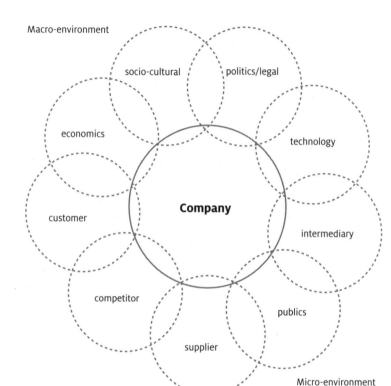

Figure 3.2 Situational analysis

effectively and quickly. Remember, all audits are inherently
political, so the team will need support from the top.

Let's consider the PESTEL framework in more detail:

- *Political*: including areas such as tax policy, employment
  laws, environmental regulations, trade restrictions and
  reform, tariffs and political stability.
- *Economic*: economic growth or decline, interest rates,
  exchange rates and inflation rate, wage rates, minimum
  wage, working hours, unemployment (local and national),
  credit availability, cost of living, etc.

- *Socio-cultural*: cultural norms and expectations, health consciousness, population growth rate, age distribution, career attitudes, emphasis on safety, global warming.
- *Technological*: new technologies are continually being developed and the rate of change itself is increasing. Things that were not accessible until recently are now mainstream, eg mobile phone marketing, blogs, social networking websites.
- *Environmental* aspects: changing expectations, eg use of fuel, recycling, waste.
- *Legal*: may impact employment, access to materials, quotas, resources, imports/exports, taxation, etc.

Having carried out a thorough analysis of your macro-environment, you must also monitor your micro-environment to identify recent strengths and weaknesses with which you can address identified macro-opportunities and threats (Figure 3.3).

This illustrates how the components of the SWOT impact upon one another. Your analyses should produce a wealth of useful, detailed information (Figure 3.4).

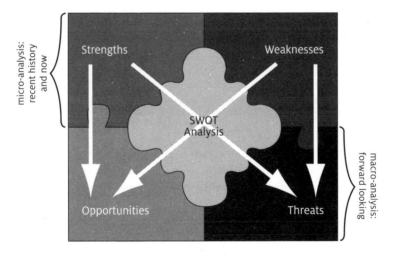

Figure 3.3 SWOT analysis showing how elements are interlinked

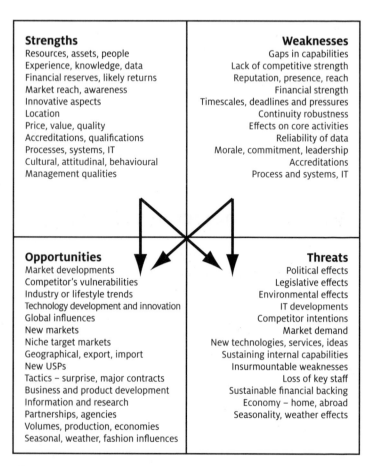

Figure 3.4 Populated SWOT analysis showing how elements interact

From Figure 3.4 you can start to see how the SWOT analysis could identify patterns and trends that will influence your PR programme. It can be used for strategic planning (eg acquisition opportunities, entering new markets, investment opportunities) or marketing planning (eg product development and launches, research). It can be from departmental or individual perspectives, looking at what you deliver to whom and how you do it. To be effective, it needs to be undertaken regularly as organisations that carry out regular SWOT analyses often spot trends before others,

thus providing competitive advantage. It's worth remembering that SWOT analyses are snapshots at one specific time.

Analysis at this broad level will inform the direction you choose to work towards, helping to set clear objectives at corporate, campaign or project levels. PR may be one element used to help you fulfil your objectives at a corporate level, hence PR objectives must be aligned with corporate objectives. Many PR practitioners contribute to the bigger picture. This is when PR is at its most effective, fully integrated into the strategic direction of the organisation.

Setting PR objectives (Stage 2)

Identifying key objectives provides a platform and achievable goals for your PR activities; they are most effective if small in number, concise and SMART (Table 3.1).

Table 3.1 SMART objectives

Objective	Comments
Specific	Avoid being either too vague or too tightly focused.
Measurable	Always ensure you can measure the success of the objective.
Accurate (some say 'Aspirational' or 'Achievable')	Don't set a wish-list as nothing demotivates staff more quickly than imposed targets that can't be met.
Realistic	How probable is it that the objective will effect changes?
Timely (some say 'Targeted')	Depending on resources, identify the time when your objectives need may mean modifying, simplifying or being made more specific.

PR objectives are usually set at one of three levels:

1. *Raising awareness.* The family history website findmypast.com launched a service with The National Archives which made 36 million census records of people living in England and Wales in 1911 available online. Its PR objective was to generate public awareness of the launch of 1911census.co.uk.
2. *Altering attitudes and opinions. Collins English Dictionary* wanted to change the way dictionary editions are launched by showing that people, not academics, are able to create words that appear in the dictionary, hence making them more accessible to the general public.
3. *Changing behaviour.* The climate change charity Global Cool launched a PR drive to get more people to use public transport by targeting festival-goers.

Examples of PR objectives might include:

- **raising your profile;**
- **altering the attitudes and opinions of key stakeholders;**
- **increasing your market share.**

Developing PR strategies: creating the message (Stage 3)

Strategies are the broad methods chosen to achieve your objectives. They do not include details of courses of action that will be followed on a daily basis; these are tactics. It is important to understand what strategies are and how they differ from tactics.

Strategies can be derived from the SWOT analysis (Figure 3.4) in the form of a TOWS analysis (Table 3.2). Typical strategies could be:

- **SO1: raising your profile in the media by engaging more with journalists as part of a media campaign;**

Table 3.2 TOWS analysis

Strategies	Urgency	Probability	Impact	Total
SO1	3	3	3	9
SO2	3	3	2	8
SO3	3	2	3	8
WO1	2	2	2	6
WO2	2	2	1	5
WO3	2	2	1	5
ST1	3	2	3	8
ST2	2	2	2	6
ST3	2	1	1	4
WT1	2	2	1	5
WT2	2	1	1	4
WT3	1	1	1	3

- SO2: lobbying MPs to change the tax rates for small businesses;
- SO3: boosting product sales or service take-up, eg increase podcast downloads;

- ST: engaging more people in your online newsletter;
- ST2: educating your staff regarding new products;

- WT1: engaging in research that will allow you to use your strengths to counter weaknesses;
- WT2: developing a social media campaign to target hitherto unreachable youth segments.

Key messages

Every PR campaign or strategy needs a set of messages that convey the main focus of the communication. They will help to inform and influence opinion, so must be clear, concise and easily understood. When deciding what your messages should say, you must first identify your target audience. This will determine how technical or simple the messages should be. You may be required to develop a suite of messages to suit a range of different audiences. In each case the underlying message will be similar or the same, just said in a different way to appeal to the relevant audiences.

Messages must also be highly credible, and are often delivered alongside advertising to reinforce the messages. Any hint of verbose claims or badly researched statistics will damage the credibility of the message and the overall campaign, and subsequently your reputation.

Sub-messages can be used to reinforce the main message. For example, Tesco's 'Every little helps' message is reinforced with product-line messages on value; Marks & Spencer's message on quality is reinforced with product-line messages on quality.

Consideration must also be made on how to present the message. What tone, context and format you choose will each impact on how the message is interpreted. You won't be able to control all of these elements but should consider them as part of your situational analysis.

Example

In spring 2009, Waitrose advertised its 'branded products', which are 'value' products in consideration of the public mood during the credit crunch. This advertising message was reinforced with articles in the press about Waitrose's range of value products. Similarly, the car industry is attempting to appeal to the environmentally conscious public with ranges of 'fuel-efficient' vehicles.

Developing PR tactics (Stage 4)

The strategy is 'how' you will achieve your objectives. Having a clear strategy will keep the tactics focused on a particular area such as media relations, internal communications, social media or community relations. The tactics may have been tried and tested or create an opportunity to experiment within a focused environment.

Messages must be credible and able to match your levels of persuasion as identified in your objective setting. You must consider the following:

- *Format.* **Consider how messages are to be delivered – using words, songs, slogans, photos or images? What font and size? They must fit your overall identity and existing profile, unless you are undertaking a radical relaunch.**
- *Tone and context.* **Adopt an appropriate mood, which, depending on your audience, may be upbeat or sombre. It may reflect the general mood of the nation. For example, in a recession, banks are showing restraint by sending out messages about safe investments, rather than encouraging people to take out irresponsibly large loans.**
- *Newsworthiness.* **Your messages must communicate something worthwhile and of benefit to your audience. What may interest you (say a message full of jargon) may not be appropriate to a mainstream audience, but may be suitable for a trade or technical audience, including clients, suppliers, investors and the like.**

Developing tactics could be considered as the creative, fun part of the planning process and implementation. Indeed, many PRs' reputations are gained from the success of their creative ideas and tactics. The key question to ask, once you've established your aims and objectives, is 'What are we going to do to achieve them?' Your strategy might identify the need for a media campaign, but 'what are we actually going to do?' to achieve a successful media campaign involves developing tactics.

Basing tactics on a media campaign – for example, where you are going to increase your coverage in trade publications or the quality newspapers – involves asking yourself a series of questions:

- **What can we do to stand out from our competitors so journalists will notice us?**
- **Is a simple press release enough or does it need some sort of gimmick, incentive or product sample to go with it?**
- **Who are the journalists we want to target and why?**
- **How are we going to contact them?**
- **What shall we do to make sure they have received and understood our message?**

Setting timescales (Stage 5)

Consider the events surrounding your messages. For example, if you're launching a campaign with messages of festive cheer via the media, you'll need to be know when to send them as monthly publications have a three-month lead-in and come out the month prior to their dated publication. By August it may be too late to send out messages of Christmas cheer via monthly magazines, but it will be too early for weekly and daily publications.

Allocating resources (Stage 6)

If you don't have a dedicated PR practitioner in your organisation, you'll need to identify who is going to implement and monitor the strategy. Maybe you're confident enough to have a go yourself, or you could use existing staff within marketing, sales or broader communications roles.

An alternative is to speak to local or national PR agencies, depending on your sector. Many companies work with agencies because of their good contacts with the press, or their understanding of specific sectors or industry knowledge. In Chapter 10 we'll discuss PR costs further.

Implementing the creative (Stage 7)

You must know your audience – that is, at whom you're aiming your messages. This might include different stakeholder groups from customers (existing and potential), investors, competitors, staff, local communities, trade unions and decision-makers such as MPs, councillors and professional bodies. Stakeholder mapping is regularly used to identify different groups of individuals who form your stakeholder profile. You need to consider who has, and who might have, influence and power over your business and objectives.

Many companies rightly focus much time and effort on customers. However, PR covers a broad range of stakeholders, including groups who are 'dormant', 'active' and 'passive'. The role of engagement with these groups may change and evolve, depending on both your and their activities. If your business wants to expand its premises, it will need to consider not only existing customers but also your staff and the communities you might impact on with building development, as well as town planners and councillors (discussed in more detail in Chapter 6).

Evaluation and reflection (Stage 8)

You must understand the benefit of your PR activities, and hence your investment of time and money must be evaluated to ensure that you're achieving your PR objectives and that your strategies and tactics are effective. In Chapter 10 we'll discuss costs and evaluation in more detail. However, the following examples provide insights into evaluation and how to conduct it effectively. You'll notice there's a value to the PR activity that has taken place that's based on how much it would cost to advertise in the publications that featured the free coverage.

Example 1: 'The pigs are worth it'

Objective: To save the British pig industry following a disastrous wheat harvest that meant pig farmers faced high feed prices and crippling losses.

Strategy: To reflect the very high standards of animal welfare in British pig farming, the crisis the industry faced and to put pressure on supermarkets to raise the price they paid for pigs via a PR-led campaign that included lobbying the relevant minister and the public.

Tactics: Activities ranged from a report into the effect of feed prices, to pig farmers recording an anthem. The 'Pig-o-meter Tour' featured a giant pig counting farmers' mounting losses, and a rally on Downing Street involving hundreds of farmers. 'Winnie the Pig' culminated in the presentation of a 13,000-signature petition. Media backing underpinned widespread support from MPs. There was a London Underground poster campaign. A report on high feed prices was presented to journalists and MPs. The report *Is the Government Buying British?* called on the public sector to buy British. There was a 'Celebrity chefs "choose pork"' promotion, with trade publication coverage to put pressure on retailers. There was support from Jamie Oliver with the Channel 4 documentary *Jamie Saves Our Bacon* in January 2009.

Evaluation: The price paid for pigs rose from £1.06 per kilogram to the target £1.40 per kilogram, with consumer purchases remaining strong. This amounted to an extra £5.1 million per week for the industry. The campaign reached an audience of 104 million through the print media coverage alone and an additional 18.6 hours of television and radio coverage. The government established a 'Pig Industry Task Force'.

Example 2: Relaunch of football pools by Sportech
Objective: To relaunch the 85-year-old brand, communicate the social responsibility message of £1.1 billion donated by the organisation to the arts and good causes
Strategy: To reach to a new mainstream using a media campaign that brought the arts and football together.
Tactics: Teamed up with English National Ballet, who choreographed and performed *The Beautiful Game*, which was showcased to the media following a poll by fans of the top 10 iconic moments of football history. More than 20,000 football fans took part in the poll, via The New Football Pools website, which was also seeded or linked into 180 websites, fan sites, blogs and online forums.
Evaluation: Sportech reported a 39 per cent increase in full-year profit for 2008 due to the relaunch activity. Over 100 pieces of coverage, including spreads in five national newspapers, with a media value of £1.1 million.

Summary and activities

Key points

- You must continuously monitor your macro- and micro-environments in order to identify patterns and trends that will influence your PR programme.
- Use PR to engage your employees through consultation, newsletters, e-mail updates, events and meetings; they'll be more likely to achieve competitive advantage via increased customer satisfaction.
- Good planning will help you to understand why you are doing what you are doing, whether you are involved with short- or long-term PR programmes.
- Every PR campaign or strategy needs a set of messages that convey the main focus of the communication. The

strategy is 'how' you will achieve your objectives. Tactics should be closely linked to the strategy. Having a clear strategy will keep the tactics focused on a particular area.

- Having a set of clear messages aligned with the corporate or campaign objectives will also help to evaluate the success objectives. Measuring media coverage in relation to whether the key messages are being or were conveyed is a great way to determine success. A set of vague or numerous messages may result in vague results.

Questions

1. What are the factors in the macro-environment?
2. Identify the parties that create your micro-environment.
3. Why is the micro-environment partly controllable?
4. Why monitor the macro-environment?

Activities

Always look at the BBC website (http://www.bbc.co.uk) and the national broadsheet newspapers (eg www.timesonline. co.uk) to keep an eye on movements in the environment. Reading magazines/books/articles such as *The Economist* (http://www.economist.com) is also helpful.

4

Working with the media

Anyone who regularly reads or listens to the news will be aware that it's a bit like storytelling in a very restricted amount of time. The biggest challenge in working with the media is understanding what makes a news story and how to communicate it to journalists. For many PR practitioners, media relations and writing for the media is the main focus of their work, taking up most their time. Much effort goes into developing good relationships with journalists. Media relations is highly valued as a PR tool because of its impartiality; journalists are largely impartial and objective, they look at a story from all angles and generally their reporting is considered to be factual and credible.

For companies wanting to be featured in newspapers, trade publications, radio or television and, increasingly, online news pages, the two main options are to pay for advertising or to generate free coverage through PR or media relations.

Advertising

Advertising may be regarded as 'pay to play' and PR as 'pray to play'. Advertising involves guaranteed placement, using the words

and images supplied by the individual or organisation that is paying for the advert.

Media relations

PR involves working with journalists to generate news items that are verified and edited by journalists. Journalists usually write the news article based on a news release or news story that may require further investigation and is usually more considered, more objective and written by a third party, lacking in biased information. The placement of the news item in this form is free.

As more of us get our news online and watch delayed TV, merrily skipping adverts, more companies are switching from advertising to PR. The public have grown up with advertising and are increasingly cynical about the messages they receive via adverts. Today's public are more inclined to trust words written by a journalist.

The media

Newspapers and consumer magazines

Journalists are very busy, working to tight deadlines in an increasingly challenging environment with many newspapers experiencing declining sales and readership. The internet is the main challenger to the newspaper industry; as soon as a newspaper is printed, many of its news stories are out of date. They are increasingly becoming opinion papers, with journalists commenting on the news rather than 'breaking' the news. However, they are still influential and many have invested heavily in their online news websites, which are increasingly interactive and dependent on 'citizen journalism', with the public often reporting the news as it happens.

Trade publications

Trade newspapers, of which there are thousands, include weekly, fortnightly, monthly and quarterly magazines and specialise in a particular subject, sector or trade. Whether your business supplies pigeon feed to pigeon fanciers, nuts and bolts to the building trade or hair products to supermarkets, there'll be a trade publication for you. It will be supplied to and read by your target audience, customers and prospects alike, reporting industry news and developments, new entrants or alternatively businesses in decline. It will report on industry trends and opinion leaders' views on the future, and will generally provide a forum to review and report on what matters to its readers, who are its key stakeholders.

Television and radio

'Broadcast' media offers a variety of opportunities for publicity, from daytime chat shows to current affairs news programmes and a range of options in between. The huge number of different programmes on radio and television available through satellite and cable channels, as well as more specialist programmes, means these options should be targeted carefully. Consideration must be given to the 'lead-in time', meaning how much notice is required by editors for the development of programmes, and to how the programme makers gather their content. Most news channels, for example, will have a forward features desk with events and dates pencilled in well in advance, but there's always the opportunity for more current news to 'bump' or 'push' these features off the agenda. A phone call to the news editor is advisable. For example, for a 6 pm TV news programme the news agenda will often be decided at a morning planning meeting, so put a call in early to make sure your news item is discussed.

How to gain media coverage

News releases

Most journalists receive hundreds of e-mails daily containing 'news stories' or news releases. Many are full of grammatical and spelling errors, while others lack relevance for the media outlet or region they target, or simply are not newsworthy. Yet despite the challenges journalists face in dealing with huge numbers of news releases, they offer the most effective way to get media coverage for your company.

A news release should not be any longer 300 words, with any supplementary information being placed at the end of the release. A clear heading should explain to a journalist succinctly what the main theme of the story is, for example 'Barack Obama voted first black US president'.

The first paragraph should contain the main elements of the story – the five Ws: who, what, where, when and why as well as how. If all these elements are relevant, the journalist should be able to answer them via a combination of the headline and the first paragraph. Supporting information will then be contained within the remaining text. PR practitioners refer to the 'inverted pyramid' (Figure 4.1) to help identify and prioritise the crucial elements of a news release.

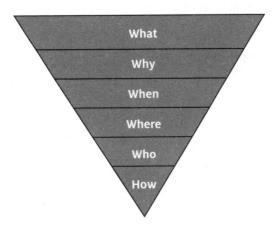

Figure 4.1 Inverted pyramid

Testing the five Ws

The following details a headline and opening paragraph for a variety of news releases issued by recognised brands:

Example 1: Olympic Park opens its doors to 4,000 Londoners for Open House Weekend

11 August 2009   The Olympic Delivery Authority (ODA) is aiming to break last year's record number of visitors to the Olympic Park as part of Open House London, the capital's largest architectural showcase.

Example 2: HSBC raises stake in Bank Ekonomi to over 98 per cent

HSBC has completed a mandatory tender offer (MTO) for the remaining 10.11 per cent of the shares of PT Bank Ekonomi Raharja Tbk (Bank Ekonomi).

Example 3: Over 500 voluntary organisations helped through the recession by £15 million fund

Today, 26 Aug 2009, 558 frontline charities and voluntary organisations across the country will receive grants worth up to £40,000 to help them provide vital community services during the recession.

News is about human interest

Most news stories have a human interest element, especially those used in the consumer media. Give your release a human element by including quotes or include a human angle by including a relevant experience of, say, a customer, employee or MD/CEO. You may want to include more than one quote, which is quite common, but any words you add to a release, whether in the general copy or attributed to an individual, must add to the news element. Do not simply repeat within a quote what you've already said in the main body of the release.

When using quotes, make sure you have the permission of the quoted individual. They'll want to see what you've attributed to them or may want to write it themselves. It's also important that the person quoted in a news release is available to talk to the press in case the press want to verify the quote or gain some further information from them.

Using bullet points or diagrams can be useful to present information more succinctly and also help to break up the paragraphs of a release. Note that news releases:

- **must be brief and well written;**
- **unlike most storytelling, start with the conclusion;**
- **must contain a clear title, date and contact information of the sender, including e-mail address and phone number;**
- **use quotations to give a human interest angle;**
- **use bullet points or diagrams to display information effectively;**
- **must be checked for errors before sending.**

Practical hints and tips

Structure of a news release
The following represents a typical news release:

- **Date: current – even yesterday is dated!**
- **clear heading – factual, not too creative;**
- **tense: present tense – is rather than has;**
- **200–300 words, double line-spaced;**
- **quotation in third or fourth paragraph;**
- **short paragraphs with short, sharp sentences;**
- **clear 'end' of news release;**
- **clear named contact details;**
- **further notes to editor.**

Five things you should not do
Figure 4.2 summarises common key mistakes that you should avoid. Let's discuss these in more detail:

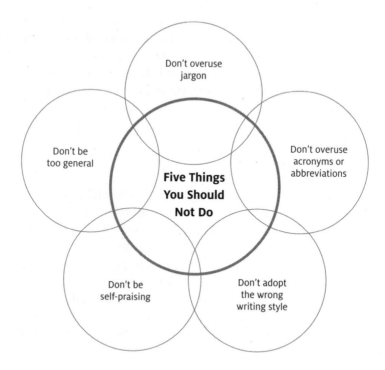

Figure 4.2 Five things you should not do

- Don't overuse jargon, except perhaps in small-circulation academic, scientific or industry journals that have very exclusive readerships. The use of jargon should be avoided as it prevents understanding.
- Don't overuse acronyms or abbreviations. Use them only where they are essential. They must always be written in full the first time they are used unless they are so commonplace that their meaning will be immediately understood, for example MP, CEO.
- Don't adopt the wrong writing style. Releases, case studies, features, reports and trade literature all have characteristic writing styles. Copy length, tone and presentation must fit the style of communication.

- **Don't be too general.** Copy written for a general audience cannot appeal to personal experience and will not retain the attention or engage the thoughts of readers.
- **Don't be self-praising.** Copy that is heavy on adjectives and self-praise often creates the opposite impression because of its lack of substance and credibility.

Feature articles

Most printed publications run feature articles as well as news articles. Often written by PR people in conjunction with journalists, feature articles are longer than news releases. They vary from 500 to 1,500 words and usually involve more comment and opinion as well as being accompanied by photographs or other visual aids. They are often more considered than a news item, so it's advisable to discuss the development of a feature article with a journalist in advance. Features are usually exclusively written for a target audience via one media outlet, for example a trade magazine or a particular national or regional newspaper.

Phone or e-mail a journalist?

How are you going to make sure the journalist reads your news release? Writing a news release can be the easy part; targeting it effectively so you get some coverage is more challenging.

As news releases are usually included in the main body of e-mails to journalists rather than as attachments, they must be brief and written effectively. It's important that your release stands out with an attention-grabbing headline in the e-mail title to entice them to open your e-mail. More important still, make sure you target your release to the correct journalist. As well as a general news desk, most media outlets have journalists working on specialist areas such as business, science, education, health, features and sport, to name but a few. It is worth becoming very familiar with the format, and names of journalists who will be most interested in your area of business.

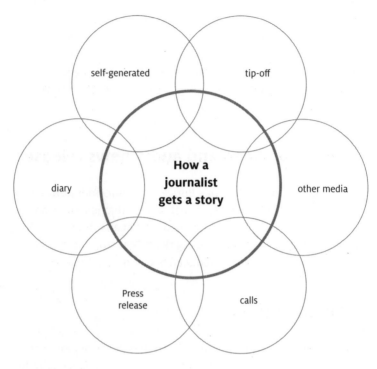

Figure 4.3 How a journalist gets a story

Building relationships with journalists is a good investment of your time as it will maximise opportunities of media coverage. Most journalists will welcome a phone call to introduce yourself or your organisation. If they're busy with deadlines, they'll usually tell you so and suggest a better time to call. They may also welcome the opportunity to meet you, either formally or informally to discuss how you can contribute to their news gathering.

Once you have made these contacts and built these relationships, it can be beneficial to have a chat with your contact to discuss up-and-coming news items in advance of sending or even writing a news release. You can ask their opinion as to what is most likely to be covered and they will advise on what you should focus on in order to maximise your coverage.

It is always worth considering what else is being discussed in the news, what's topical! Can your company or colleagues comment on national or regional issues, or can they bring a regional angle to a national story? Remember, journalists may be busy on other news stories, in which case don't waste your story. Save it until it's more appropriate.

Timing of video and audio news releases

If it's the day of the Chancellor's Budget announcements, don't send a release or call a journalist with a story that isn't relevant to this important event. Your item may not be of any interest to the journalist and it may get lost among the bigger story. It may not gain any coverage at all or be reduced to a NIB (news in brief).

Whom to target?

Most SMEs will have a news publication that they'll aspire to be featured in; this could be the regional or local newspaper, a trade publication or a business magazine. The most effective way to get your company featured is to understand what the journalists are seeking, what sort of stories they write about, what writing style they use and how frequently the publication appears.

Example
Netto saw 6.6 per cent growth between August 2007 and August 2009. It overcame its discount image of a store stocked with unexciting, unfamiliar European products. The store targeted journalists on consumer magazines and national newspapers with new products and requested that the store be referred to as a 'supermarket' rather than a discount store. New stores were opened, with special events

to attract local shoppers. Consumers were educated to view Netto as a contender to the established supermarkets via targeted PR activities.

What to say?

Having identified your target publication, you must consider what you want to say. Keep it simple! Don't overcomplicate things by trying to say too much; one or two key messages are most appropriate. Most news articles are of fewer than 250 words and aimed at audiences with far less knowledge of your product or service than you, so make sure you use appropriate language. The use of technical words and phrases might be appropriate for a trade publication but considered as jargon and over-complicated if targeted at the regional newspapers.

How to say it?

Reading the publications that you want to feature in will help you to understand what sort of stories are featured, how long the items tend to be, how frequently the publication is printed, what sort of variety of articles are usually featured and any special features that are coming up that you might want to contribute to or comment on.

Ask yourself questions like: What will the readers already know? How much background information do I need to supply to help them understand the value of the story? How long will they be prepared to spend reading my story?

When to say it?

If a publication is printed daily, then it's essential that you understand the deadlines a journalist might be working towards

and when he or she will be most receptive to your e-mail or phone call. For weekly, monthly and quarterly publications it's advisable to speak to journalists and find out what their deadlines are.

Whom to say it to?

Most journalists like to receive information by e-mail, although it is a challenge to make sure your e-mail is read by them, because of the large volume they receive every day. A way to overcome this is to ring them in advance to let them know you are sending them an e-mail. Take this opportunity to discuss the content of your story with them and to check they'll be happy to receive it. They may advise you to send it to a specific journalist or ask for some key bits of information to be included, such as a quotation from a named person in the company or a photograph to go with the story.

Why are you saying it?

A news release must be relevant and current to the reader. Newspapers survive on being able to target stories appropriately to their audiences and they are dependent on receiving a good supply of information in order to maintain their edge over their competitors. Stories must include elements of news or surprise as they must inform and enlighten the reader. Reflecting on the value of your news story is very important, and it's always better to wait until you really have some news rather than sending regular news releases.

Use of photography and images

You can maximise the impact of your news release by illustrating it with images or photographs. Take a good look at the publication

you want to feature in; what sort of images does it use, how are photos or images used?

Most readers of news publications glance at the photo and headline before deciding whether the article is worth reading, so make your photos stand out! A good photo or image can mean your story is featured in a more prominent place within the publication. Readers' attention will be drawn towards a photo story within the first three pages and in a central position or at the top right hand of the page, rather than as a NIB. NIBs are the short articles with no images, featured in a column down the left- or right-hand side of the page.

Many companies have a selection of stock images which they may use regularly to go with news stories, or they may commission a set of photographs to go with a specific story. The key is to make the photo illustrate the story accurately and creatively.

Before you send a journalist a photograph, make sure he or she has the capacity to receive it; the journalist may ask you to send it directly to the 'picture desk'. You must make sure the photo can be identified. Give it the same name as your news release, and provide a list, from left to right, of the individuals in the photos. Check that their names are spelled correctly!

Dos and don'ts for photography

Let's now consider some best practices and typical pitfalls.

Further to the pitfalls (Table 4.1), don't fall foul of the 'lamp-post effect' in which respected managers are unwittingly turned into comedy figures with antennae coming out of the tops of their heads. Also try to avoid the 'James Purnell' effect; he was famously Photoshopped into a photo after he missed an official NHS photoshoot in Manchester in 2007. It looks tacky and very obvious when you try to amend or alter images in this way – not to mention being a PR own goal, as the press made hay at the time.

Table 4.1 Dos and don'ts

Dos

- Think about who and what you want to feature in the photo.
- Consider the backdrop carefully. Office shots can be boring; logos and backdrops can be over the top and more appropriate for advertising material than news stories.
- Make the photo as interactive and relevant as possible. Have people doing something relevant to the story rather than simply posing.
- Consider paying a professional photographer to take the photo; they usually have an hourly charge, so it's worth getting a variety of photos taken to make it worthwhile.
- Negotiate standard hourly charges for photographers. These can range from £100 for general professional photographers to several thousand pounds for specialist photographers.
- Ask what else the photographs could be used for, such as your website, corporate literature and publications, promotional materials, exhibition displays, posters and recoil stands for events or the reception area.
- Make the photo work hard for you!

Don'ts

- Don't have too many people in the photo; three is usually sufficient.
- Don't try to please everyone who might want to be in the photo. You can always have a group photo at the end of the photoshoot to please those who feel they should be included and perhaps include these images in corporate literature or on the intranet or website.
- Don't have people standing in a line, handing over a cheque or certificate. Photos like this are banned from most publications as too hammy, and they look very dull.
- Don't take photos inside if they could be taken outside. Most photos come out better if set up outside where the lighting is usually better, so be flexible. Have your photos taken outside if possible but inside if the weather is unsuitable.
- Don't take photos of people sitting behind a desk. Again these are very dull.
- Don't have a backdrop that lets down the photo. Consider the surroundings carefully.

Working with celebrities

As the media and the public continue to be intrigued by 'celebrities' and the consumer magazines continue to thrive, many companies are using celebrities to promote their products or services. This approach can work well for many brands, especially if there is a real synergy between brand and celebrity.

Example 1

Outdoor retailer Berghaus opened its first retail store in September 2007 with explorer Sir Chris Bonington abseiling and unzipping two pieces of branded fabric covering the store frontage, revealing it to the crowd. While this created an exciting opportunity for the shoppers, it primarily provided a great photo-opportunity for the media, and the story was used widely in the press, with 'higher than expected' footfall in the store as well as increased takings recorded in the first month.

Example 2

The Meningitis Research Foundation has a number of high-profile celebrities who act as patrons, including the actor Ewan McGregor, James Dyson, TV doctor Hilary Jones, soccer legend Pat Jennings, and David and Victoria Beckham. Patrons agree to support the charity and get involved in fundraising activities and promotions. All of these celebrities will have a good understanding of the condition from personal contact with those affected by meningitis. Victoria Beckham contracted viral meningitis in 2000.

Example 3

Sir Clive Woodward helped Johnson and Johnson Vision Care promote eye testing with its Hero Campaign for Hero Brands

awareness campaign, which aimed to spread the message that an eye examination can help people perform 'to the best of their ability'. The company also did a TV tour with heptathlete Kelly Sotherton and a radio tour with mixed doubles badminton pair Gail Emms and Nathan Robertson. The campaign was covered by the BBC programme *Breakfast*, Sky News, *The Times*, the *Daily Mail*, the *Daily Telegraph*, *The Guardian*, *Metro*, Eurosport and Setanta. The magazine *Optician* reported a 4 per cent annual rise in eye tests in 2008.

Example 4
Shelter Scotland lobbied the Scottish administration and generated a 'gift for journalists on a tabloid paper' when it developed a campaign fronted by bands Idlewild and the Wombats to encourage 18- to 24-year-olds to press for the enforcement of legislation that every homeless person in Scotland will have the right to a permanent home by 2012.

This celebrity culture has provided a healthy income for celebrities from all walks of life; contenders on *Dragons' Den*, *Big Brother* and other reality TV shows are used to promote a range of businesses and products as well as speak at events. Their degree of success affects how much they charge. Expect to pay anything from their train fare to a photoshoot to £30,000 for their involvement in endorsing your brand.

If you can build a relationship with these individuals and create a real synergy with them, you should be able to find a celebrity who will recognise the opportunities that their contribution makes to your organisation and their reputation without your having to pay too much for their services.

Celebrity endorsement can also damage your reputation, and organisations must be quick to back away from a celebrity who might bring them into disrepute by association. A drunk sportsperson, a cocaine-snorting model or an actor swearing publicly can quickly become headline news for all the wrong

reasons, so you must make sure your celebrity has a squeaky-clean record and no skeletons in the closet!

Summary and activities

Key points

- The biggest challenge to working with the media is understanding what makes a news story and how to communicate it to journalists.
- Journalists are busy people who work to tight deadlines in an increasingly challenging environment. However, they offer the most effective way to get coverage for your company in the media.
- Most news stories, particularly those in the consumer media, include human interest elements by incorporating one or more quotes, or a human angle such as customer or employee experiences.

Questions

1. What are the key elements that help to make up a news release?
2. How would you approach the media to cover your story?
3. What sort of visuals help to make a good story great?

Activities

When you're reading the newspaper, distinguish between news articles and feature articles. See whether you can spot which news articles are driven by a news release. Test this out by taking a look at the websites of those detailed in the article to see whether there is a press release to match with the newspaper article. It may not be exactly the same but it may have prompted the article.

Vary the newspapers and news websites you read so you can get a feel for the types of articles that appear to appeal to different audiences.

Explore how many trade publications are relevant to your sector and which ones most fit your line of business. Read them on a regular basis and identify key journalists you might like to target with a news release.

Look critically at the photographs that accompany news articles. Can you spot why they have been used? Do they tell the story without your having to read the article?

Take a look at some FTSE 100 companies or competitors in your sector to see what sort of media relations they are engaging in. Most will have a press or media website from their homepage website.

5

PR and developments in online communications

The internet, especially Web 2.0, has revolutionised how companies communicate with stakeholders. Websites are not like 'brochures' any more; they're about engagement and constantly develop to ensure visitors are kept interested. Their reach and ability to be personalised mean that those who have recognised the potential are busy engaging with global communities.

The newspaper industry was among the first industries to appreciate the benefits of the social media era. Nowadays, companies are increasingly utilising online PR activities via blogs and social media sites, such as Facebook, LinkedIn and Twitter. Engaging with stakeholders via interactive websites generates feedback and consumer contributions via discussions that may influence their brand choices. While there is a definite set of 'most popular' social media sites, we don't know what tomorrow's technology or 'fad' may be – but we do know that companies which do not engage with stakeholders online risk being discussed on social networking sites for all the wrong reasons.

Managing your reputation online

The risks associated with a lack of online engagement include publics discussing your brand in a negative way, which may gather pace, attracting large global audiences and ultimately damaging your brand. It's impossible to stop people talking about your brand. Indeed, it could be just the sort of positive PR you require, but in order to maximise it you must monitor and contribute to discussions, correcting errors and acting on feedback, both good and bad. It can take companies many years to build reputations that can be destroyed in minutes by disgruntled bloggers. Managing your reputation online is essential to protecting your brand and business from criticism and scrutiny.

In 2007, Google added blogs to its search engine criteria. Blogs allow users to write web pages and make them available to the public. Some companies have internal blogs or member-only blogs. There are millions of blogs that have been created by people who understand that with a bare minimum of knowledge they can make any information or view public. Most blogs allow readers to add comments to their blog 'posting'. Blogs are updated more regularly than websites, hence when someone 'Googles' a subject, the websites that appear on the first page are usually a selection of weblogs. Subsequently, any disgruntled clients who 'blog' about your business will come higher in Google searches than your own 'static' website. This encourages others to enter these blogs before they enter your site, especially if they are looking for reviews, hence the seeds of damage have been sown. Prospects who read bad reviews may avoid purchasing your products or services.

Maximising your reach

You'll seek to maximise your Google ranking to draw consumers to your site. This requires regular editing of your site, linking it to other sites, including blogs and social network sites. The resulting increase in 'hits' raises your Google ranking. The most obvious way to manage your online reputation is to Google your name, website name or

product name frequently, making sure that nothing undesirable appears. Use online tools like Google Alerts to automate this process. Constantly enhancing and updating your website, developing links to other active social sites, will see your address increasingly embedded in a range of sites, and so the links grow, as do the opportunities to reach new audiences. Remember, you must maintain your Google ranking by updating and interacting with such sites regularly.

The power of bloggers

Transparency is crucial in order to be credible and earn respect. Some PR practitioners have rightly been criticised by internet users for contributing to online discussions that support their products or clients without declaring their interest. This is seen as unethical behaviour by the CIPR. Customer feedback is highly desirable and you must engage in these relationships in sincere, transparent and consistent ways. If you come across unwanted negative comments, you must act quickly and professionally. Engage with the blogger, either by e-mail or by responding to their blog online. Customers will forgive isolated failings and respect companies that learn from these incidences.

Example
Virgin didn't react quickly enough to a disgruntled blogger whose comments on his in-flight cuisine became an overnight hit, owing to the blog's witty and engaging style. It took just two days for it to feature in printed and online news outlets. Finally, Richard Branson responded in person to the individual, congratulating him on his blogging success and inviting him to advise on the company's in-flight menus.

The key is to respond quickly, address the situation, apologise if necessary and, above all, prevent it from becoming the lead story in the news for all the wrong reasons.

Microblogs

A microblog is modelled on a blog but allows only very limited space for writing a message. These messages can be followed both online and via mobiles. Twitter, launched in July 2006, allows signed-up members to write comments up to 120 characters long. Social networking sites like Facebook are remodelling themselves on this popular development and allowing members to update regularly with short comments or 'status updates'.

Example 1
News of the US Airways passenger plane crash into the Hudson River in New York in January 2009 was communicated around the world in real time more quickly than any news channel could keep up, as a witness to the crash recorded the incident and updated his 'Twitter' page, sending pictures and news of the crash around the world in seconds.

Example 2
Sheffield International Venues successfully uses Twitter to update its clients on class changes, opening times and unforeseen occurrences that mean its leisure centres have to close (because of flooding, electrical faults, etc). When one centre was recently closed owing to an electrical failure, clients were able to go straight home without the inconvenience of parking at the centre or getting stuck in traffic or becoming frustrated at the centre, demonstrating the immense value of immediate communication to its customers.

Really Simple Syndication (RSS)

Web users frequently sign up to receive information from selected blogs, social websites or public websites by clicking on the RSS link on relevant pages. News websites provide RSS feeds so that viewers can receive automatic updates on selected topics. This is a great way for PR practitioners to follow information on their industry, sector and even company or organisation.

Example
Neil regularly uses an RSS site to follow the ups and downs of his beloved football team (website: http://www.newsnow. co.uk/h/Sport/Football/Premier+League/Sunderland). It offers a useful insight on how stories often have different takes in the global media, as well as often providing entertaining comments from supporters.

New media release

News releases have adapted to the online environment and evolved into 'new media releases' that are e-mailed to journalists for use in online and printed publications. The new media release is complete with live links (hyperlinks), RSS feeds, photographs, videos and other social media.

Pay per clicks

The online advertising opportunity offered by pay per clicks is the fastest-growing form of advertising worldwide. Companies that place advertisements within websites are charged for the number of clicks on the advert. Pay per clicks can also be used as a PR tool

to encourage clicks onto your website or key message, and can be easily monitored (using readily available software) and evaluated.

Search engine optimisation (SEO)

Many companies invest time and energy into enhancing their position in the listings that search engines produce. When people seek new sites, they'll enter key words into the search engines, usually Google, Yahoo! or MSN. Search engines continuously develop and constantly monitor popular sites that fit the key words. The opportunity to maximise search rankings has led to a strong growth in SEO agencies, or search marketing agencies, which use a combination of good copy (written words) and strong technical IT skills.

Example
Numbering an estimated 175 million, worldwide retailers' websites are among the most visited. Tesco is ranked 32 and BT at 39 in the world, with billions of online interactions, far more than any high street outlet could cope with, making the online marketplace the most economically efficient in the world.

How PR uses social media

The main changes affecting PR are the speed, transparency and interaction of modern communications. What you may have previously discussed with journalists is now available to everyone at the click of a button, including customers, competitors, staff and other stakeholder groups. Companies that depended on static websites are now upgrading them to offer visitors much more interaction and entertainment. Rather than being merely a

repository of information, Web 2.0 allows discussion and the adding and sharing of information. It is taking the concept of e-mail, original websites and message boards and putting them together into one central site that is more efficient, effective and essential to many developing businesses.

Many PR practitioners are harnessing this opportunity and making it work for their clients, using a combination of RSS feeds, embedded links to and from websites, updating microsites and social media sites. All of these activities direct 'traffic' to and from relevant websites that aim to develop two-way communication with stakeholders.

The Long Tail of PR

The Long Tail of PR is a way to demonstrate that the use of the internet and social media extends the lifespan of a story, compared to traditional forms of media. Chris Anderson devised the Long Tail theory in 2004 and published it in the magazine *Wired*, of which he is currently the editor-in-chief. He says:

> The theory of the Long Tail is that our culture and economy is increasingly shifting away from a focus on a relatively small number of 'hits' (mainstream products and markets) at the head of the demand curve and toward a huge number of niches in the tail. As the costs of production and distribution fall, especially online, there is now less need to lump products and consumers into one-size-fits-all containers. In an era without the constraints of physical shelf space and other bottlenecks of distribution, narrowly targeted goods and services can be as economically attractive as mainstream fare.

Anderson uses online music and video to further illustrate his point, explaining that songs not played on the radio on a daily basis and video not available on the television can be accessed via the internet at any time, even years later. This contrasts with

traditional print media, which tend to be disposed of within 24 hours of reading. He argues that 'social media management will quickly grow into a big deal for all organizations' and that 'the days of worrying about only your own website ended in 2007'. Online coverage can be recovered from the bottom of search engine rankings with a bit of effort and some intervention and inclusion of hyperlinks and generating of relevant online discussion.

HR Media Ltd, like most modern media and PR agencies, recognises the importance of social media. Martin Webb, senior account executive at HR Media Ltd, says:

> Our job is to raise and protect the profile of our clients. We would have used traditional media to do this previously. However, social media allow us to reach an even bigger, more varied and ultimately more immediate audience. It would be ludicrous to ignore this... The media have changed dramatically in the last five years. In ten years' time, not only will the media have changed even more dramatically – but so will the people who use it. The generation which engage with social media are getting to the point where they are becoming the influencers, the buyers, the advisers, the sellers – so public relations needs to follow suit if this is where public relations is happening!...When we discuss social media with our clients, we are always very keen to stress the importance of a solid website. Social media can perform (if done properly) a very cyclical purpose, in that they can reinforce a message, or allow the user to reinforce the message, but ultimately if someone is reading that message and wants to find out more, the central web presence is the final destination. It can be frustrating if a company is active and visible in social media, but invisible (or poor) as an end product (from our client's perspective).

Every day, clients ask practitioners like Martin, 'How do I set up Facebook groups?', 'Is it worth setting up a Twitter account?', 'What do you think of a YouTube channel?' Martin judges the platform on its merit, the purpose of the coverage and the

audience the client is trying to reach before engaging. The biggest danger is to set up a social media platform paying lip-service to the latest fad and not keep it going. That is far more damaging than any negative comment on a social media platform.

Example
Increasingly, PR agencies are offering a web-video service that can be uploaded to YouTube, the second most used search engine in the world. HR Media won a video competition for WhizzGo cars. The video was used on WhizzGo cars' website, Twitter, blogs and Facebook pages. Anyone searching for WhizzGo would find lots of ways into its services via the web and vice versa; the services would find them.

Challenges in the workplace

While you may think you're controlling the reputation of your organisation on the internet via your corporate website, a range of different, sometimes conflicting, messages may be being made public by employees, as well as customers and other external stakeholders. Comments about employers have appeared on sites like Facebook and Bebo, many with very positive outcomes, but where a company's reputation is brought into disrepute by a disgruntled employee, you may be faced with a challenging situation: how to deal with negative comments appearing publicly, and how to deal with the employee.

A set of expectations is commonly being implemented into employee guides to advise employees of the consequences of misusing the internet in work time, as well as posting negative messages about employers. Some of the negative comments could be a case of whistle-blowing, where a company claims to operate in a certain way and the employee feels compelled to dispel any

misrepresentation, especially if these concerns have been ignored through formal internal channels. So the message is to always 'practise what you preach'. Don't claim on your website to be highly ethical if, for example, your recycling policy is weak or you suspect that your suppliers are bypassing rules on child labour.

As discussed, some blogs may appear above your company website in search engine listings. The key message is that organisations are no longer able to control the messages or discussions about them and they need to engage with online debate or disgruntled employees to overcome any challenges. The answer may be as small as making improvements to communication internally so all staff are fully aware of the company's objectives, or at the other end of the spectrum it may mean making fundamental changes in the way you do business.

Example

In January 2009 an environmental group challenged Starbucks to stop running cold water taps constantly during opening hours, at points where staff would rinse utensils. This request went unheeded by Starbucks until it was brought to the attention of journalists via a series of blogs. The story became a top national news item and Starbucks was forced to agree that it would stop such practices and revise its policy in order to save water. This story conflicts with Starbucks' website, which claims that the environment is at the heart of its corporate responsibility agenda.

It is very difficult to stop information leaking out, but guidance to employees and transparency in your business practices is essential to minimise any risk of negative comments on the internet. Don't be panicked if you find your company is being discussed online; it may not always be bad. You must engage in debate and overcome negative perceptions through positive consultation and demonstration of business practices.

Using the internet to gain a competitive advantage

The internet is truly remarkable, and essential for commercial success. It has changed the way businesses operate. Online information is dominated by content developed by those external to the organisation. Online users are inquisitive and questioning, with an increasingly high proportion of purchases now being made online, and information provided online affecting purchasing decisions. The PR profession, as well as search marketing agencies, are very aware of the opportunities and are working hard to convince clients that while print coverage is still very important, it is being dwarfed by the relevance of online communication, owing to its reach and opportunities to engage with stakeholders.

> **Example: Best job in the world – you can't have failed to miss it!**
> In January 2009, Queensland Tourism promoted the Barrier Reef islands via a job add for 'the best job in the world' as an island caretaker. Although a real job opportunity, it was designed to attract interest and visitors to the region. It became one of the most successful viral campaigns, winning the Cannes Lion Award and attracting nearly 10 million visitors to the tourism website, 34,684 applicants from 201 countries, and more than $100 million worth of media coverage (advertising-equivalent free publicity) from a budget of $1.2 million.

To protect information excessively can be a big turn-off for stakeholders, and pose questions like 'What have they got to hide?' It also shows a lack of expertise and understanding of the

increasingly transparent external environment. Companies that have embraced the internet now compete on online exposure and are judged by their transparency and online engagement.

> Life can only be understood backwards, but it must be lived forwards.'
>
> Søren Kirkegaard, 1967

Hence, the future is unknowable yet recognisable, and the outcome of everyday online interactions among people, entities and environments will increasingly provide your greatest opportunities for customer satisfaction and corresponding competitive advantage.

Summary and activities

Key points

- **The internet has revolutionised the way that companies are able to communicate with stakeholders, and the newspaper industry was one of the first industries to react to the potential of the social media.**
- **Companies are engaging with stakeholders via blogs and social networking sites, such as Facebook, LinkedIn and Twitter, and developing interactive websites to gain feedback and engage in discussions that may influence their brands.**
- **Managing your reputation online is essential in protecting your brand and business. Reputations painstakingly built over years can be destroyed in a few minutes by disgruntled bloggers, negative comments and poor results on either comparison or social networking sites.**

Questions

1. Why are companies moving on from static websites?
2. Why does the online coverage of your business last longer than printed coverage?

Activities

-   Visit Chris Anderson's site to read more on the Long Tail (http://www.thelongtail.com/about.html).

-   Set up a social media microsite like Twitter and see how many people you get to follow you by discussing developments in your sector. Can you become an online industry expert?

6

Stakeholders and customers: how to develop and maximise relations

Have you ever stopped to consider why you are working in the manner that you are? Why are you attending particular meetings? What have you gained from the interactions you've had with colleagues? What have you learned that's new? How have the meetings moved things forward (if at all?) How do your internal relationships compare with those that are external?

A useful tip is to keep a diary (or critical incident log, if you prefer!) of how meetings have helped you to achieve your company's objectives. After a few months, reflect on your entries and ask yourself some questions. Are you attending because:

- **it's voluntary or obligatory?**
- **because of the apathy of others?**
- **it's routine or a crazy impulse?**

You'll find that your drivers are complex, vary with time, change depending on circumstances and are completely different from those of your colleagues. Having a better grasp of your own drivers, you'll be better placed to understand how stakeholders react to your communications, and will be able to

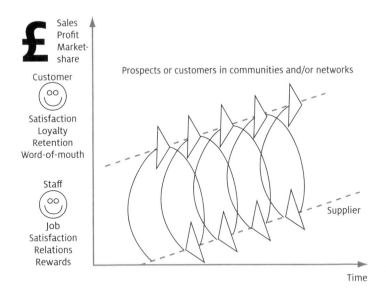

Figure 6.2 Benefits of a healthy dialogue

Macro- and micro-environments

Wherever and whenever you see changes in your business environments (Figure 3.2, page 28), you must change and adapt, otherwise you risk being left behind and could suffer quite serious consequences. Being a consumer yourself, you will appreciate that we often value goods (or services) that appeal both socially and psychologically. Often, consumer issues are highly charged with emotion as well as clear thinking. Consumers attach varying degrees of symbolism and values to their purchases. Increasing numbers of consumers pay premium prices to buy products, say those identified as Fairtrade, that match their value systems.

The risks of not understanding such issues are twofold: first, if your product offer doesn't align with consumers' values, then increased customer losses are likely; and second, consumers these days not only 'vote with their feet' but contribute to the plethora of social media sites. As discussed previously, you need to consider

how you can use PR to influence them in the right direction – that is, your company.

The decision-making process

No one is saying that price is not an issue for consumers, but it is rarely *the* issue in decision-making. Historically, campaigns sought to encourage customers to buy a product or service – that is, close the deal. In doing so, marketers too often simply listed the product's features without relating how they helped solve customers' problems. Pre-Web 2.0 this may have been enough to satisfy customers, but these days online consumers expect much more than just the traditional transaction; they expect service, reliability, website personalisation, easy use and fun. Yes, instead of the traditional notions of purchasing, customers are seeking information on benefits while enjoying themselves in the process. Indeed, the thrill of the auction is a key element of eBay's business model.

However, the advent of Web 2.0 user-generated communications tools, such as social networking sites, has shifted the emphasis (from the supplier simply closing the deal) to helping consumers to make decisions prior to the purchasing decision itself. Answer this: are you now engaged in trying to sell what you think they want? Or is it a case of finding out what information consumers need to make better decisions?

If you're simply focused on closing the deal, you could be in trouble. Figure 6.3 shows the traditional business-to-consumer (B2C) decision-making process. The transition between each stage could be affected by feedback from social networking sites, blogs and other user-generated tools. Bear in mind that the time dedicated to the various stages differs, depending on whether the purchase is:

- **A routine or repeat purchase of something bought many times before, such as bread, milk or other fast-moving consumer goods (FMCG) items. This is a quick process with low risk and hence little monitoring of the decision.**

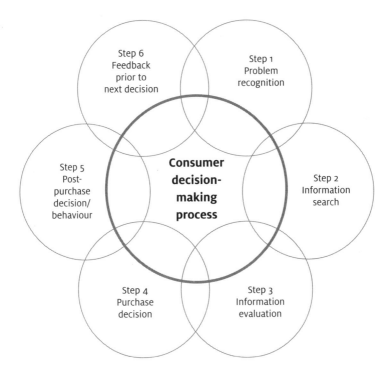

Figure 6.3 Consumer decision-making process

- A purchase with medium or limited risk, where the item is bought infrequently with a higher degree of risk, say an annual holiday or a flat-screen television for home use.
- A rare, high (or extended) risk where if it goes wrong the implications may be long-term – for example, buying a house, a wedding dress, a new high-value car, etc.

Simply put, every stage of the decision-making process presents opportunities for prospects or customers to seek opinions or input from a blog, forum, social networking site and/or price comparison site. Wherever possible, your company can use PR to provide the information needed to help customers make the right decision – that is, buy your goods and services!

The decision-making unit

Traditional marketing has always advocated awareness of the decision-making unit (DMU) (see Figure 6.4).

The DMU is a simple model that implies passivity – that is, all the actors simply sit there, not interacting with each other. Experience tells us, however, that the DMU stakeholders can impact each other greatly, in some cases energising each other, in others providing constraints. In small to medium-sized enterprises (SMEs), different stakeholders can form part of multiple scenarios, for example as initiator and user but not buyer. With the advent of Web 2.0 the concept of the DMU still

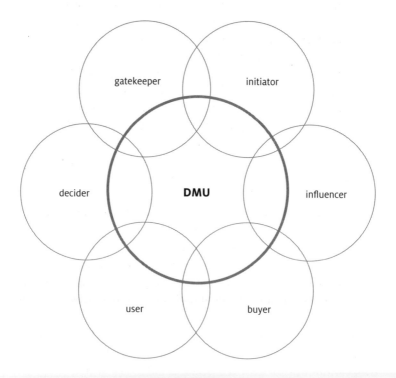

Figure 6.4 Decision-making unit (DMU)

applies. However, different stakeholders not only fulfil differing roles but often contribute to online debates via a forum (or indeed multiple forums), blogs, social networking sites or comparison websites. A further complication is that these stakeholders may also use multiple media channels simultaneously. Such people are known as media multi-taskers.

SMEs

Marketing within SMEs is different from that in larger companies. SMEs tend to adopt the characteristics of their owners or managers and tend to be more intuitive. This lends itself well to social media sites such as LinkedIn. SMEs are economically of increasing importance. In the United Kingdom there are 2.5 million enterprises, of which 99 per cent are SMEs. However, marketing texts have largely ignored SMEs, as they predominantly focus on larger companies. This trend is now changing, with increasing numbers of SMEs buying and selling goods and services online. The business-to-business (B2B) decision-making process (Figure 6.5) applies to both SMEs and larger organisations.

Some barriers to adoption of e-commerce by SMEs do exist, such as the following:

- **SMEs lack awareness of sources of assistance, such as grants.**
- **They perceive IT skills problems.**
- **They feel their company is of too small a size to benefit.**
- **They perceive the required technology to be too expensive or too complicated or incompatible with in-house systems.**

Try to anticipate these issues when communicating with SMEs. It is not always easy to find information on the latest social media tools, as was proved during a discussion at the Academy of Marketing conference. A room full of distinguished marketing academics (who among them have written hundreds of different

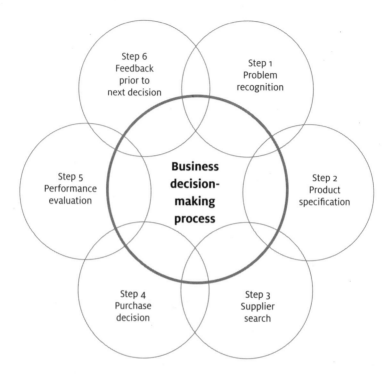

Figure 6.5 Business decision-making process

titles) expressed concerns regarding discussing the latest Web 2.0 tools; such as Twitter, in their texts. They felt that things move so fast that by the time their texts are published, the tool might have become passé. This attitude is too product oriented when what is needed is a more customer-centric approach. The tools are indeed changing, but a constant is that customers need to know the benefits of what you offer them. That never changes!

Customer satisfaction

As exchanges bring suppliers and customers together, relationships are formed, and you need to develop the initial

relationship by finding out as much as you can about the client's needs. Put simply, if you give customers what they want, they'll return to buy your goods and/or services. Servicing existing customers is much cheaper than attracting new ones, therefore customer satisfaction enhances sales turnover and profitability as well as increasing your market share. Satisfied customers tend not only to be repeat buyers but also to tell their friends, families and colleagues. Conversely, if they have a poor experience, they tend to tell even more people about it! Think 3:10. Everything good your company does will lead to customers telling three people about their experience, whereas for everything bad it's 10!

You probably now better understand the need to move away from single transactions and towards effective management of long-term customer relationships.

Emotional intelligence

How many times have you sent an e-mail and as soon as you've hit the 'send' button you've regretted it? How often has someone misinterpreted the tone of an e-mail? Or has your humour been misconstrued? As a manager, you may have explained difficult decisions to your staff and still they've not reacted the way you'd anticipated. Well, you're not alone, and many, often highly intelligent, people suffer the same malaise. Communication is not simply an intellectual exercise, it's social and emotional.

Increasingly, consultants are referring to emotional intelligence (EI) as complementing the traditional IQ form of intelligence. When communicating with your stakeholders and publics, you essentially need to devise an engaging message that will have a positive impact on the audience – that is, increase interest, desire and action among the target audience. EI helps with identifying, understanding, integrating and managing emotions – both one's own and those of others.

EI is highly useful in teamwork, particularly in complex multidisciplinary scenarios. The EI of a team is not merely the sum of individuals' EI. Rather, EI is generated within the team as

norms are created, mutual trust develops and a group identity is formed – qualities that promote cooperation and collaboration. In short, EI provides understanding of how the emotions experienced by individuals affect the work of the team. EI is 'more than just a passing fad... [it has] captured the long-term interest of employers and educators' (Grewal and Salovey, 2005: 339).

Summary and activities

Key points

- **In order for you to be successful in your communication strategies, it's crucial that you listen to what stakeholders are saying and actively encourage their participation in the process. That said, not all stakeholders are equal.**
- **Customers should be at the heart of all business decisions and activities. However, organisations should be both inward and externally focused to truly understand and react to changing trends.**
- **Anticipating your customers' needs is a start to developing a relationship with them. Providing them with what they require by satisfying their needs will entice them to come back time and time again. Over time, customer needs change and your communications activities need to change with them.**

Questions

1. Why do some consumers take a long time moving through the consumer buying process?
2. What are the key factors that influence a consumer's buying behaviour?
3. How does purchasing differ between a consumer and a business?

Activities

- Map the different needs and motivations of different 'actors' in your DMU? What are the key benefits that your organisation can attain by recognising the different roles within the DMU?

- Reflect on the impact of social media sites on your decision-making process (DMP). How does your company tailor its communications to address DMP variations among your customers? Do you know what your key customers want now? In 18 months? Or in 3 years? If not, why not?

- Think about your behaviour. How have your needs changed as you've grown older? Can you think of any organisations that satisfy your needs really well in a way that encourages you to go back time and time again? Likewise, can you think of any organisations that have disappointed you? If you have been disappointed, how would you advise them to improve? How have you reported your disappointment to your networks and communities?

For the more academically inclined, the following article on SMEs is useful:

Gilmore, A, Carson, D and Grant, K (2001) SME marketing in practice, *Marketing Intelligence and Planning*, 19 (1), pp 6–11

For light reading (?) on SMEs, look at the following:

EC (2005) [accessed 25 August 2009] European Commission Recommendation 2005/361/EC [Online] http://europa.eu.int/ISPO/ecommerce/sme/definition.html.

7

Crisis, what crisis?

Often, managers are judged on how they deal with both unexpected and expected issues that arise. Crisis management is big business for many PR agencies, which build reputations on helping businesses out of sticky situations. This chapter considers some of the measures that may save you from having to bring in the agency experts, with the added associated costs.

Planning

You can plan for dealing with a crisis. Many organisations devote huge resources to simulating crises in order to understand how they might deal with the real thing should it happen. If a damaging scenario may arise, then it's far better to anticipate it than to ignore it. The risk may seem insignificant. However, you must ask yourself what the outcome might be should it arise.

While you could try to plan for all identifiable eventualities (eg fire, flood, contract breaches, financial mismanagement, flaky customer services, flagrant abuse of staff, etc), it's more realistic to consider crisis as a risk element that can either be anticipated or

take you completely by surprise. PR can help you through a crisis or assess elements of risk by understanding what the implications might be, for both your internal and your external audiences. It can be used to support strategic planning as well as implementing tactics to minimise the risk of a crisis.

Who to communicate with during a crisis

Your stakeholder mapping analysis (Chapter 6) will shift dramatically during a crisis. Dormant or latent stakeholders may become very active during a crisis. Consideration must be given to their perspectives and possible activities; will they support you in a conflict, and your efforts to minimise risk during your damage limitation activities?

Communicate with key stakeholders proactively before they read about your organisation in the media or on social media sites. You must know how to engage them in order to win their support. The danger of ignoring some stakeholder groups is that doing so could result in the period of crisis being extended, or the crisis escalating and becoming even more difficult to manage.

Saying sorry... *mea culpa*

Too many organisations deny any wrongdoing during a crisis or are too slow to admit responsibility. This leads to further scrutiny and criticism, and a protracted period of crisis. Stopping, or killing, the story may be crucial to managing the situation. This might not mean saying sorry as an admission of guilt, but simply apologising for the inconvenience caused, while you investigate further. The media and other audiences will be more sympathetic to your situation and be more inclined to work with (rather than against) you to come to a speedy conclusion of the situation, especially if you're sincere!

Demonstrating your sincerity may require further evidence that you're addressing the situation and investigating bad and good practice. This should include a thorough investigation of any wrongdoings. This doesn't mean going on a witch-hunt to find someone to blame, but responsibly addressing the situation and monitoring the public mood towards your organisation.

Being proactive as well as reactive

Keeping the communications lines open may mean opening up your organisation to further investigation. Responding to media enquiries in a professional, timely manner is essential, as is considering ways of rebuilding confidence in your brand or organisation. Many organisations experienced in dealing with crises understand the value of being proactive as well as reactive in the face of adversity.

Example

In July 2005, following the London suicide bombings in which 56 people died and over 700 were injured, Leeds Metropolitan University (LMU) had to respond to intense media interest as journalists tried to uncover information about the bombers. As the police investigation to find the bombers led them to communities in and around Leeds, the world's media followed.

The media, equipped with only the bombers' names, scoured the region for clues to where and when they may have met. This put immense pressure on LMU as rumours spread that the bombers had studied at the university. With the police still to release the identity of the bombers, the university would have breached Data Protection Act 1998 if it had confirmed the names as those of students, current or past.

This gave LMU's communications team much-needed time to work with local stakeholders to establish as many facts as possible, including scouring its own database to establish whether the names being quoted in the media matched any on file. Meanwhile, the country was in shock as details of the devastation caused by the bombers were made available, as well as the tragic stories behind those who had lost their lives.

LMU proactively contacted Leeds City Council as well as other higher and further education institutions to establish whether they were under the same pressure and whether there was anything they could do to support each other. From this consultation, LMU established that a large number of local residents were being made temporarily homeless while the police investigation was under way. LMU's communications team arranged for members of the displaced communities to stay in the university's halls of residence.

By the time the police confirmed the bombers' identities, LMU was able to announce its contribution to the displaced communities, at the same time as confirming that at least one of the bombers had studied there. The news release and subsequent press articles led with news of the displaced communities being accommodated in the university's halls of residence. News that a bomber had been a student was barely mentioned in the press. Despite being drawn into the crisis unexpectedly, LMU took control of the situation. It established a crisis team early on with the following key objectives:

- Manage the flow of information.
- Avoid distortion.
- Actively promote positive stories but be sympathetic to the mood of the nation as the country was in shock following the horrific bombings in London.

- Identify and communicate with priority stakeholders.
- Operate on a business as usual basis.

The communications team brought in colleagues from other departments to help manage the huge number of media calls. It created teams to monitor developments in the press, to communicate proactively with stakeholders and to continue with ongoing projects.

LMU's communications team had established protocols for dealing with the media, which included regularly reminding colleagues not to respond to media enquiries directly but to refer journalists to the communications team, who had good working relations with the regional media. This enabled them to work with the media in a number of areas, including finding out what themes of the crisis the media were concentrating on, to establish how LMU could contribute proactively as well as reactively.

This example clearly demonstrates the need:

- **to develop a crisis team who can be objective, not dealing with front-line queries from journalists;**
- **for good relations with the media during calmer times, which can help during a crisis;**
- **to know your key stakeholders during a crisis;**
- **to understand where and when it's appropriate to be proactive;**
- **for sensitivities around issuing positive news stories in crises;**
- **to use legislation, for example that on data protection, to give you much-needed time, even if it's only a few hours;**
- **to take control during a crisis, if possible.**

Never say 'no comment'

Saying 'no comment' when questioned on a situation can give the impression of being guilty. It infuriates the media and the public when organisations respond in this way, and it can make a bad situation worse. Companies that refuse to engage with the media and the public will encourage them to seek other sources for the information they need. Journalists are especially sophisticated at using contacts and tools to get the answers they require, often at the expense of those who refuse to engage in discussion with them. Other sources include the internet, the emergency services, industry experts, local MPs and councillors, employees current and past, neighbours, customers and clients.

Talking to the media during a crisis

You must quickly establish your key objectives, which initially may focus on damage limitation. Whatever your objectives, it is important to communicate clearly, concisely and confidently, and to maintain control of the situation. It is not always necessary to put a spokesperson forward to face the media. If you're worried that he or she might not be able to deal with a barrage of questions from an aggressive media, simply issue statements via e-mail or your website.

During a crisis, large numbers of journalists want answers, hence it is often more effective to issue a holding statement, simply stating that you're investigating the situation and will issue more details shortly. This will buy you time and reduce the need for you to organise press conferences or provide opportunities for journalists to come to your premises during the crisis. Such visits are inadvisable as they can add an unwanted element of stress to a tense situation. Issuing regular statements via e-mail or your website can help to feed the media's insatiable appetite for news without letting them take control of the situation.

Journalists are trained to persist with their enquiries and can put people on the spot with questions they won't or can't answer. Statements reduce the opportunity for further questions to be fired at individual representatives.

Example
When a London to Glasgow Virgin train was derailed near Carlisle in February 2007, Virgin boss Richard Branson was on the scene within hours of the accident, talking to the press, empathising with the passengers and generally being a great ambassador for the Virgin brand. He praised the train driver, Iain Black, for his bravery in supporting his passengers at the crash scene. Branson knows exactly how the press works and how to manage a crisis situation sensitively and sympathetically. His approach generally lessens negative speculation and poor publicity.

Crisis manuals and simulation

Many practitioners refer to crisis manuals as 'king' in managing a crisis effectively and many produce lengthy documents full of great ideas and action points, which in reality are rarely used during a crisis, owing to their static nature. An effective crisis manual will contain details on communications systems to implement when needed, including basic messages, identifying key stakeholders or audiences, up-to-date contact details and protocols. It should be easy to use and provide clarity in often confusing times.

Conducting a crisis simulation is a useful exercise that can create the atmosphere of a crisis in a controlled environment. It should also highlight gaps in procedures and provide the opportunity for staff to understand the important roles they would play in a crisis. Repeating the simulation at regular intervals will

make sure that any weaknesses are identified. A simulation may involve inviting external parties, including the media and the emergency services, to take part. This will ensure that all key parties recognise the role they play and all key players can be acknowledged as crucial to the process.

Summary and activities

Key points

- **A bad situation can become a crisis if not recognised immediately. Crises can be sudden (the cobra effect) or slow-burning, rumbling on (the python effect). How you deal with the situation will depend on how long the crisis lasts.**
- **Organisations need to take control of matters as quickly as possible. Developing a crisis team to respond to the situation and develop proactive as well as reactive responses is crucial. Identifying quickly the roles people will play in dealing with the crisis, from the receptionist to the MD or CEO, will ensure that resources are used effectively.**

Questions

1. What are the crucial elements of dealing with a crisis?
2. Who should address the media during a crisis, and in what way?
3. What role can staff play during a crisis?

Activities

1. **Consider how well prepared your organisation is for dealing with a crisis.**

2.   Review your crisis procedures and simulate a crisis situation on a regular basis.

3.   Think of the current crises that are facing businesses and organisations – you just have to read the news to see examples of good and bad crisis management.

8

Internal communications

Employees must be viewed as ambassadors for your business and should have a real stake in making your business a success. Keeping them well informed and engaging in two-way communication, which allows for them to feed back their constructive views on the business, will enhance the relationship and add value to your business.

As well as being essential for large employers, where two-way communication between staff and management is deployed at a global as well as a local level, internal communications is beneficial for small companies to share information and allow staff to feed back ideas and issues that will help the business to perform better. It is also essential for companies that want to rebrand, so that management have a clear understanding of how stakeholders view the business, with internal stakeholders being a very important group.

Traditionally based in human resources (HR) or personnel, internal communications has developed into a thriving discipline in its own right. It has grown in size and stature as management recognise the important role that staff play in the success of an organisation.

Key strategic areas that internal communications can affect include:

- **supporting major change;**
- **communicating messages from the management;**
- **communicating the business's mission or vision or values;**
- **raising awareness of business issues and priorities;**
- **increasing and maintaining the credibility of the management;**
- **motivating employees;**
- **allowing feedback from staff;**
- **improving the communications skills of management.**

Example
Tesco recognises the value of its employees, stating that they are as important as customers with regard to the success of the business. It regularly asks staff what is important to them, and responds accordingly, treating them with respect, providing managers who help them, and creating interesting jobs and opportunities for progression. In return, Tesco's staff are fully aware of the company's objectives through its 'Every little helps' strategy. Tesco understands that if staff have rewarding jobs, they're more likely to go that extra mile to help customers.

Controlling the message

Internal communications is the discipline that engages with staff through a series of tactics, including notice boards, meetings, intranets, events and newsletters. It is important that you listen to staff and let them know that you acknowledge and value their opinions and, where appropriate, act on them.

In order to communicate with staff effectively it is important to understand the business's overall strategy so that you can share with staff your vision and how they can help you to achieve it. Too many employees work in silos, concerned only with their area of expertise or discipline, and lack awareness of, and even interest in, how the wider business functions. However, with a bit of effort from management to help them understand how their role contributes to the 'bigger picture', staff will take pride in their work, which in turn benefits the organisation.

Schemes such as profit sharing, comments boxes, share options, as well as pension contributions from employers and holiday allowances that go beyond statutory provisions of employment law all add to the well-being and satisfaction of employees. Conditions in the workplace that go beyond health and safety legislation and ISO 2001 also help to make employees feel valued. As employers, you will be judged by benchmarks set by law, as well as by other employers. Generous employers understand the value of respecting their employees and providing a 'better than satisfactory' working environment.

Getting to know your employees

Too many employers have assumptions about how to make employees feel valued, often based on their own experience rather than on research. To really get the best out of your staff, you must invest time and effort in getting to know them and in understanding their needs. The most effective way to gain an understanding of and empathy with staff is to conduct an audit.

The audit

Find out what your employees understand about your business and identify gaps in their knowledge, and issues with their moral engagement and motivation. You can conduct an audit via a number of routes:

- Focus groups, although they are best conducted anonymously by a person impartial to the business.
- Questionnaires. Keeping them brief and offering an incentive to complete them usually maximises the quality of data being returned. They can be conducted via online surveys or on paper, with employees being given a deadline to complete them.
- Team meetings conducted by line managers as part of a team-building exercise or scheduled update meeting.

Evaluating an audit

You must demonstrate a commitment to the process of gathering information to understand your staff's perceptions of the business and issues affecting their job satisfaction. If staff don't feel they're being taken seriously, then you must address this by making more of an effort to listen to them. As Tom Peters famously said, manage by wandering around: walk the floor, shadow the workforce, spend one day a month in their workplace doing their jobs to appreciate their perspective more effectively. The knowledge you gather will identify patterns and inconsistencies that you can act upon in a positive way.

Frequency of staff auditing

Best practice would recommend an annual formal audit with regular discussion going on throughout the year. Audits should always be voluntary, to ensure staff provide honest and considered responses. To maximise participation, you must act quickly on recommendations and comments by staff. Report the highlights of the audit as well as any negative issues raised. Consistent criticism must be addressed to reach a positive outcome in order to keep morale high throughout the year.

Remind staff of the impact the previous audit had on the company and how their input led to positive changes. There are

standard audit questionnaires you can use or adapt for your business, most offering a selection of qualitative and quantitative questions. Survey Monkey offers a free online questionnaire service for questionnaires of up to 10 questions, with a great tool for analysing results quickly. Examples of questions in a standard questionnaire are shown in Table 8.1.

Table 8.1 Sample questionnaire for a staff audit

	Strongly Agree	Agree	Somewhat Agree	Somewhat Disagree	Disagree	Strongly Disagree
I know what's expected of me and my job						
I have clear information about how I do my job						
I feel comfortable with what I'm asked to do in meeting my job expectations						
My supervisor and I have a clear understanding of what I'm expected to do and how I'm to carry it out						
Management do a good job communicating their decisions to everyone						
Management allow me to execute my work responsibilities with little or no supervision						
I understand the company's priorities						
I feel I'm given opportunities to contribute to the direction of the department						
I'm given opportunities to comment on the company's direction						

What if you don't like the feedback?

Even during a strong economic climate in which the job market is buoyant, it's equally important to maximise engagement with employees to minimise the costs of recruitment and employee turnover as the choice and competition from employers increases. The messages may differ depending on the economic climate. However, a truthful and open approach is always essential. As previously discussed, people are the most important asset in your organisation and it's vital to retain their talent as long as possible.

Whatever the outcome, you must address it personally and professionally. It's no good ignoring issues, as they're unlikely to go away without your input. Addressing the issues raised may be an uncomfortable experience, but once they have been dealt with, everyone should feel more valued and respected. If you engage with staff and reward them for their efforts, you will reap the benefits of having a committed and focused workforce, on message and on your side. So, don't hide in the office. Get out there and meet the teams that help you to make your business what it is.

Example

A survey published in June 2009, conducted by the financial communications agency FD, polled 524 white-collar workers and found worryingly high levels of employee dissatisfaction as bosses dealt with the tough recessionary times. A minority of employees (44 per cent) felt that their CEO showed strong leadership, and only 28 per cent trusted messages from their CEO more than 'a little'. Businesses expect people to work harder, often for less money, during a recession, and this is a tough act to balance for any boss. The focus on employee engagement is never more important than during difficult times.

FD's survey found that 33 per cent of employees will look for another job if the boss fails to address concerns and 67 per cent do not have common face-to-face contact with bosses. Eighty-one per cent said face-to-face contact with their line manager was the most trusted form of communication.

Resources for internal communications

Large companies have dedicated internal communications specialists who will constantly audit, evaluate and communicate with staff on behalf of the senior management. Internal communications is a growing specialism that has developed alongside the need for organisations to communicate strategically with all their external stakeholders. Internal communications practitioners will also ensure that senior management are fully engaged in communicating with staff via events, meetings and, increasingly, video casts and audio casts broadcast on the company intranet or in-house TV screens.

Tactics for internal communications

Company newsletter or magazine

An internal communicator's role usually involves producing and editing newsletters, both online and paper copies. Companies may release a weekly, fortnightly, monthly or even quarterly publication to staff, made up of regular news items, and a notice

from the boss. Regular items might include articles on staff achievements, both professional and personal, outstanding performance in the workplace, and a regular item from the senior manager on business matters. Newsletters should be colourful and easy to read, with lots of photos to break up the text and illustrate the articles.

Intranet

Establishing an intranet involves developing a web-based forum for communication with staff, and is restricted to access by staff. Staff must make an effort to view this sort of medium, and it should not be relied on as the sole way to communicate with staff.

Events and meetings

Most staff would rather see managers face to face than only see their faces in newsletters and on websites. A combination of formal and informal opportunities for staff and management to meet should be staged throughout the year. The content of the events will depend on their degree of formality, but such events should not be underestimated as regards their role in developing great employee relations.

Notice boards

A much more traditional way to communicate with staff, notice boards are still very effective, especially for organisations that have staff who do not regularly sit at the same desk or have access to the internet. Very often the content is used to signpost staff to other sources of information, as the level of detail you can post on a notice board is usually fairly minimal.

The water cooler effect

Informal channels of communication, such as employees gathering around the water cooler, photocopier, corridors and post room, are where the latest gossip tends to be shared. Rather than frowning on these 'natural' phenomena, employers should recognise them as useful opportunities for staff to feel engaged, and as adding satisfaction to their jobs. These informal channels can be used to communicate messages, often more quickly and effectively than the formal channels.

Staff use of the internet

Most companies will have a website and encourage staff to read notices from management via it. Increasingly, companies are developing their own social networking sites for staff. These are aimed at reducing the amount of time staff who use computers spend on 'non-work-related social networking sites', and they have a role in gathering feedback and the latest trends from staff.

While there have been incidences of staff abusing the internet at work, even posting offensive comments about employers, many employers are recognising that this can be due to poor internal communications, employee dissatisfaction, and a lack of transparency and clear protocols by employers. It is perfectly acceptable for employers to discipline staff for such activities, but they should question why staff feel the need to 'go public' with their views. Often it is a lack of good two-way internal communications that leads to this situation.

Employee communication needs

The basic requirements for good internal communications are built around the needs of employees. As a guide, these needs include:

- general information about the organisation;
- specific information about their role in the organisation;
- clarity around their role;
- a clear understanding of the organisation's vision;
- information on workplace practices;
- opportunities to be involved and consulted;
- feedback on performance;
- access to training and development;
- access to communication channels.

An internal communications strategy that addresses these needs effectively should produce an engaged workforce who enjoy their work because they feel valued.

Organisational culture

It is widely accepted that organisations need good leaders to provide a clear direction for the success of the business. This success includes recognising the need to engage with staff at all levels of the business. Good leaders define the culture of the organisation, and the very survival of the business depends on their commitment. The leader's ability to communicate effectively is important to the credibility and quality of internal communications.

David Thomas, from Harvard Business School, stresses the importance of multimodality in communication, saying:

> What you say is only the beginning... Your behaviour, your actions, and your decisions are also ways of communicating, and leaders have to learn how to create a consistent message through all of these. It's been said many times, but leaders lead by example... Communication can't always follow the top-down model... With the fluidity of information in business today, leaders need to be masterful listeners; they need to be able to receive as well as send. Individuals at all levels of an organization need to be able to take responsibility

for their decisions. They've got to feel they have a sphere of influence that allows them to have their own version of enacting the organization's vision and strategy.

Rosabeth Moss Kanter, also from Harvard Business School, puts it another way: 'Leaders must wake people out of inertia. They must get people excited about something they've never seen before, something that does not yet exist.'

There needs to be an alignment of the interests of the organisation and the interests of the individuals. Incentives must be meaningful, whether they are monetary or intrinsic.

Ethical employers

Employees are just as keen to work for an organisation they believe in as they are to earn money. Graduate surveys consistently reveal that the type of company they work for is more important than salary for most. So make sure you appeal to the best and can make them as committed to the business as you are, so that you retain them for as long as possible.

Don't fall into the trap of feeling that a job is 'just a job' for your employees. The psychological contract between employer and employee is complex and multi-layered. As employers streamline activities, contracting services and products from abroad, jobs are rarely considered secure. With a much higher turnover of staff than ever before, companies must acknowledge the complex relationship with staff.

The new 'psychological contract' with staff is based on offers of training and development, to keep staff employable not just by their current employer but for the future, as well as fair pay and treatment in return for employee commitment.

We'll discuss ethics more in Chapter 11.

Summary and activities

Key points

- Staff should be one the greatest assets of an organisation. They must be treated well and engaged with to ensure they contribute to the success of the business.
- Conducting annual audits on employees' understanding of the business's aims and objectives will allow management to understand what is important to staff and to implement change where appropriate to improve employer–employee relations.
- Many tools are available to ensure you communicate effectively with staff. Using a combination of tactics that will allow management to communicate with all staff and allow them to feel valued will reap rewards in terms of employee engagement, which in turn benefits the organisation.

Questions

1. Why do companies engage with internal communications?
2. How important is internal communications to the overall PR/ marcomms efforts of an organisation?
3. What sorts of tools are available to use to communicate well with staff?

Activities

- Consider the tools that you have found most effective during your career in allowing your employer to communicate the key values and strengths of the business to you.

- Put yourself in the position of employees across your organisation, at a range of levels of seniority and ask yourself what would make them feel more engaged. Are they already fully engaged and do they understand the key objectives of not just their department but the wider organisation?

- Have a look at surveys like the *Sunday Times* 100 Best Companies to Work For (http://business.timesonline. co.uk/tol/business/career_and_jobs/best_100_ companies/). What sort of internal communications do they use?

Getting the facts right: using research to create a competitive edge

As discussed previously, before you can satisfy customers and add value to their experience, an understanding is needed about who they are, what they require and what influences them. The way we acquire this information is through marketing research.

> Fortune favours the prepared mind.
>
> Louis Pasteur, 1854

Pasteur's observation seems obvious, and yet business history is littered with examples of ill-prepared communications campaigns for product launches or repositioning efforts failing owing to a lack of research. Carrying out good-quality research is undoubtedly the best way to prepare for any communications strategies that your company will undertake.

Consider the number of decisions you make on a daily basis. Some decisions may be fairly minor; others may be important, with far-reaching consequences. Good-quality information helps to reduce risk and create more certainty when making decisions. You'll be well aware that there are often a variety of answers or solutions when making decisions. Marketing communications

research can provide information to support you when making decisions within a given set of circumstances or parameters.

Types of research

The term 'marketing research' is very broad and encompasses many different 'types' of research which you may be able to use, so let's consider some alternatives.

Market research

Market research is research specifically undertaken on the market type (ranging from monopoly through duopoly and oligopoly to the theoretical perfect market), barriers to entry, market size and market condition. This type of research is particularly useful when your objectives are geared towards entering new markets and you have to design a communications campaign that is fit for purpose. You can use a number of frameworks to provide a structure. For example, Porter's 'five forces' model looks at aspects such as the competitive intensity, new entrants, the power of buyers, the risk of substitutes and the role of suppliers. This type of research can really focus in upon the key features of the actual market in which you operate.

Product research

Under the heading 'product research' you'll seek information specifically on the product, the product's features or the desirability of the product. As previously discussed, you can use PR to improve your feedback from social media sites. This approach is often used in new product development where you're seeking consumer insights and perceptions of the actual and potential product(s). It can also be used if you start to encounter any problems with your products. As discussed in Chapter 2, when

a company is moving from maturity to the decline stage (Figure 2.4, page 19), you can use PR to identify means of extending the maturity stage research by engaging users in feedback exercises on social media sites. Remember, all audits are inherently political, as they can involve parties having to be self-critical. To overcome the bias (of a supplier asking for comments on its own products), you can use a third party such as your local business school or PR consultants.

Distribution research

Distribution research is a key area for your company as you must identify where the consumers and/or customers think your products ought to be sold. During the development of your entire marketing communications strategy, decisions regarding how to support the distribution of your products are key. Again, this could be a central piece of your communications research: How do you use your distribution network in order to maximise your competitive advantage? How do you use PR to communicate benefits to retailers who may stock competitors' products alongside your own? To an extent, manufacturers lose control of the communications process when their goods enter the retail space and you can use PR to maintain contact with the end-user and the retailer. In the 1970s a major retailer would stock, say, 5,000 product lines. Now it will carry 50,000 lines and you can use PR to differentiate your goods once the research has indicated the possibilities.

Research methods

Research by its very nature is often systematic and scientific. Don't let this put you off! You don't have to collect the data yourself; your PR practitioner, consultant or agency will gladly liaise with a marketing research agency to do it on your behalf. You still need to fully understand the benefits that the research

process offers and how it works. Why? Because once the data are presented to you, it'll be your decisions that will lead to implementing changes in your company.

Generally speaking, all research should follow a logical approach (Figure 9.1).

Let's consider in more detail what is involved in conducting research.

First, it is important to define the research question. Just why are you conducting this research? You will be trying to solve a particular problem or answer a particular question, for example 'Why are the sales of this specific product falling?'

Be as specific as you can about the question you wish to answer. This is important as it provides focus for the whole

Figure 9.1 The systematic marketing research process

research project. You can't afford to be too broad with your question as this could create a research project that's too woolly to produce meaningful answers. But nor do you want the research question to be too tightly focused, as this could constrain the research and you may miss unplanned opportunities. It's not easy!

Once you've identified the research problem, you then need to set your research objectives. As in Table 3.1 (page 32), objectives should be SMART.

Example
Research problem: To increase brand awareness of Leeds Business School by more than 3 per cent during 2010.

Create the research plan

As in Figure 3.1 (page 28), research is better if it's planned. You'll need to think about the different types of data that you'll need, resource demands, access and so on. Let's consider the type of data required. There are two types: secondary and primary.

Secondary data

Generally speaking, most researchers tend to collect secondary data before primary data. This is because secondary data are data that already exist. Such data can come from internal sources such as company reports or previous market research reports. External sources such as government publications, newspapers, magazines and directories are also useful. The internet enables secondary research to a greater extent than ever before, although its scale is problematic, given recent (already out-of-date) estimates of 65 billion pages in the web. Large research agencies, such as Mintel and Nielsen, also publish

research reports which you could purchase or commission. However, they can be costly.

Secondary data are not specific to your research question, nor will they be up to date or particularly accurate, which are the key disadvantages. However, they may give you a starting point, or a feel, for the optimum direction. Although there are these disadvantages, the reason we often use and start with secondary data is because doing so is cost-effective (the data already exist), you do not need to be a skilled researcher to collect or use them and they are relatively quick to collect. Therefore, if you work as a sole trader or in a small organisation, the use of secondary data to try to find the solution to your problem is realistically the starting point for you.

However, using secondary data will get you only so far. As the data are not specific to helping you answer your research problem or question, and because they may be out of date, and therefore slightly inaccurate, the chances are that you will need to collect more up-to-date and relevant data. The data you collect for the first time, which are commissioned to be specifically focused upon solving your research problem and objectives, are known as 'primary data'.

Primary data

Primary data are based upon specifically answering your research problem and objectives. Therefore, they are specific, relevant, timely and, if collected and analysed properly, accurate.

There are different ways you can collect primary data. One of the factors that plays a part in deciding which technique you use to collect the data is whether you wish the research to be structured using quantitative data or qualitative data. These two terms sound intimidating but in fact they are very simple and straightforward.

Quantitative data

Quantitative data are data based upon numbers that are representative of a larger population. Care has to be taken as it's

easy to generate superficial figures that suggest trends that may not be there. That said, well-designed 'quant' research, based on either secondary or primary data, can provide useful information on consumer trends.

Example
When psephologists Ipsos MORI carry out research to predict the result of UK general elections, they often use quantitative data that seek to represent the whole voting population. They typically poll a sample of 1,500–2,000 prospective voters and generate results that are accurate to plus or minus 3 per cent. When it's a close-run thing, 3 per cent may not be accurate enough and they would need a much larger sample. Alternatively, they could triangulate their findings with those of other surveys.

Questionnaires

Ipsos MORI would use a questionnaire as the method to collect raw data. You would then analyse the data to deduce information, in this case the public's voting intention. Raw data are not the same as information.

Questionnaires can be administered in a number of ways:

- **face to face, with the questionnaire being completed by either yourself or the respondent;**
- **by telephone;**
- **by post;**
- **by e-mail;**
- **online, via a pop-up.**

Each of these techniques has strengths and weaknesses. You need to acknowledge these to avoid bias, which is the bane of good research. Consider posing the following question to male respondents:

Have you used, or would you use, a condom?   Yes/No

You can be fairly confident that the answer is honest and lacks respondent bias. You could ask this using any of the above methods.
The follow-up question is:

What size?

As you can imagine, this poses a number of questions that need to be addressed to avoid bias. You must consider the sensitivities of the researcher *and* the respondent. Hence, this question would probably be better asked in a non-face-to-face way, such as by e-mail or by phone.

Respondent bias can also result from over-long questionnaires. Table 8.1 (page 101) is typical of a questionnaire that uses a Likert scale (that is, with responses ranging from 'strongly disagree' to 'strongly agree') in an attempt to avoid the shallow nature of some quantitative research. The example provided is fine, but try to avoid pages of questions.

Questionnaires are very useful if you need to collect data from a large number of people. A key issue to consider is that if you're looking for trends in a large body of people, you will not have the resources to question them all. Hence, you'll need to question a representative sample of your target audience. It's a balancing act, as the more people you question in your target audience, the greater the degree of accuracy your results will have.

Questionnaires do provide you with the opportunity to also ask open-ended questions to collect qualitative data. An example is 'What is your opinion on banning smoking in public places?' However, if you're using lots of these in your questionnaire, then you probably should have used a qualitative research design in the first place.

Qualitative data

If you are wishing to collect data that are based upon people's attitudes, opinions, feelings or perceptions, then a qualitative approach is required. Often, how we feel is a greater force than how

we think cognitively. Any long-standing football fan knows that the heart rules the head, particularly for supporters of the majority of teams that rarely win trophies! Qualitative research is often used to ascertain consumers' feelings regarding new products or services.

However, the choice is governed by your research problem and objectives. You then have to undertake the collection of primary data, which is quite a skilled task with a variety of methods or techniques. The two most common methods used to collect qualitative primary data involve the use of focus groups and interviews.

Focus groups

To set up a focus group, you select 6–12 respondents from your target audience and ask them questions. Focus groups are very useful when you're developing new products or services, as you create the opportunity to interact with a selection of your target market and perhaps show them a prototype of the product. What do they think about its design? Size? Colour? Weight? Name? How much would they pay for it? Where would they buy it? A lot of useful qualitative data can be collected.

Interviews

An in-depth interview is just with one respondent. Therefore, the interviewer can really probe for in-depth answers, feelings, opinions, etc. However, the technique can be costly, as it is time-consuming and done on a one-to-one basis – but the results are both timely and, hopefully, accurate.

Choosing the most appropriate method to use can be difficult. The trick is to really understand what it is you're trying to find out – hence the reason you need to understand your research question and objectives very well and also understand which methods are useful for collecting which type of data. You also need to consider your limitations and circumstances. It's also important to understand whether instead of using qualitative or quantitative data, you may actually need a blend of both, which in reality is often the most suitable.

Analysing and presenting the findings

Once you have collected the data, you then have to analyse them. What do they all mean? How can your company use the data? This can take time and skill, hence many PR consultants use specialist research agencies to plan their research and collect, interpret and analyse the data.

Quantitative data are easier to analyse as they are well suited to statistical analysis, spreadsheets or simple graphs. Packages such as SPSS exist to facilitate complex analysis of large amounts of data. Qualitative data must still be analysed to identify themes and trends. Simply offering a few respondent quotes is not usually enough.

Once the analysis is complete, your PR representative will want to coordinate the presentation of the findings to the appropriate stakeholders. This may include your manager, director, customers – not just yourself! Rest assured that good knowledge gained from well-designed research can only strengthen your company's position, so don't be surprised if others may find the results and conclusions interesting as well. Hence, you should put some effort into making the report stand out.

A common mistake is that researchers and marketers make the report easy for themselves, not the reader. Have a beginning, middle and end, with a logical flow from start to finish. Don't start discussing things in the conclusions section for the first time!

Marketing research is at the heart of most marketing decisions. To remain competitive, innovative and attractive to the customer, we must constantly evolve our products, services and organisations. Marketing research is central to providing us with the data and information to help us to do this successfully. It goes without saying that the research should be conducted in an ethical fashion. If in doubt, refer to the Market Research Society's code of conduct.

Summary and activities

Key points

- Marketing research is used to provide up-to-date, accurate information to help companies solve problems and lower the risk in important decision-making.
- Marketing research is systematic in nature and a basic process is to be followed.
- Secondary data are data that already exist. Such data are cheap to collect and readily available, and a non-skilled marketer can collect and use them. However, they are often dated, therefore inaccurate and not specific enough.
- Primary data are data that a marketer collects for the first time. They are therefore specific, timely and accurate. However, they can be time-consuming and expensive to collect. A degree of skill is also required to collect and analyse the data accurately.
- There are a variety of techniques available to collect primary data including questionnaires, focus groups and interviews.

Questions

1. Why do marketers need to invest in marketing research?
2. What are the risks associated with marketing research?
3. Why is the setting or research objectives so crucial?

Activities

Look at the material in your office: past research projects, sales statistics, competitor information, pricing initiatives – they could all be regarded as secondary data and could be useful to refer to in the future. So, create a

simple information system in your office. Ensure that you file these documents (don't throw them away!). Even if you don't find them useful initially, somebody else might!

For an excellent introduction to social and market research, have a look at the following textbook:

Adams, K and Brace, I (2006) *An Introduction to Market and Social Research*, Kogan Page, London

Also look at a variety of websites. The Market Research Society's code of conduct is essential reading for those involved in marketing research (website: http://www. mrs.org.uk). Others to peruse are:

http:// www.mintel.com

http:// www.datamonitor

http:// www.marketing-intelligence.co.uk

10

How much should good public relations cost?

While today's new technologies offer exciting communications choices, there are also challenges. When marcomms work well, they can provide many benefits for the brand, the company and, more importantly, the customers. However, when they go wrong (and they go wrong with worrying regularity!), they can have devastating effects. Not only can precious time, money and resources be wasted, but your brand name, brand equity (the value of the brand) and the reputation could all be adversely affected. Because many of your comms activities will be in the public domain, your mistakes are there for all to see: your intended receivers, your competitors and (in some cases worst of all)... the media!

Which marketing strategies do you wish to drive with PR?

Marketing communications

You may wish to complement your traditional PR activities through generating buzz in other ways, such as guerrilla

marketing or getting bloggers to write about your company. We need to acknowledge this and remember it when we are creating, planning and executing our comms activities. When faced with making purchase decisions, consumers often seek information to support their decisions, particularly when making larger, riskier purchases. They'll read magazines (eg sector-specific publications or consumer-friendly titles such as *Which?*), use the internet to glean more information (from social networking sites, public forums, comparison sites, opinion leader sites and blogs) and, above all else, turn to the people around them for advice and guidance. They'll ask colleagues, friends and, most of all, family. It's a common practice for a consumer to access all of the aforementioned sophisticated communication materials and still heed the advice and opinions of those closest to them more than the supposed 'experts'.

Positioning

Positioning is simply about how your customers (and prospects) perceive your company in relation to the competition. Hence, you need to consider how good their communications are. As a matter of course and practice, you should always be monitoring your competitive environment (see Chapter 2). What communication tools do your customers use? How often? Are they successful?

Product portfolio

Are you centring your messages on a product or service? If so, what points do you need to exemplify? After considering the above factors, you also need to think about the customers in more detail and then select the most appropriate strategy to reach them with your message.

How much to invest in PR?

The answers will very much depend on your situation and how you interact with your marketing environments (see Figure 3.2, page 29). Let's assume that you're looking for a PR agency to handle a new product launch. You approach four agencies and their quoted 'budgets' range from £10,000 to £200,000. How do you evaluate their plans?

The cost of hiring a PR agency varies greatly, depending on how established the agency is and the level of service that you require. Large companies can pay hundreds of thousands of pounds on generating PR, an amount of money that would put many SMEs out of business. Many PR firms will also act as a media centre, taking enquiries from journalists, and may offer a guarantee of some kind, which can reduce the risk of spending thousands of pounds for no end product. So it really depends on:

- **What marcomms tactics are you using already and how are they working?**
- **How much do you need to do?**
- **How much can you afford to do?**
- **What is your marketing budget overall and how much of it are you willing to devote to PR?**

Consider the budget allocation decision you'll have to make; PR may take 5 per cent of your budget or it may be 100 per cent. It depends! So take a look at your overall marketing budget, your target audience and your goals. While it's true that you usually get what you pay for, should you automatically discount the lowest budget (or the highest, for that matter)? Remember, you're looking for your PR to be efficient *and* effective.

So we now need to reflect on the key question: How much are you going to spend? This is a key determinant of your communication choices. Indeed, whether strictly correct or not, the decision is largely driven by your budget, which in turn impacts on whether the choices of communication tools open to you will widen or, conversely, become extremely narrow.

What is your budget?

First of all, asking how much a PR campaign should cost is a lot like asking how much an advertising campaign or a sales promotion campaign costs. An ad campaign can cost £5,000 or it can cost £250,000,000. Likewise, PR is a tool that can be used by all organisations and hence can benefit them in different ways. So how much your organisation needs to do is a question that has to be judged on its own merits. A PR campaign can range from:

- **being free: many PR practitioners carry out *pro bono* work for charities or causes with which they're sympathetic;**
- **very low cost: at Leeds Business School we're always looking for clients who are willing to offer internships (eg a day a week or in blocks of weeks), placements or work experience for PR undergraduates; companies new to PR may seek an initial 'one-off' project to test the water;**
- **medium cost: use of a dedicated consultant with high-sector experience; retaining a small to medium-sized agency with limited resources; ad hoc use of a larger agency when fit for purpose;**
- **higher costs from large, possibly multinational agencies that will take on all of your communications efforts with truly global reach.**

Naturally, these different approaches will have a range of costs (Table 10.1).

Ad hoc PR, like ad hoc marketing in general, is to be avoided as it's a lottery more than it's social science. Once you've worked with an agency or consultant, you'll be satisfied that PR is effective and you may want to commit to hiring a PR agency on an ongoing basis. For this the agency will put together a couple of press releases each month, and develop a longer-term PR strategy. The cost for this typically starts at £1,000 per month.

Table 10.1 Costs of PR

Company Type	Daily Rates	Budgets
Independent PR practitioner/ consultant	£75–£150 daily	Up to £5,000 for monthly retainers
Independent PR practitioner/ consultant (10 years' experience)	£150–£300 daily	£3,000–£10,000 for monthly retainers
Small PR firms (5–25 employees)		Up to £5,000– 10,000 per month
Large PR firms: junior representative		£7,000–£25,000 per month
Large PR firms: senior partner		£20,000–£100,000 per month minimum up to £1 million

Time is money

Remember that even if your company isn't investing time in generating material, your agency or consultant will be! Pascal has often been quoted as writing 'I'm sorry for writing such a long letter but I didn't have time to write a short one.' Experience shows us that writing a 200-word piece of PR copy can be as taxing as 'knocking off' 1,000 words. Certainly CIPR and CIM professional students recognise the challenge of writing to a word limit. Typically, a 1,500-word case study or feature article may require 20 hours of the creative department's time; this involves researching and polishing off after numerous revisions. As discussed in Chapter 4, press releases are the building blocks of PR programmes, and two-page releases may easily require 5–10 hours to write and distribute to the appropriate outlets.

Even the smallest PR programmes should budget 20 hours per month for basic media relations. Larger companies often budget hundreds of hours per month! A guide is to map all of the publications you (or even better, those that your customers) deem to be useful and allocate a proportional time for media relations activities. Hence, if your company needs regular exposure through, say, 20 key reporters, reviewers and analysts, consider budgeting approximately 20 hours per month.

Remember that there are many incidental 'out-of-pocket' expenses (for postage, photography, long-distance phone charges, couriers, etc) to be factored in. These could range widely, from £100 to £2,000 per month. Distribution costs, assuming the release will be mailed to, say, 50 media outlets, should not exceed £250. On a one-off basis, some companies will simply put together a press release, send it out and hope that it delivers results. This costs in the region of £200–£400 and is low cost but risky in that results are far from guaranteed. To keeping mailing costs as low as possible, companies have increasingly moved towards e-newsletters.

> **Example**
> EFL is a leading UK-based supplier of hubs and routers to ISPs. It e-mails a monthly newsletter to 5,000 prospects and customers at a cost of £75. The content is designed in-house, so naturally the company has some HTML experience. Its scheduled PR programme is highly effective as its staff strive to keep the material therein of high quality. There is always a demand for news of benefits and means of adding value, particularly if featuring testimonials where products or services have helped a company solve a key business issue.

Large PR firms can charge anything from £1,000 to £5,000 for a single press release. However, for this they'll drill down into your company (hence understanding your aims and objectives) and

sector before creating and distributing a press release. Large PR agencies will want to follow up their efforts as a matter of professional etiquette.

As Table 10.1 illustrates, £3,000 a month will retain a good PR company. However, you must ensure you're getting value for money, and set aside a number of days or hours for the effort needed to do so. You need to be confident that the agency or consultant you engage has access to the media contacts that relate to your company. PR is like every other walk of life (and business) in that people buy from people, and PR consultants generally have only limited outlets where they have excellent relationships and can get you coverage. Beyond their sphere of influence they may struggle to provide the reach and access your company needs.

Many clients believe that it is imperative to understand exactly what PR is delivering to their bottom line, arguing that PR agencies (and staff) need to comprehend the financial aims and objectives of the company as well as barriers to achieving competitive advantage.

You'll certainly want to know whether your clients perceive your media presence favourably over a period of time. If they don't, ask them what is needed to improve their perceptions. If any of their suggestions are adopted, use this as a powerful tool. Clients simply love to know that their advice has been taken on board. Is your agency providing the right coverage, frequency of release or improved positioning in the media? Try to come up with measurable parameters for evaluating the effectiveness of your PR from the clients' perspectives. Bear in mind the following:

- **Favourability of coverage is not the same as volume of coverage.**
- **Advertising value equivalents (see page 132) and Opportunities to See (see page 136) are not easy to measure.**
- **Qualitative information is often more useful than quantitative measurement.**
- **Measurement of changes to your company or brand reputation may happen over a long timescale.**

- **It's not simply how many times your company is mentioned; rather, it's about how your customers' (and prospects') views and behaviours have changed.**

If you try to skimp on publicity efforts by budgeting only a couple of hundred pounds per month, don't expect the world. The publicist will be able to spend only a few hours working on your account, so don't expect to be on television and in the best newspapers around. The old adage is true: you get what you pay for!

The do-it-yourself option

There are plenty of examples of people who are not PR professionals but practise PR as a matter of course to ensure their business or organisation maintains and develops a healthy profile and reputation. Bill Gates, Richard Branson and, more recently, Barack Obama are just a few of the high-profile people who understand the power of PR. Never ones to say 'no comment' or turn away from a difficult situation, they have earned respect based on transparency and a willingness to engage with the public.

As an ambassador for your organisation, you and everyone who represents your business, because they are employed by you, buy your products or use your services, have the ability to influence the reputation of your organisation. It is important therefore that you harness PR opportunities, recognise who your brand ambassadors are and build and maintain excellent relations with all parties involved. You can do this informally as well as formally but you must always do it in the knowledge that whatever you and your ambassadors do and say about your organisation may impact on its reputation and success.

You may look to hire a PR agency on a one-off or an ongoing basis. PR should be a continuous process but you may be happy with generating some initial media coverage but subsequently managing your PR activities in-house. Doing your own PR costs you nothing but your time, although you'd be wise to do a lot of reading on the topic before you start, speak to your local business

school, study a CIPR-approved course or even pay for a few hours of coaching from a PR professional.

There is a news medium where you can circulate press releases yourself: PR Newswire (www.prnewswire.co.uk). It offers a range of services and targeted release mechanisms. It is a bit 'scattergun' but does work. Last time one of us used it, the cost was about £250 to go to thousands of news desks.

Make sure the chemistry is right

Entering a new relationship with a PR firm should be a very positive experience for both parties. Good PR agencies and consultants will be willing to work with you to establish a realistic budget at the beginning of the relationship. The odds are very good that the two companies will work well together, almost seamlessly. When business partners respect and trust each other, everyone benefits. Isn't that what building a relationship is all about? It is important to take care of your PR team. These are the people who will tirelessly promote your company and seek ways to improve your competitive advantage.

Evaluation

Whenever you seek to communicate benefits to customers, whether it's a piece of PR, a sales promotion, an ad or a direct mail letter, you must always be able to measure its effectiveness and decide whether the communication has worked and achieved its objectives. You can easily spend large amounts of time and money on your communication activities, so you need to know whether they're working. If they are... great! But why have you got it so right? What can be taken from this success to create another? Conversely, if the communication is failing... why? Is the message unclear? Is it the media chosen to carry the message to the receiver? Is it down to noise? Is the encoding incorrect? With potentially high costs involved, you must be able to rectify

mistakes quickly and learn so that future communications will hit their intended marks.

The process of evaluation can be quite simple, especially if you have set SMART objectives for your PR activities (see Chapter 3). SMART objectives might include changing legislation or ensuring that a set number of delegates attend an event. But they could be as subtle as changing people's views and attitudes. Whatever your objective, it is essential that you identify from an early stage how and what you are going to evaluate to measure the success of your PR activities.

Building evaluation into your programme of activities from the outset ensures good accountability and effective management. In practice, evaluating campaigns and PR activities can be fraught with challenges and disagreements. PR is a discipline in which experienced practitioners regularly debate the value of various types of evaluation, and purchasers of their services may challenge the benchmarks drawn up for purposes of evaluation.

The CIPR has produced guidelines and toolkits on evaluation but there is no defining common standard. PR is subtler and more difficult to quantify than other communication disciplines, such as direct mail or advertising, and the evaluation methods, while varied, are essential. They are often dynamic and flexible to enable change where required and reflection at all stages of implementation.

Evaluation of media coverage

Still the most common form of PR activity, media coverage can be evaluated in a number of ways to create some meaningful understanding of the success of your coverage.

The crudest, yet still the most commonly used, is to compare the size of a piece of coverage gained with how much it would have cost to place an advert in the same media outlet. Advertising value equivalents (AVEs) are used by PRs to demonstrate to clients and business that PR is more cost-effective than advertising and a more credible way to get your message across to readers or viewers.

A quarter-page advert in your trade publication or regional newspaper might cost £1,000. If you gain a quarter-page article, whether through an interview with a journalist, via your news release or self-generated by a journalist, you might compare the value of the coverage gained with what you've saved in terms of advertising.

Example 1
In 2008, Ultragen wanted to launch an anti-ageing skincare device called Stop, at a high price and with no confirmed retailers on board.

Objectives:
Launch the product and build awareness of the technology behind it.
Secure credible retail partners.

Tactics:
With research, the PR team gathered endorsements from credible medical and cosmetic professionals. Trial products were offered to beauty bloggers. The supermodel Marie Helvin was secured as the 'face' of Stop and a photocall was staged in the window of Selfridges. Local press events were held around the country, receiving regional coverage, and product samples were sent to celebrities.

Evaluation:
A total of 116 articles appeared in titles such as *The Sunday Times Style*, *Grazia*, *She*, *Harper's*, *Tatler* and the *Mail on Sunday* as well as regional media. GMTV's *LK Today* programme gave a product demonstration.

Result:
Both Selfridges and Harvey Nichols were secured as distributors, along with smaller retailers. Harvey Nichols

reported that Stop was flying off the shelves, and placed emergency repeat orders in the run-up to Christmas 2008.

From this example we can see that Ultragen knew the market it wanted to launch its product at, it knew which publications would help it to do this, and it recognised that gaining endorsements from credible sources, using an appropriate celebrity, would maximise the results. Evaluation was ongoing, as monitoring the media was essential to keeping the story alive. The PRs would have been contacting relevant, targeted journalists as the coverage grew, using the hype around the product to create more coverage, as beauty journalists don't want to miss out on the latest technology.

Example 2
In January 2009, ancestry.co.uk acquired the rights to publish the London Metropolitan Archives, a collection of records detailing more than 400 years of London history.

Objectives:
To raise awareness of the online launch of the London Metropolitan Archives.
To drive visitors to the website www.ancestry.co.uk.
To boost subscriptions.

Strategy and tactics:
Research by the PR team worked out that more than half of Britons could trace a relative within the collection. They pulled out key facts concerning celebrities, and TV historian and actor Tony Robinson launched an event at the Guildhall

Crypts with a launch news release going to more than 200 national journalists.

Evaluation:
More than 30 journalists attended the launch event, leading to 108 pieces of media coverage, including 25 broadcast items and 40 websites that covered the story.

Results:
The Campaign led to a 30 per cent increase in traffic to the site and a 57 per cent increase in new membership over the two weeks following the launch.

Getting to the detail

This rather crude way of measuring the success of your media relations or news release is still considered to be very effective for most campaigns. However, it does not take into account whether the media coverage you gained was good or bad.

We know that on average only one in seven articles in a national newspaper is a positive news story. It would therefore be foolish to assume that all the coverage about us or our company is always going to be positive.

Key questions by which to test your media coverage will depend on the objectives but might include the following examples:

- **Has the article reached the most appropriate audience? It's no good celebrating coverage of your new service or product if the newspaper or magazine it has featured in is not read by your target audience.**
- **Have the key messages you wanted to convey been included? Does coverage of your new organic locally sourced product mention these key product characteristics?**

- **Has your brand name or company name been represented accurately?**
- **If you are launching a new website, does the article feature the address?**
- **If there are two named individuals included in the news release, are they each recognised, or are you going to have to explain to a key investor that they were not mentioned in your press coverage?**

In order to gauge media coverage most effectively, it is useful to develop a grid listing the key messages you want to communicate as well as assessing any negative comments and the overall tone of the message.

PR Week regularly conducts a survey to gauge which methods of evaluation PR practitioners have used. On average, 60 per cent use media content analysis or press cuttings to evaluate their activities. The next most popular technique is one called Opportunity to See (OTS), which is the number of occasions on which an audience has the potential to view a message.

Most 'cuttings agencies' – companies that scan the press looking for key words or names – include the circulation numbers of the relevant media. The circulation figure is usually three times the distribution figure. So if a newspaper sells 250,000 copies a day, its circulation figure is 750,000, as it is assumed that each copy is read by an average of three people.

Surveys and focus groups are also used to evaluation PR programmes. But it is generally accepted by practitioners that a range of tools and techniques is needed to properly assess PR impact.

Barriers to effective evaluation are also common, so avoid falling into the trap of not planning it into your programme of PR activity. Typical reasons for poor evaluation include lack of time, lack of personnel, lack of budget, cost of evaluation, doubts about its usefulness, lack of knowledge and exposure to criticism.

Summary and activities

Key points

- The cost of your PR will depend on the overall comms budget and campaign currently used. PR must be coordinated with your other marketing activities.
- The cost of hiring a PR agency varies greatly, depending on how established the agency is and the level of service that you require.
- Building evaluation into your programme of activities from the outset ensures good accountability and effective management.

Activities

- The Chartered Institute of Public Relations' website (http://www.cipr.co.uk) has useful sections. 'Looking for PR' includes definitions, a glossary and a guide to hiring a PR consultant, plus a PR directory.

- MediaUK is a forum for discussion and information for PR professionals in the United Kingdom plus an excellent media UK internet directory and a listing of the latest media news (website: http://www.mediauk.com).

- If you're interested in integrating PR into your marketing planning, buy Malcolm McDonald's book (*Malcolm McDonald on Marketing Planning: Understanding marketing plans and strategy*, Kogan Page, London, 2007). It hits the nail fairly and squarely on the head. For those teaching marketing planning it's an invaluable resource. Many of the lessons in general marketing planning apply to planning a comms campaign.

11

PR championing ethics and sustainability

When you are considering the challenges facing your company, a key question is 'Why would clients buy my products rather than those of a competitor?' Finding good answers to such thoughts is crucial. One answer is that consumption is social, in that when 'buying', we take on attitudes, beliefs, opinions and values from others, hence companies that are not aware of changes in society run the risk of alienating customers. This is the case with sustainability, which despite being missing from most marketing texts is increasingly important to key stakeholders.

The business of business is business...?

Sustainability is based on mutual benefit – that is, both parties benefit and can work together long term. Milton Friedman challenged the idea of mutual benefit, arguing that the business of business is business. That is, a company's only moral responsibility is to make money for its shareholders. He even

argued that 'the social responsibility of business is to increase its profits', which somewhat dismissively alluded to the growing roles of social and societal marketing. Yet despite Friedman, more and more companies have espoused their green credentials while recognising how a widening range of societal issues, such as ethical practices, has gained importance with consumers.

It has been argued that Friedman's libertarian position leads to the establishing of non-sustainable structures, as was the case with the 2008–09 economic meltdown. Assuming Friedman's viewpoint to be one end of a sustainability continuum, its opposite can be deemed to be 'pure sustainability', which is philosophical, arguably spiritual and wholly dedicated to improving the human condition (Figure 11.1).

All companies are located on the continuum (knowingly or otherwise) and need to be aware of their position. Companies need to be able to position (or reposition) themselves within their markets in order to make effective decisions. If your research shows that your customers' perceptions (of your sustainability positioning) don't match your own, then you need to implement changes.

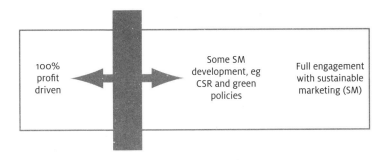

Figure 11.1 Sustainability continuum

Using PR to overcome barriers to sustainability

In the future, you'll probably need to operate in an increasingly sustainable fashion and you'll need to identify and remove barriers to adopting sustainability (Figure 11.2).

While it's unlikely that all of these apply to your company, you need to consider some of the following factors.

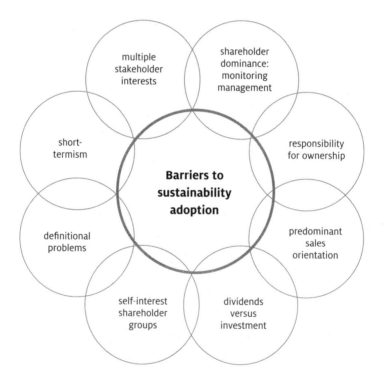

Figure 11.2 Barriers to the adoption of sustainability

Definitional problems

We live in fast-changing times and it's not surprising that many terms are used to represent new concepts. Even terms you'd think were well established, for example 'the environment', are used in myriad ways between differing texts and in some cases by the same author. It is prudent to consider such concerns since consumers often connect with broader environment issues. Their environmental interaction is important, intensely emotional and can affect their purchasing decisions.

It is therefore worth reflecting on key relatively recent developments that have shaped the sustainability agenda. The 1987 Brundtland Commission defined sustainability as 'development that meets the needs of the present without compromising the ability of future generations to meet their own needs'. In 1997 the issue was brought to much wider audiences (ie business academics and practitioners) when Hart coined the phrase 'sustainable development' in the *Harvard Business Review*. Soon afterwards, Elkington's 'triple bottom line' (TBL) appeared in the same publication. In the TBL the traditional economic focus (ie the company's bottom line) is complemented by the addition of new foci, namely social and economic responsibility. The Hart and Elkington texts are two of the most important recent contributions on the subject of business and sustainable development.

Since the concept of the TBL was coined, the sustainable business development concept has grown, often being referred to as 'People–Profit–Planet'. This may still be new to many practitioners (and academics!). However, elements of it have been practised for centuries. One often-cited example of sustainability in practice is the Co-operative movement, which has been practising a recognisable form of sustainable retailing since the 1840s.

One of the difficulties of defining sustainability derives from the multidisciplinary context. For example, town planners have a different take compared to marketers, who in turn differ from

accountants. Even within disciplines there are many different definitions, with one study identifying over 500 attempts at developing quantitative indicators of sustainable development.

For a workable definition, consider the following:

> Sustainable Marketing (SM) involves principled marketing predicated on the tenets of the Triple Bottom Line. Hence marketing decisions should be ethical and guided by sustainable business practices which ultimately are the only way to resolve the tensions between consumers' wants and long term interests, companies' requirements, society's long run interests and the need for environmental balance.
>
> Richardson, 2008

This definition should act as a springboard for your company. Make sure that it is reflected in your mission and vision statements, and then use PR to ensure that all publics and stakeholders are aware of your position.

Shareholder dominance: monitoring management

Principals (ie shareholders and institutional investors) are aware that agents (ie directors and managers) may act out of self-interest and position the company in such a way as to reduce returns and share value. Hence, the principals incur the cost of monitoring the directors via annual audits, which are obligatory for all UK plcs. Too often, agents communicate with their shareholders only in the run-up to the AGM. This approach should be avoided and replaced by treating shareholders in the same way as you would customers. Use PR to build relationships, keep them informed, build loyalty and enhance shareholder satisfaction – and remember, loyalty is not the same as satisfaction!

Responsibility for ownership

One of the myths regarding business is that it's part of the problem, not the solution, and that issues such as sustainability should be the concern of politicians and governments rather than 'business'. On reflection, this approach is seen to be contradictory. 'Business' needs to be at the forefront of the 'sustainability' debate as trade largely takes place among companies, not governments. Also, it's not simply trading that is huge, but also the flow of capital in the form of foreign direct investment (FDI). In 2004, global trade ($7 trillion) was dwarfed by FDI ($17 trillion). Hence, 'business' has enormous potential to promote sustainable trade patterns. Also, 'business', rather than government, has the knowledge and skills to trade sustainably as well as helping to shape global sustainability guidelines and practices. If the Co-operative movement can thrive for 160 years, then other businesses can.

Example
Brownfield developments have found increasing favour among planners. However, retailers seeking development opportunities have complained about a lack of cooperation by local authorities, citing severe delays in winning planning approval. This macro-environmental interface is interdisciplinary in nature (being between the domains of retail marketing and the built environment). Retail developers may benefit from an improved PR role with the local community if it is their interest to gain advantage 'by favourably influencing the opinions of planners and the local community... [by] communicating the benefits of a proposed store to the relevant public' (McGoldrick, 2002: 267).

It is easy to see how sustainability 'ownership' can be fuzzy in some companies and hotly contested in others. Corporate social

responsibility (CSR) is often controlled by human resource departments. Some organisations recognise the importance of CSR with elements in their mission statements (a strategic management decision), which may include 'green' issues (possibly a quality control issue), ethical supply policies (the purchasing department) and charitable links (all of the above!).

This corporate 'bun-fight' is reflected on the larger stage, where proponents of sustainable development differ widely in terms of emphases – for example, what to sustain or to develop, and when? In B2C sectors you could argue that responsibility lies with the service provider, the consumer, the community, the regulator or even the government. An example of governmental influence in the United Kingdom is the Companies Act 2006, which heavily affects CSR. Increasingly the environment will be used as a launch pad for governmental initiatives and legislation. PR can be an invaluable tool for informing the different parties and managing expectations.

Undoubtedly, when things are going well, everyone wants to stake their claim. However, when it goes wrong, where does responsibility lie? Recent studies have discussed corporate social irresponsibility, where CSR is abused by organisations seeking competitive advantage through misinformation. It is no wonder that we're increasingly sceptical of environmental claims, hence the rise of accusations of 'greenwashing'. Ultimately you must act in an ethical way and communicate transparently with your stakeholders.

Dividends versus investment

This question of whether to emphasise dividends or investment is more likely to apply to larger companies or those with active shareholders who seek maximum returns on their investment. As discussed, there are many tensions within companies, some of which are exacerbated by the (mis)use of the word 'sustainability' itself. For some, shareholder sustainability is the main corporate driver, featuring returning dividends and maximising share value for owners. Principals demand regular, stable dividend payments.

However, funds needed to pay dividends detract from the agents' ability to undertake new (sustainable) projects; principals want to sustain dividends to maintain market value. Shareholders' concerns (having funded the company through investment) should be acknowledged in conjunction with those of the stakeholders that enable the company to continue and thrive. Progressive managers should naturally cater for the lives and well-being of its micro-environmental stakeholders, such as employees, suppliers and the community in which the company is located. Hence, for most commentators shareholder sustainability does not equate to 'sustainability', and undoubtedly PR can serve a function regarding informing, and managing the expectations of, publics, including shareholders and institutional investors.

Self-interest shareholder groups

It may be stating the plain and obvious, but the terms used so far, namely 'business', 'company' and 'organisation', are somewhat nebulous. There are many differing types of multi-stakeholder businesses, including single proprietorships, partnerships, co-operatives, non-profit enterprises, social enterprises, private limited companies (ie those with 'Ltd' after their name) and public limited enterprises (plcs). Each of these categories differs in terms of aims, objectives, vision, culture, structure, and so on. In some companies, principals (aka shareholders) were deemed to be a key 'public' in that they had influence; however, they were largely deemed to be passive. Increasingly, shareholders are being referred to as key stakeholders in that they actively participate in the running of the AGM. Some principals acquire shares specifically to affect the running or direction of the company, which would usually be the domain of the agents (ie directors and managers). This may lead to strategic shift and/or drift, not to mention the potential for diminishing returns. Recently, shareholders have formed well-organised pressure groups in order to maximise their influence on corporate policy. These groups are often adept at using PR as a key tool in promoting their agenda.

Multiple stakeholder interests

Organisations do not exist in isolation, which renders Friedman's philosophy somewhat redundant. Simply put, companies affect the lives and well-being of their stakeholders and publics (Figures 3.2 and 6.1, pages 29 and 76). Managers have to interact with said stakeholders, such as employees, unions, suppliers, intermediaries, government and, most importantly, customers. Each of these may have their own agenda and/or be motivated by self-interest. In business schools we often preach the mantra of improving customer perceptions of added value. However, shareholder 'value' may come at the expense of customer 'value' and satisfaction. Companies could certainly use PR as a tool to address issues such as diminished job security, higher unemployment and poorer (perceived) products and services.

Short-termism

The economic difficulties of 2008–09 illustrated clearly that, for example, many financial institutions do not operate in a free market where they can do as they wish. Governments will always bail out financial institutions if the alternative is economically damaging. Cases such as Northern Rock should serve as an invaluable lesson in the danger of short-term approaches. In Northern Rock's case the business model was changed (after demutualisation) to an unsustainable model which strove for higher returns than had been the case in the company's long history as a mutual 'friendly' society.

In some cases, managers may wish to adopt policies beyond those demanded by legislation or regulatory bodies, such as being listed on the FTSE4GOOD index. This could incur costs that diminish market value or returns. Such action is often watered down if not prevented outright by fear of over-reaction by the short-termist markets. Hence, those with vested interests (such as institutional investors and free-marketeers) encourage managers to ignore investments in longer-run drivers of success such as

sustainability. Many of these investors lost substantial funds in Northern Rock, which could have taken a different trajectory if they'd adopted a more sustainable approach... irony upon ironies!

Predominant sales orientation

A popular misconception is that PR promotes the (short-term?) selling of products to the target groups. Such sales orientations are now cited as contributing to consumers' increasing awareness of 'greenwashing'. Certainly Friedman's libertarian position contributes to the assumption that businesses advocate 'selling more', while 'sustainability' is about consuming less (Howell, 2006); therefore the two paradigms are diametrically opposed. Friedman's 'dominant' paradigm of free trade is increasingly criticised for being inherently unsustainable. However, economists still measure 'sustainability' by emphasising accounting approaches that focus on the maintenance of capital stocks and supply-side controls. Customers rarely feature in sustainability models discussed at the highest levels, such as the United Nations, the European Union or UNCTAD (the United Nations Conference on Trade and Development).

PR as an internal marketing tool

As previously discussed, internal marketing is a well-established concept (Figure 2.2, page 17) but is largely poorly practised. PR is the obvious tool to help promote internal marketing *and* the adoption of sustainable practices internally. After all, a key foundation of the TBL is 'people', and there are hundreds of studies that demonstrate the benefits of treating your people well. There has been a sea change in consumer opinion regarding the TBL and it is likely that marketing academics are trailing consumers, progressive organisations and other disciplines. Kotler now argues that marketer's lives will become more complicated. Meeting 'planet' costs may necessitate raising prices!

This does not automatically mean that the product will be harder to sell. However, you'll need to sell the benefits and add value. Also, you'll need to consider where your company should be on the 'sustainability continuum' (Figure 11.1). You may choose to commit heavily or to a lesser extent. One thing's for certain: in terms of sustainability there's no turning back.

Many managers have let operational effectiveness supplant strategy, particularly in scenarios where constant improvement is often seen as the route to superior profitability. Naturally, operations have to keep pace with customer change, and the move to sustainable marketing could be one such change. What is needed is not change for its own sake but the right change, and many examples exist of companies that have benefited by moving towards adopting TBL. What's needed is a framework for benchmarking (Figure 11.3).

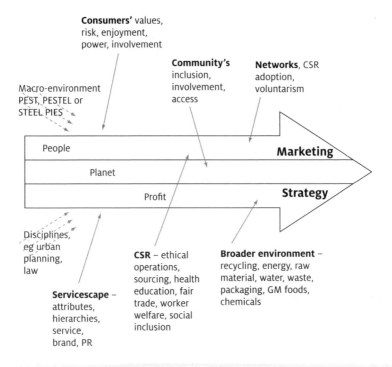

Figure 11.3 A framework for sustainable marketing

Managing change... or is it changing management?

Companies are made up of different systems that interact with each other and their respective environments. You won't be shocked by the notion that many managers protect their fiefdoms jealously and lack a vision of the bigger picture. A severe challenge for operations managers of 'non-enlightened' companies would be to operationalise the move towards sustainable marketing, as few models or theoretical constructs exist. It can be argued that too many companies are process or systems driven when they should be customer driven. Think about the term 'customer relationship management' (CRM). Surely this is a misnomer and we all should be seeking customer satisfaction management!

Anyway, you need to measure your effectiveness in all of the zones in Figure 11.4. There are already many tools out there. However, if you're struggling, you should contact your local business school, which will be more than happy to help you. Once you have your findings, plot them on a chart (Figure 11.4). Once you have done so, you can quickly ascertain the areas where you need to make strategic and/or operational changes. In the example provided you'd have to work on your communications with the networks and communities. Let's briefly consider how you might approach this challenge.

PR, networks and the community

Patterns exist in the adoption of CSR across differing organisations. Companies that are highly motivated may adopt an idealistic stance or even one of enlightened self-interest, whereas stakeholders on whom they rely may adopt CSR practices only when coerced. This potentially poses a risk for some companies. For example, Nike's poor PR resulting from allegations of child labour generated negative publicity that spread rapidly on social

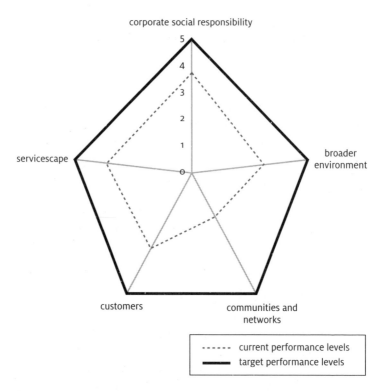

Figure 11.4 Sustainability polar diagram

networking sites. Reputations are easily tarnished by supply-side scandals concerning emotive issues such as child labour.

Hence, with your success depending on suppliers, it's important to ask yourself to what extent you can trust your supply network (a term preferred to 'chain') to act in ways you deem to be sustainable. Retailers, for example, are undoubtedly interdependent, networking organisations and will need to trust their partners. Trust can be shaped by previous experiences and cooperative efforts, and by the more general reputation firms build up. Sustainable marketers may also engender trust in like-minded consumers, and that trust can be grown, say through PR as a means of promoting positive word of mouth. Hence, it's logical to recognise the case for measuring trust within your network.

Developing trust within communities

Larger organisations often engage with the community only reluctantly. This attitude reduces the site of a new development to 'a plot' and something apart from the community. More progressive companies seek to establish relationships with local firms, consumers and regulators. Rather than simply complying with the minimum expectations, marketers need to be more inclusive and sensitive to stakeholders. You may easily benefit from improved PR with the community – not to mention enhancing your chances (as previously discussed) of success by favourably influencing the opinions of planners who receive positive feedback from the local community.

> **Example**
> Tesco's expansion into the United States with its Fresh & Easy chain has been based upon successfully engaging the host communities, often adopting a 'softly softly' approach that has contributed to its success. It describes the new chain as 'American stores for American people'. Even Tesco's UK tag line, 'Every little helps', is socially inclusive. Undoubtedly Tesco's success is underpinned by long-term research into the needs, wants and desires of its customers.

Using support mechanisms

Codes of conduct

You should use the wealth of good advice that is freely available simply by tapping into the codes of conduct of various bodies. They'll cover different aspects; for example, the Market Research Society provides a comprehensive code available from its website (www.mrs.org.uk). This covers any ethical research-based issues you may

have. As we said in Chapter 1, the leading professional PR body is the CIPR. In signing up to its code of conduct, all members agree to:

- **maintain the highest standards of professional endeavour, integrity, confidentiality, financial propriety and personal conduct;**
- **deal honestly and fairly in business with employers, employees, clients, fellow professionals, other professions and the public;**
- **respect the customs, practices and codes of clients, employers, colleagues, fellow professionals and other professions in all countries where they practise;**
- **take all reasonable care to ensure employment best practice, including giving no cause for complaint of unfair discrimination on any grounds;**
- **work within the legal and regulatory frameworks affecting the practice of public relations in all countries where they practise;**
- **encourage professional training and development among members of the profession;**
- **respect and abide by this Code and related Notes of Guidance issued by the Institute of Public Relations and encourage others to do the same.**

Standards and guides

As well as codes of conduct, you'll find a range of 'standards' available to help you to measure your sustainability. For example, BS 8901:2007 provides a specification for a sustainable events management system. ISO 14001 is an internationally accepted standard that provides organisations with a planned set of criteria required for implementation of an effective environmental management system (EMS).

Also, you'll find that trade bodies and special interest groups have refined their own codes. As service industries make up approximately 85 per cent of the United Kingdom's GDP, it's fair to

assume that some of the support materials for the event management sector will chime with other areas. Raj and Musgrave (2009) provide excellent coverage of event management and the sustainability challenge, and suggest the following support tools:

- **Sustainable Events Guide;**
- **SEXI: The Sustainable Exhibition Industry Project;**
- **The Hannover Principles: Design for Sustainability: Expo 2000;**
- **Staging Major Sporting Events: The Guide;**
- **The Sustainable Music Festival: A Strategic Guide;**
- **Green Tourism Business Scheme;**
- **The Eco-Management and Audit Scheme (EMAS).**

Frameworks to measure societal change

Governments, companies and charities use PR to promote campaigns that influence attitudes and behaviour towards issues such as health, tax rates, education and charitable giving. PR is valued by its success in altering societal views and behaviour. The ethical marketing, social PR and design agency Forster has developed Forster's Evaluation Framework to help clients recognise what is trackable and identify what they are prepared to track. The framework involves three stages:

1. *Audience Reach.* This measures where your message is being received, for example the number of hits in targeted media, search engine rankings, website hits, how many partners are involved in the coverage, attendees at an event. This can be measured via monitoring the progress of the campaign in a relatively simple way.

2. *Audience Engagement.* This involves asking questions of the 'reached' audience – for example how involved did they get, did they click through to your website, how long did they stay on your website, did they contribute to the event or meeting? This can be measured by getting feedback from the audience

by running focus groups with a sample of the audience, or using technical data to monitor websites.

3. *Audience Action*. This involves tracking progress on awareness and development levels and will involve more detailed research with the targeted audience prior to, during and after completion of the campaign activities.

Example

Research commissioned by the Disability Rights Commission (DRC) revealed that young disabled people lacked confidence to use public transport. Forster designed a communications campaign, GOJO, to address the issue among 16- to 25-year-olds in five UK regions. The aim was to increase confidence levels, leading to more journeys by young disabled people on public transport, as well as raising awareness of new rights in discrimination laws.

The main focus of the campaign was a website that provided practical information and details of how to complain to transport operators. It encouraged interaction via a blog where users recorded their travel experiences and offered tips. Forster also undertook stakeholder relations targeting transport providers and those that worked with disabled people.

Evaluation of the website during the 11 weeks of campaign activities showed that 78 per cent of website sessions (21,597) did not come through a referral website, reflecting on the success of online PR. It also showed that the link that achieved the most referrals to the site was from the Direct Gov website. Forster's qualitative and quantitative pre- and post-campaign research found that 70 per cent of respondents said that GOJO had influenced them to use public transport.

These examples illustrate how good sustainable practices utilise the People element of TBL (Figure 11.5) in conjunction with the Planet and Profit elements.

Figure 11.5 Fundamentals for good PR practice

Ultimately the demand for sustainable business practices is here to stay and is going to increase with every passing year. As Kotler says, 'There's no turning back.'

Summary and activities

Key points

- **Buying is always guided by consumers' thoughts, feelings and actions, and since we take on attitudes, beliefs, opinions and values from others, companies that are not aware of changes in society run the risk of alienating customers.**

- All companies are located on the sustainability continuum and need to be aware of their position in order to be able to position (or reposition) themselves within their markets by making effective strategic and operational decisions.
- You will need to look towards operating in an increasingly sustainable fashion. Hence, you may need to benchmark your current performance and identify (and remove) barriers to adopting sustainability
- There are many support mechanisms available to you, including codes of conduct, trade bodies, guides, business standards and business schools, not to mention PR agencies and consultants.

Activities

There's precious little on sustainable marketing even in the key marketing texts. To look at a range of academic conference papers (which cover a large range of industries around the world), go to the Corporate Responsibility Research Conference website (http://www. crrconference.org).

The following book contains a number of informative studies on sustainability, including the key Hart and Elkington studies:

Welford, R and Starkey, R (2001) *The Earthscan Reader in Business and Sustainable Development*, Earthscan, London

Have a look at the Co-operative's CSR platform; it's as good as any in the world. It's transparent and independently audited, and the Co-operative refuses to take business that contradicts its ethical policies. Also look up the FTSE4GOOD index.

Answers to questions

1   Public relations in business: an introduction

1. PR operates at all levels of any organisation, as all employees are ambassadors for your brand. PR can operate tactically, working across all functions of the business, promoting the organisation internally and externally. It can contribute to the boardroom discussions. PR is most effective if it is understood and endorsed by the senior management and if it underpins business objectives. At its best, it permeates every decision the business makes and every strategic aim it has.

2. The Data Protection Act 1998 restricts the amount of information PRs are able to release about individuals who may be being investigated by the press. It also helps PRs protect vulnerable people from public scrutiny. The Freedom of Information Act 2000 means that journalists can ask questions of public-sector organisations, but it gives PRs the time to investigate the requests thoroughly, as you can have up to 20 working days to respond to FOI requests. Privacy laws, including the Human

Rights Act 2000, provide rights to privacy and confidentiality for individuals that protect them from being exposed in the press.

3. PR can be implemented by an individual in an organisation who maybe already does marketing for your business. Courses run by the CIPR and institutions like Leeds Business School can help embed good PR understanding and practices. Consultancies and PR agencies are also available to offer more comprehensive, tailored PR for your business.

2 Where PR sits with advertising and marketing

1. Noise involves understanding and interpreting the plethora of distractions that your messages may face when transmitted through differing media. This ultimately can affect the decoding or customers' interpretation of your message. If the customer can't see the wood for the trees, you'll need to encode your message in a different way.

2. Because we're wired up to continuously communicate in a range of ways: audio, visual, textural, smell, and so on. These stimuli are happening all of the time and the combination of fragmented markets and oversupply means we all have to work at how we communicate with our stakeholder continuously.

3. An opinion leader is someone whom the target market sees as having a social standing and influence generally. An opinion former is such owing to their actual expertise, usually through their profession, which means that they have credibility.

3 Understanding strategic public relations

1. The PEST factors constitute the key forces in the macro-environment: social, technological, economic,

environmental, legal, political, informational, ethical and sustainable.

2. The micro-environment consists of customers, competitors, suppliers, distributors, publics, facilitators, employers, employees, unions, shareholders, financiers, manufacturers, agents, franchises, intermediaries, lawyers, agencies, journalists, investors and plumbers!

3. The micro-environment is partly controllable and influenced because of the relationships that the organisation has with the relevant parties. The influence varies depending on circumstances, for example in a crisis.

4. The monitoring of the environment is very much dependent upon the nature of the industry, market and environment you see yourself operating in. Ideally, you should be monitoring the environment daily, even in a stable climate. The macro-environment is turbulent and dynamic; anything can happen!

4 Working with the media

1. Remember that most news items have a human element angle, even if this involves including a quote from a credible source. Make sure you can address the who, what, where, when, why and how of each news release. If you can answer these questions and your release is newsworthy, then you've the basics of a news release.

2. Journalists are busy people, under huge pressure to meet tight deadlines and engage their audiences. Getting to know your key journalists is a good way to develop a professional relationship with them. Try to create an opportunity to meet them to introduce your organisation and explore how you can help the journalist to deliver great news articles to their target audience.

3. Good photography and graphics are well worth investing in to enhance your news stories. Consider the content of the photograph to enhance the story and create more coverage of your story. Think of the composition; more than three people in a photo can get too busy. Giving a photographer a brief that

is clear but allows for creativity is important. Increasingly, PRs are developing video news releases and audio news releases to sell in their stories to the media.

5 PR and developments in online communications

1. As audiences and technology become more sophisticated, the need to generate two-way communication and interactive websites is increasing. No longer is it relevant to post new pages on your website without creating the opportunity for visitors to the site to respond in some way. This relationship with visitors to your site is more meaningful and more likely to generate repeat visits and collection of data regarding visitors to your site which you can use for future communication and relationship development.
2. Online coverage lasts longer than printed coverage because it is still available days, months and often years after first appearing. The opportunity to develop links to other websites and generate RSS feeds adds to the Long Tail effect, identified by Chris Anderson. This is great if all your coverage is positive, but not so good if there is some negative coverage. To overcome this you must keep posting new positive articles on your social media sites and websites.

6 Stakeholders and customers: how to develop and maximise relations

1. When consumers are making a risky decision, whether it be financially risky or personally or socially risky (or all these!), they tend to take their time making the decision, searching for information and weighing up the pros and cons.

2. Factors such as sex, age, occupation, income, their personality type, sense of motivation and perception, and past experiences will all serve to influence consumers' choices and behaviour.
3. Businesses purchase in significantly larger volumes than consumers. They also have a degree of specialised purchasing skill which the average consumer does not tend to have. The procedures and policies of purchasing by a business also tend to be more formal and often include several people.

7 Crisis, what crisis?

1. During a crisis the key element is to ensure that the organisation maintains an element of control of the situation. It can do this by establishing a crisis management team early on. Proactively looking for sensitive ways to overcome negative media and public reaction can reduce the impact, as can keeping in touch with the media on a proactive and reactive basis.
2. Good relations with the media during calmer times can be very useful during a crisis. Issuing statements rather than putting a person up for interview will help you to control the messages and reduce the need for journalists to come onto your premises looking for answers.
3. Staff should be fully trained in the role they will play during a crisis, and the importance of not speaking to the press. All media enquiries should be handled by a dedicated team or an individual who has seniority and experience of dealing with the media.

8 Internal communications

1. Companies that engage in internal communications recognise the benefits of having an enthusiastic workforce. Effective internal communications can increase productivity and profitability. It can reduce sickness rates, absenteeism and

staff turnover. As Rosabeth Moss Kanter says, 'Leaders must wake people out of inertia.'

2. Organisations that have good internal communications usually have good external communications or PR, but the same is not always true in reverse. Internal communications is a growing discipline within public relations, traditionally practised by journalists or the HR function. It is a highly strategic discipline that commands experience and a strong track record of success among employers. It is one of the areas of growth within marcomms as employers strive to reduce employment costs and increase productivity.

3. A range of tools is available to internal communications specialists. As a strategic discipline, internal communications requires research, via for example audits, including focus groups and questionnaires, to ensure that employees are able to engage effectively with a range of means of communication such as weekly newsletters, video and audio messages, events and intranets and to maintain overall satisfaction. On a local level it encourages discussion among department teams, with the opportunity to feedback good and bad practice within the organisation without fear of reprisal, and acknowledgement of the value of the contributions being made by staff.

9 Getting the facts right: using research to create a competitive edge

1. Investment in marketing research is crucial to provide accurate data to help make more informed decisions, lower risk and generate greater knowledge. Secondary data are data that already exist in some shape or form. The use of past sales or market research reports, articles and government statistics are all examples. Primary data are data that are collected first-hand to help solve the actual research problem and fulfil the research objectives. The use and creation of a questionnaire, in-depth

interviews, focus groups, observation and experimentation are all examples of how primary data can be collected.

2. Research can be time-consuming and costly, both financially and through the use of additional resources. A degree of expertise is also required at times.

3. Research objectives serve to provide focus, a sense of purpose and direction to the research. They tend to govern the choice of secondary and primary data and the overall design of the research itself.

References

Elkington, J (1998) The 'triple bottom line' for 21st century business, published in R Welford and R Starkey (eds) (2001) *The Earthscan Reader in Business and Sustainable Development*, Earthscan, London

Grewal, D and Salovey, P (2005) Feeling smart: the science of emotional intelligence, *American Scientist*, **93**, pp 330–39

Hart, N A (ed) (1996) *The CIM Marketing Dictionary*, 5th edn, Butterworth-Heinemann, Oxford

Hart, S L (1997) Beyond greening: strategies for a sustainable world, published in R Welford and R Starkey (eds) (2001) *The Earthscan Reader in Business and Sustainable Development*, Earthscan, London

Howell, R [accessed 20 February 2008] Global trade and sustainable development: complementary or contradictory?, paper for Corporate Responsibility Research Conference, Dublin, July 2006 [Online] http://crrconference.org

Imber, J and Toffler, B (2008) *Dictionary of Marketing Terms*, 4th edn, Barron's Educational Series, New York

Ivanovic, A and Collin, P H (2003) *Dictionary of Marketing: Over 7,000 terms clearly defined*, Bloomsbury, London

0 1341 1381894 9

Kotler, P, Wong, V, Saunders, J and Armstrong, G (2005) *Principles of Marketing*, 4th European edn, Prentice Hall, Harlow

McGoldrick, P (2002) *Retail Marketing*, 2nd edn, McGraw-Hill, Maidenhead

Raj, R and Musgrave, J (2009) *Eve...   ent and Sustainability*, CABI, Wallingford

Richardson, N (2008) To what extent have key retail and generic marketing texts adopted sustainability?, *World Journal of Retail Business Management*, **2** (4), 47–55

Shannon, C E and Weaver, W (1963) *The Mathematical Theory of Communication*, University of Illinois Press, Urbana